# ADVOCA
# FOR SQE2

*Advocacy for SQE2: A Guide to Legal Practice* is the first in a new series of books aimed at those preparing for SQE2, providing a comprehensive overview of everything you need to successfully pass the SQE2 advocacy assessment.

Split into the two practice sections that candidates may be tested on – dispute resolution (civil) as well as criminal litigation – the book covers the basics of court procedure in both areas, so that you fully understand the role, duties and responsibilities of an advocate. In line with the requirements of SQE2, it also tests the competency skills required of an advocate in legal practice such as planning and organisation, drafting, legal research, presenting a reasoned argument, witness handling, observation, exercising judgment and the application of knowledge and decision-making. It also includes a range of supporting features, including:

- In Summary sections
- Key Practice Cases
- Practice Tips
- Practice Risks
- Problem Based Exercises
- Realistic Case Scenarios
- Self-Reflection Checklist

Further supporting materials are also provided on the companion website.

Written by an author with practice experience and early involvement in the planning and development of the SQE itself, this unique book will be essential reading for any candidate wishing to be fully prepared for their SQE2 advocacy assessment.

**Dr Rita D'Alton-Harrison** is a senior lecturer, solicitor, author and legal education trainer and adviser and has been teaching in Higher Education for over 20 years both on undergraduate and postgraduate professional courses. Rita has over ten years' post qualification experience as a solicitor and previously practised in the field of civil and criminal litigation. Rita is also the series editor for the Routledge Legal Practice SQE2 series.

# Legal Practice for SQE2

Series editor: Rita D'Alton Harrison, Royal Holloway, University of London

The Legal Practice Skills for SQE2 series maps out key legal skills against five main areas of practice, and the Statement of Solicitor Competence, providing candidates with a set of concise, practical volumes to help them prepare for the examination. The style of each book is precise, with bullet-point lists summarizing key information and revision points concluding each chapter. The books also feature multiple choice questions with answers, example problem questions and realistic case scenarios.

**Advocacy for SQE2**
Rita D'Alton Harrison

# ADVOCACY FOR SQE2

## A Guide to Legal Practice

Rita D'Alton-Harrison

Routledge
Taylor & Francis Group

LONDON AND NEW YORK

Cover image: © Getty Images

First published 2023
by Routledge
4 Park Square, Milton Park, Abingdon, Oxon OX14 4RN

and by Routledge
605 Third Avenue, New York, NY 10158

*Routledge is an imprint of the Taylor & Francis Group, an informa business*

© 2023 Rita D'Alton-Harrison

*British Library Cataloguing-in-Publication Data*
A catalogue record for this book is available from the British Library

*Library of Congress Cataloging-in-Publication Data*
A catalog record has been requested for this book

ISBN: 978-0-367-68224-8 (hbk)
ISBN: 978-0-367-68087-9 (pbk)
ISBN: 978-1-003-13477-0 (ebk)

DOI: 10.4324/9781003134770

Typeset in The Sans
by Deanta Global Publishing Services, Chennai, India

Dedicated to Angela and every heart that she touched.

# Contents

# List of Figures

# Series Editor Introduction

Recognising that competencies are developed over time and increase with experience, this SQE2 series helps to 'grow' the legal professional using guided exercises, self-reflection and elements of independent study. Each textbook in this series is designed to help the reader to master the six legal skills assessed in the SQE2 in the context of specific fields of practice whilst also preparing them for entering a new life in practice. In this way it is hoped that the textbooks will serve as both a workbook and a reference manual to help the reader to build upon and improve their skills at the early stages of their legal career. Each book in the series contains commentary explaining why and how the legal skills are relevant to practice as well as signposting when the inclusion of additional information would increase the quality and effectiveness of the legal professional's work and when the inclusion of certain irrelevant or incorrect information would not. In addition to the six SQE legal skills, the exercises in each book are designed to help with the development of additional skills such as observation, decision-taking, judgment, drafting and retention of information as well as taking the reader through the essentials of procedural rules and practice tasks.

# Acknowledgments

I am grateful for the patience of my family whilst writing this book and for their encouragement and support. I would like to thank the editorial team at Routledge for giving me the opportunity to develop the pedagogy that underpins this book and the series itself and for sharing my vision and commitment to provide learning opportunities for non-specialists entering a specialist field. In particular, I would like to thank Russell George and Emily Kindleysides. I also acknowledge the invaluable resource of cases accessed using the online repository of the British and Irish Legal Information Institute ('Bailii') and other case repositories. Finally, my thanks go to all my past students who have helped me to understand the different ways in which students learn and how they learn best.

# Abbreviations

| | |
|---|---|
| **ADR** | Alternative Dispute Resolution |
| **BSB** | Bar Standards Board |
| **CILEX** | Chartered Institute of Legal Executives |
| **CJA 2003** | Criminal Justice Act 2003 |
| **CJPOA 1994** | Criminal Justice and Public Order Act 1994 |
| **CPIA 1996** | Criminal Procedure and Investigations Act 1996 |
| **CPR** | Civil Procedure Rules |
| **CRIMPR** | Criminal Procedure Rules |
| **ECHR 1950** | European Convention on Human Rights 1950 |
| **MCA 2005** | Mental Capacity Act 2005 |
| **PACE 1984** | Police and Criminal Evidence Act 1984 |
| **PD** | Practice Direction |
| **QOCS** | Qualified One-Way Cost Shifting |
| **SDT** | Solicitors Disciplinary Tribunal |
| **SOSC** | Statement of Solicitor Competence |
| **SQE** | Solicitors' Qualifying Examination |
| **SRA** | Solicitors Regulation Authority |

# PART A
## The Competent Advocate

# Introduction

In writing this guide to advocacy I hope that I have been able to demonstrate how skills and academic knowledge are interconnected and interdependent and how practice and theory can work hand in hand to develop leadership skills and confidence in future advocates.

Whilst this companion textbook is intended to help prepare students for the national Solicitors Qualifying Examinations ('SQE'), it also provides useful information on evidence and procedural rules that will take students beyond their studies to entry into the profession. It is a companion and reference text that the novice advocate can use whilst in practice by referring to discrete parts and sections of the textbook.

The book also clearly signposts where SQE advocacy assessed skills are covered within the text. Using exercises, problem-based scenarios and case studies, the reader is encouraged to learn by doing and to build their confidence through role-play and 'confidence exercises'. The textbook emphasises the importance of engaging with the court procedural rules and professional conduct rules throughout the various stages of advocacy.

The skills and knowledge that an advocate will need are explored in the context of criminal and civil litigation only. Therefore, the focus is on the Civil Procedure Rules ('CPR') and the Criminal Procedural Rules ('CrimPR'). Other procedural rules such as the Family Procedure Rules and the Supreme Court Procedure Rules are beyond the scope of this book. The textbook examines how and when the criminal and civil rules may arise in the day-to-day work of an advocate.

An advocate is not expected to learn the procedure rules verbatim, but they are expected to familiarise themselves with the framework of the rules and understand how they connect. This book aims to assist with this task but is not meant to be a definitive summary of the entirety of the rules, which are themselves numerous and are updated on a regular basis.

DOI: 10.4324/9781003134770-2

## 0.1  What Is an Advocate?

An advocate is a person who conducts a case in a court or tribunal. Part of an advocate's role is to represent a party in legal proceedings by speaking on their behalf and putting forward evidence and legal arguments. An advocate is expected to advance their whole case at trial and to ensure that they advance the best evidence possible to support and prove that case. However, speaking is only one part of an advocate's role. Conducting a case also involves preparation, legal research and a focused strategy to achieve successful outcomes. At all times, an advocate is expected to be competent and adhere to certain standards. For this reason, advocacy is a 'reserved activity' under the Legal Services Act 2007 and only qualified legal professionals can undertake this role in the court system.

Advocacy is in essence a craft and one in which the public and the judges must have faith. Research by Gillian Hunter and others (2018) found from their interview of 50 circuit and High Court judges, that the judiciary considered the attributes of a good advocate to be an ability to communicate well, to focus on the case by taking a structured and strategic approach and by undertaking detailed preparation in readiness for attendance at court.

## 0.2  What Does Competence Mean?

Competence is the ability to do something successfully and effectively to an expected standard. In a professional setting, this relates to the ability to provide an appropriate standard of service to members of the public. To reflect the differing levels of competency expected of advocates, the Solicitors Regulation Authority ('SRA') have developed a competency statement.

## 0.3  What Is the SRA Statement of Solicitor Competence?

The SRA has identified the skills, knowledge and behaviours expected of solicitors (including advocates) and these are set out in the *Statement of Solicitor Competence* ('SoSC'), together with the levels ('threshold standards') that a solicitor is expected to meet upon qualifying to practice as a solicitor. The standard for newly qualified solicitors (Level 3) will be competence to an 'acceptable standard', rather than an excellent standard of mastery.

The *Statement of Solicitor Competence* helpfully sets out the type of tasks and activities that a competent advocate would be expected to perform (see A–D in Figure 0.1) and these tasks are explored in this book together with other practice skills and knowledge that an advocate will need during case preparation and analysis.

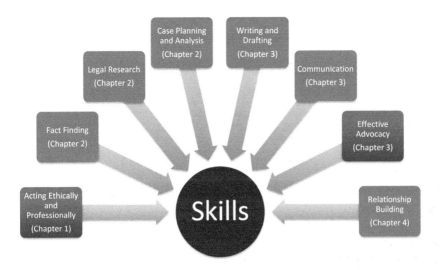

**Figure 0.1** Book Skills Content.

## 0.4 How Do I Use this Book?

The book is divided into three parts. **Part A** will focus on how to become a competent advocate within the meaning of the SRA *Statement of Solicitor Competence*. Exercises will incorporate aspects of 'embodied 'earning' – loosely defined as a somatic approach to learning that involves the perception of learning through senses, body and mind and responses. This recognises the need to 'grow' the advocate and that competencies increase with experience rather than being gained immediately. **Part B** introduces the reader to both civil and criminal litigation put in the context of knowledge-based case studies in order to make interim applications, pre-trial applications and post-trial sentencing and appeals. **Part C** contains the answers to the exercises and case studies in Parts A and B. At the end of Part B you will find two helpful appendices. The first (**Appendix A**) cross-references the most common civil and criminal applications to their specific procedural rule and any accompanying legislation. The second (**Appendix B**) cross-references specific evidential rules to their relevant procedural rule and legislation and a 'synopsis case' that summarises the origins and key aspects of the rule.

Parts A and B are further divided into individual chapters.

In Chapter 1 we will examine how an advocate acquires professionalism by managing their behaviours and acting ethically. We will examine the SRA Standards and Regulations and principles which govern the behaviours of legal professionals. These align with the 'SoSC' A and D.

In Chapter 2 we will consider the essential skills necessary to plan, analyse and produce a focused strategy in case preparation including legal research. This section will cover the 'SoSC' B1, B2, B3, B6 and B7.

In Chapter 3 we will focus on how an advocate communicates with others through effective written and communication skills. We will explore writing, drafting, oral presentation and communication skills of an advocate. These align with the technical legal practice under the 'SoSC' B4 (drafting effective and accurate documentation), B5 (effective spoken and written advocacy) and C1 (effective communication).

We will consider the remaining competency aspects of C (C2 and C3) in Chapter 4 when we consider how to work with others by building relationships both with clients, the court, witnesses, experts and other legal professionals and litigants in person.

We will cover various skills within the chapters in Part A as shown in Figure 0.1.

All the advocacy skills that are assessed as part of SQE2 are clearly signposted. However, the book is intended to deal with all skills that an advocacy will be called upon to use during their time in practice. As such, the learning outcomes at the end of each chapter, whilst including the skills examples given by the SRA in the SoSC, focus on all the skills the reader will be expected to have gained at the end of each chapter.

Answers to all exercises (except confidence exercises) can be found in Part C.

In addition, Part A includes some helpful 'Dos and Don'ts' for practice and some key practice cases are explored in each chapter together with other relevant cases, legislation and journal articles.

All competencies are further explored in the case studies to be found in Part B of the text. This enables the knowledge gained in Part A to be applied to a practice setting. We use procedural rules and evidential rules to work through pre-trial applications and interim applications in criminal and civil case scenarios in Part B. Because a competent advocate is also expected to abide by court rules and procedure, we will discuss court procedure in all chapters in Parts A and B.

All names, characters and places contained in the exercises and case studies in this book are entirely fictional and are not intended to resemble anyone living or deceased.

I have endeavoured to provide the most up to date information on the law and procedure and this includes all amendments to the civil and criminal procedure rules up to the changes made in 2022. Whilst every effort has been made to ensure the information is accurate, I acknowledge that any errors that may occur are my own. I welcome any constructive feedback, comments and suggestions from practitioners, academics, students, and others to refine the commentary, exercises and case studies for future editions.

# 1 Managing Your Behaviours
## Professionalism and Ethics

### Key Chapter Points

1.  Professionalism is about being knowledgeable with the ability to work independently whilst observing the rules, conduct and behaviour expected from the specialised group to which you belong.
2.  The SRA Standards and Regulations contain the rules, conduct and behaviours expected from trainee solicitors, solicitors and registered European and foreign lawyers.
3.  Professional rules and codes of conduct ensure that you are competent in your work and conduct yourself and your work ethically.
4.  A competent advocate carries out their role to the expected standards as set by professional bodies and the court.
5.  An ethical advocate is expected to be honest, have integrity and adhere to regulations and standards to maintain public trust and confidence in the profession.
6.  Professional bodies provide support and guidance to help advocates solve ethical dilemmas.

## 1.1 Introduction

An advocate has a responsibility to behave ethically and to provide a professional level of service to members of the public. An advocate is also expected to protect the reputation of the legal profession by avoiding unethical behaviour. This applies whether an advocate is a barrister (see The Bar Standards Board ('BSB') Professional Statement Threshold Standard and Competencies contained in the BSB Handbook and Code of Conduct) or a member of the Chartered Institute of Legal Executives (see the CILEx Regulation Code of Conduct and CILEx Work-Based Learning Portfolios known as 'Day One Outcomes') or a solicitor (see SRA Statement of Solicitor Competence).

In this chapter, we will concentrate on the competencies of ethics for solicitors under competency A of the SRA Statement of Solicitor Competence ('SoSC') (see Figure 1.1). However, acting ethically is a requirement across all types of practice and in life especially when working with the client and others. Competency A therefore in reality

DOI: 10.4324/9781003134770-3

**Figure 1.1** Chapter Content.

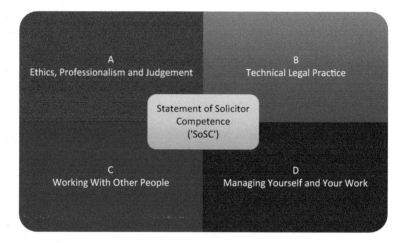

**Figure 1.2** Statement of Solicitor Competence.

overlaps with competencies C and D of the SRA competency framework, which we will also consider in this chapter.

# The Meaning of Professional Ethics

## 1.2 Professionalism and Ethics

Ethics can be loosely defined as an understanding of what society would consider 'right' or 'wrong' or 'good' or 'bad'. Ethics affects how individuals make decisions because they are dependent on the definition of others. Different people may have differing views about what is to be regarded as right or wrong behaviour. This can make decision-taking difficult. Professionalism has been defined in various ways such as belonging to a knowledgeable group with an obligation to provide a public service (Pound, 1953), characterised by individuals having autonomy, independent judgment, or being bound by ethics (Hoyle and John, 1995) and self-governing (Lester, 2014). Boon and others (2005) argue that a profession is defined and legitimised by its control over knowledge.

Regardless of differing definitions, what most professions will have in common is that their activities and behaviour will be governed by a code of conduct based on ethics.

Professional ethics can be thought of as shared principles and values that govern professional practice. It is an expectation of how a professional person will conduct himself or herself and will usually be based on principles of fairness and transparency.

Advocates are required to follow the professional rules and codes of conduct set out by their governing body in order to help them to maintain competency. In the case of solicitors these are contained in the *Solicitors Regulation Authority's Standards and Regulations Handbook*. The SRA refer to ethical behaviours in the seven 'Principles' (see below) as well as setting out the standards expected in conducting work in practice (Code of Conduct) and rules relating to holding client monies and monies from third parties (Solicitors' Accounts Rules).

## 1.2.1 SRA Principles
The SRA Standards and Regulations set out seven mandatory Principles that solicitors must follow. These are:

- *Principle 1* – act in a way that upholds the constitutional principle of the rule of law, and the proper administration of justice. This means respecting the laws passed by Parliament and following legal processes including complying with court orders and avoiding wasting the court's time or causing unavoidable delays.
- *Principle 2* – act in a way that upholds public trust and confidence in the solicitors' profession and in legal services provided by authorised persons. This principle extends beyond the solicitor-client relationship and involves protecting the reputation of the legal profession including your firm or organisation.
- *Principle 3* – act with independence. This means that you should not allow your independence to be compromised by others as this will weaken your ability to remain objective.
- *Principle 4*   act with honesty. This means that you must avoid being dishonest and instead act in a way that will enable others to place their trust in you.
- *Principle 5* – act with integrity. This means holding yourself to a higher standard than ordinary members of the public and being careful to ensure your behaviour will withstand scrutiny.
- *Principle 6* – act in a way that encourages equality, diversity and inclusion. These values are contained in legislation such as the Equality Act 2010 and should be observed in your treatment of others and in the service that you provide as an advocate.

- *Principle 7* – act in the best interests of each client. There is a fiduciary relationship between a solicitor and a client. The best interests of the client may relate to how you prepare their case to meet their goals and objectives but can also be reflected in your duty of confidentiality to the client and your duty to avoid conflicts of interest.

The Principles extend to life in practice but can also extend to an advocate's social and personal life if, for example, they engage in behaviour that is likely to damage public trust in the profession (Principle 2). Ethical behaviour towards others also helps to maintain effective and professional relationships with clients (C2) and others (C3).

## 1.2.2  Ethics, Professionalism and Judgment
Ethics should be the heart of every action and decision-making process taken by an advocate. This is important because poor standards and unethical behavior by an advocate can impact the public at large. It can also lead to a loss of trust and faith in the legal profession, especially if poor advocacy leads to miscarriages of justice with wrongful convictions or a failure to uphold the rule of law. In the case of *Medcalf v Weatherill and Another* [2002] UKHL 27, Lord Hobhouse summarised the rationale for this high standard of behaviour as follows:

> A Professional advocate is in a privileged position. He is granted rights of audience. He enjoys certain immunities. In return he owes certain duties to the court and is bound by certain standards of professional conduct in accordance with the code of conduct in his profession.
>
> *[54]*

Ethical behaviour will also help to ensure professional behaviour.

Let us now consider three principles that have commonly been the subject of cases going before the Solicitors' Disciplinary Tribunal: Principle 2 (public trust and confidence), Principle 4 (honesty) and Principle 5 (integrity).

## 1.2.3  Public Trust and Confidence (Principle 2)
The key focus here is the need for the public to trust the profession as a whole and therefore the rules place all solicitors under a duty to ensure that this trust continues. The principle can be best summed up in the quote in Figure 1.3.

The protection of the reputation of the profession is regarded as so important that the obligation to protect the profession's reputation can extend to conduct within and outside an advocate's working life, particularly when using social media. This can be illustrated by the case of *SRA v Lewis* [2018] SDT Case No. 11856-2018 where a high-profile solicitor who had received anti-Semitic abuse on Twitter and subsequently issued death threats to his abusers was fined £2,500 plus costs (this was reduced from £7,500 after taking into account the abuse the solicitor had received himself).

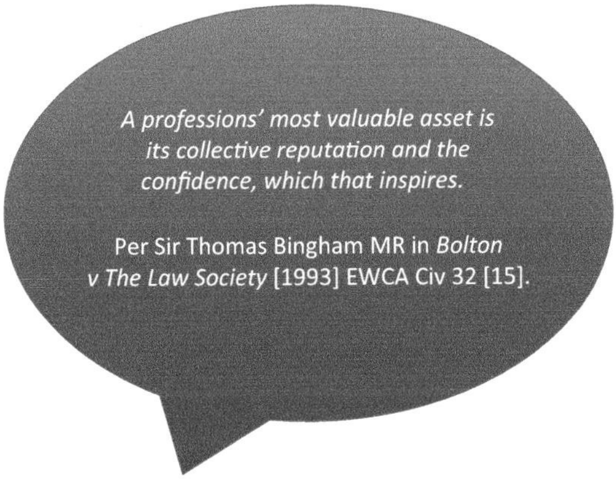

> *A professions' most valuable asset is its collective reputation and the confidence, which that inspires.*
>
> Per Sir Thomas Bingham MR in *Bolton v The Law Society* [1993] EWCA Civ 32 [15].

**Figure 1.3** Public Trust and Confidence in the Profession.

In *Beckwith v SRA* [2020] EWHC 3231 (Admin) the court stated that the principle of public trust and confidence "may reach private life only when conduct that is part of a person's private life realistically touches on...the standing of the profession" [54]. As an example, the principle of public trust and confidence was said by the courts to be capable of applying to "seriously abusive conduct by one member of the profession against another" [44].

The facts of *Beckwith* concerned allegations of sexual misconduct by a male senior partner towards a female solicitor in a more junior role. One of the questions in the original hearing before the Solicitors Disciplinary Tribunal ('SDT') was whether a senior solicitor's behaviour towards a junior solicitor could be said to amount to serious misconduct. The SDT found that it did not. The appeal itself related to an earlier ruling by the SDT that the appellant, who was a partner in a city law firm, had acted without integrity and in a way likely to breach public trust and confidence by engaging in sexual behaviour following an after-work drinks gathering. The appellant was alleged to have initiated and/or engaged in sexual activity with the junior associate solicitor who had consumed a large amount of alcohol. Whilst the SDT did not accept there had been an abuse of the appellant's position of seniority it did find that the public would not have expected a solicitor to conduct himself in that way (this was a failure to uphold public trust and confidence). The SDT found that the solicitor had acted inappropriately by engaging in sexual activity in those circumstances and therefore his conduct fell below expected standards (lack of integrity). The SDT imposed a fine of £35,000 plus costs.

The matter was referred to the High Court by way of appeal. The court was asked to consider whether integrity and upholding public confidence should apply to private sexual conduct or be confined to 'professional misconduct'. The court held that each profession's code of conduct had to be applied as written and this varied from profession to profession. The SRA Handbook (this has now been replaced by the SRA Standards and Regulations) did not extend integrity to private sexual misconduct and confined it to matters that could be said to relate to or affect professional practice as a solicitor. In terms of upholding public trust and confidence, the court accepted that this could extend to a person's private life if it touched on how the public would expect solicitors to treat each other. However, as the SDT in its own ruling had accepted that the sexual encounter in this case was consensual and that there had not been an abuse of a position of seniority, it could not be said that the public would lose trust or confidence in the profession as a result of the appellant's conduct. The appellant had affected his own reputation (for which he had been disciplined at work) but not the reputation of the profession as a whole.

It is important to note that this case is not authority to say that sexual misconduct or harassment that takes place outside work can never be caught by the rules. The SRA subsequently amended the rules after the decision in *Beckwith* and the guidance accompanying the SRA Standards and Regulations includes sexual harassment as an example of a breach of Principle 2. In addition, the decision in *Beckwith* confirmed that each case would have to be judged on a case-by-case basis. This should be done in a way that achieves a fair balance between the right to respect for private and family life and the public interest in ensuring regulation of the solicitors' profession.

## 1.2.4  Honesty (Principle 4)

The requirement for honesty can be found under Principle 4 of the SRA Principles. This is a relatively new addition to the Principles, for the first time it is a requirement rather than merely an unexpressed expectation. However, honesty is not defined in any of the SRA rules but implicitly it can be considered to be the opposite of dishonesty. Whilst honesty connotes truthfulness, this is only one aspect of honesty. As Hughes LJ explained in the case of *Ivey v Genting Casinos (UK) Ltd (t/a Crockfords)* [2017] UKSC 67 "truthfulness is indeed one characteristic of honesty, and untruthfulness is often a powerful indicator of dishonesty, but a dishonest person may sometimes be truthful about his dishonest opinion" [75].

In *Bolton v The Law Society* [1993] EWCA Civ 32, the courts indicated that disciplinary Tribunals will hold solicitors to a very high standard of honesty in order to "maintain the reputation of the solicitors' profession as one in which every member, of whatever standing, may be trusted to the ends of the earth" [15]. Honesty therefore connotes trustworthiness, not just truthfulness.

In this case, Mr Bolton was found to have behaved in a naïve and foolish manner, but his conduct was not considered dishonest. In fact, the Solicitors Disciplinary Tribunal went so far as to accept that Mr Bolton was an honest man and the Court of Appeal also accepted this view. Nonetheless the Solicitors Disciplinary Tribunal found that Mr Bolton's action was serious enough to warrant his suspension from practising as a solicitor. Why? It was because he had not been truthful. This is because he acted on a conveyancing matter in relation to the sale of a house owned by his wife. The house was to be sold to her brother. Mr Bolton acted for all the parties in this transaction, his wife, her brother and the mortgage company, even though there were clearly potential conflicts of interest. Instead of holding the mortgage monies in the client account, Mr Bolton used some of it to pay tax due on the sale of the property and to also pay out some of the monies to his wife. In the event, Mr Bolton's brother-in-law failed to pay the remaining £20,000 needed to complete the purchase price. The sale was never completed and the shortfall to the mortgage company was eventually remedied and repaid. The accounting error only came to light after an investigation by the regulator about an unrelated matter and Mr Bolton's accounts were inspected. Mr Bolton was found to have breached the Solicitors' Accounts Rules.

An advocate would be expected to be honest in terms of how they relay information to others, in particular, not to deliberately mislead or lie or withhold important information. This is important, not just in dealings with the client but also with the court and third parties such as experts. It may be more difficult to say no to a family member and for this reason an advocate should avoid acting for family and close relatives.

## 1.2.5 Integrity (Principle 5)

Integrity has been defined in the case of *Hoodless and Another v Financial Services Authority* [2003] UKFTT 007 (FSM) to mean "moral soundness, rectitude and adherence to an ethical code. A person lacks integrity if unable to appreciate the distinction between what is honest or dishonest by ordinary standards" [19].

In the case of *Wingate and Evans v Solicitors Regulation Authority; Solicitors Regulation Authority v Malins* [2018] EWCA Civ 366 (Admin) Jackson LJ summarised integrity as "a useful shorthand to express the higher standards which society expects from professional persons and which the professions expect from their own members" [97].[1]

Principle 5 of the SRA Principles requires solicitors (including trainee solicitors) and registered European lawyers and registered foreign lawyers to act with integrity. This will also ensure competency levels in terms of applying good business practice, especially in accounting and financial matters (D3).

The definition of integrity does not mean that saintliness is expected from the professional person. As noted in *Wingate and Evans v Solicitors Regulation Authority; Solicitors Regulation Authority v Malins* [2018] EWCA Civ 366 (Admin): "The duty of integrity does not require professional people to be paragons of virtue. In every instance, professional integrity is linked to the manner in which that particular profession professes to serve the public"[104]. The case of *Wingate* gives some useful examples of lack of integrity taken from previous case law, such as 'making false

1 NB These cases considered the SRA Principles pre-2019 and the question of public trust and confidence was then found under Principle 6 but is now found under Principle 2. Integrity was previously found under Principle 2 but is now found under Principle 5. Honesty is a new Principle introduced by the SRA Standards and Regulations in 2019.

representations on behalf of the client' or 'recklessly, but not dishonestly allowing a court to be misled' [101].

The facts in *Wingate* provide an illustration of how it can be easy to fall into behaviour that might be considered to amount to a lack of integrity. In this case two solicitors (Mr Wingate and Mr Evans) were partners practising in a small firm, W.E. Solicitors LLP, which had fallen into financial hardship. They were unable to repay a bank loan, even after the bank agreed to take a reduced amount.

Mr Wingate therefore sought an alternative source of funding and turned to a fund called Axiom which agreed to lend £900,000. The fund specialised in funding the cost of litigation for the clients of firms. Mr Barnett, who was a member of the Council of the Law Society and also a solicitor, managed the fund. The partners thought that they could trust Mr Barnett and relied on oral statements made by him to the effect that the loan of the monies was not restricted to litigation funding but could be used for general purposes. However, the loan agreement stated that the monies could only be used for the specified purpose of litigation funding. Mr Wingate stated in evidence that he had been told by Mr Barnett the terms of the loan agreement would be varied to make it less restrictive. However, before this could happen, Axiom went into receivership and Mr Barnett was eventually struck off the Roll of Solicitors.

W.E. Solicitors were unable to repay the loan and were investigated by the Solicitors Regulation Authority. As the firm had used the funds to pay debts, including the bank repayment and sums owed to HM Revenue and Customs, they were in clear breach of the funding agreement. Mr Wingate and Mr Evans were found to be in breach of the Solicitors Accounts Rules (these are found in the SRA Standards and Regulations) as well as other professional misconduct. The Solicitors Disciplinary Tribunal origi-nally imposed a fine of £3,000 on both Mr Wingate and Mr Evans for breach of the Solicitors Accounts Rules. The SRA appealed on the basis that this sanction was too lenient. The matter went to the High Court, which allowed the appeal, and Mr Wingate and Mr Evans then appealed to the Court of Appeal. The Court of Appeal found that Mr Wingate (who dealt with the negotiations with Axiom) should have appreciated the "highly dubious" nature of the transaction as the agreement signed by the parties did not set out the true nature of the parties' understanding of how the monies would be spent. His appeal failed. Mr Evans's appeal was allowed on the basis that his failure to obtain and read the funding agreement did not of itself mean that he lacked integrity or that he was dishonest.

Similarly, in the conjoined appeal of *Malins*, the court held that backdating a notice of funding arrangements by creating a letter after the event stating that such a notice was enclosed, could amount to dishonesty and therefore a breach of the principle that a solicitor should act with integrity. However, as Mr Malins had, on the facts of this case, created the letter but had not sent it, he was only acting without integrity but not dishonestly.

Whilst a lack of integrity might occur due to an act of dishonesty, dishonesty is not an essential requirement for Principle 5 to be breached. The case of *Scott v Solicitors Regulation Authority* [2016] EWHC 1256 illustrates why it is important to draw a distinction between dishonesty and integrity. In this case the appellant solicitor brought an appeal in the High Court against a decision made by the Solicitors' Disciplinary Tribunal ('SDT'). The SDT had made a finding that the solicitor appellant had acted without integrity. The original charges against the solicitor related to breaches of the Solicitors Accounts Rules and failure to cooperate with the SRA. The SDT held that the solicitor had not been dishonest in the use of client accounts. However, on the question of integrity, the court held that the solicitor did lack integrity by being reckless as to how he dealt with client money. Sharp LJ held that "a person can lack integrity without being dishonest" [48].

According to cases such as *Williams v Solicitors Regulation Authority* [2017] EWHC 1478 (Admin) and *Newell-Austin v Solicitors Regulation Authority* [2017] Med LR 194, lack of integrity (when it does not involve dishonesty) is to be judged objectively rather than subjectively and is therefore measured by the standards of the reasonable person.

Whilst integrity is to be judged objectively, dishonesty is judged both objectively and subjectively. Disciplinary tribunals such as the SDT will often align the test to the criminal test of dishonesty set out in the case of *Ivey v Genting Casinos (UK) Ltd (t/a Crockfords)* [2017] UKSC 67. This is a two-stage test:

1. The jury must find that the actual state of the defendant's mind was dishonest based on the defendant's knowledge and belief as to the facts (**SUBJECTIVE** limb). Any question of the reasonableness of that belief is simply a matter of evidence, what matters is whether the belief is genuinely held by the defendant.
2. The jury must then consider whether the act itself was dishonest according to the ordinary standards of reasonable and honest people (the **OBJECTIVE** limb). If the answer is no, then the defendant is not to be regarded as dishonest.

## Confidence Exercise

**Try This One on Your Own!**

Consider the following behaviours, could any of these be said to breach the above SRA Principles? If so, which one(s)?

1. You agree to lend your name to an investment fund managed by a friend. You know that the fund's claim that investors will receive high returns is a

dubious claim in the current economic circumstances. You also know that lending your name will add credibility to the scheme. You feel that this is the right thing to do to help your friend who is in financial difficulties. You have not used your firm's name in your association with the investment fund.

2.  You have a private Twitter account in which you occasionally give your own political thoughts and opinions. You have a follower who opposes your ideology and repeatedly responds to your posts by leaving insulting comments. You have tried to ignore the insults but are unable to ignore a response posted by the follower as it uses derogatory comments to describe your appearance. You post a Tweet threatening to find and destroy the follower and anyone close to them.

In considering the above scenarios, remember the following:

- An advocate is expected to be trustworthy and to protect and maintain public trust.
- An advocate is expected to avoid behaviour that might be regarded as dishonest, offensive, threatening, abusive or an abuse of their position.
- Advocates have a responsibility to protect the collective reputation of the legal profession and this is more important than the interests of the advocate.
- Helping other people to act in an improper or dishonest way can also be regarded as misconduct by an advocate.

The responsibility to be ethical requires managing behaviours and this is recognised within the SRA Statement of Solicitor Competence (see SoSC A). Competency implies ethical behaviour through proficiency and meeting standards.

## Professional Competency

## 1.3  The SRA Statement of Solicitor Competence

The SRA Statement of Competence sets out the skills, knowledge and behavious expected of legal professionals. With competency comes an assumption that advocates act both professionally and ethically. As discussed, although ethics and professionalism are found in competency A they overlap with the other competencies within the SRA Statement of Solicitor Competency. For example, A3 requires legal professionals to "disclose when work is beyond their personal capability" as well as "recognising when they have made mistakes or are experiencing difficulties and take appropriate action". This also impacts the advocate's working relationship with the client and others (D).

Standards should not be lowered simply because unforeseen circumstances arise that take an advocate by surprise. An advocate is expected to pre-empt all possible risks and alternative courses of actions. For example, under D1 (e), part of managing yourself and your work involves "dealing effectively with unforeseen circumstances". Not all matters in litigation can be foreseen but what matters is how an advocate deals with situations as they arise and finds solutions. For example, if you were acting for a claimant in civil proceedings and suing a company for negligence, what would you do on receiving information that the same company was subject to a hostile takeover by another company? You would want to act quickly to secure any assets before the hostile takeover, in which case you might think about the powers that the court has under CPR 25 to make interim remedies such as a 'freezing injunction' or an order to restrain a party from dealing with any assets whether located in the jurisdiction or not (see CPR Part 25.1 (1) (f) (ii) and for a helpful case that summarises the criteria for obtaining a 'freezing injunction', see *Kaza Ltd and Another v Akcil and Others* [2019] EWCA Civ 891).

Advocates who are new to their role may of course make mistakes but learning through repeated tasks, supervision and feedback all help to maintain levels of competence. There is an expectation in A2 of the SRA Statement of Solicitor Competence that an advocate's professionalism will include "taking responsibility for personal learning and development" as well as "reflecting on and learning from practice and learning from other people". Attending professional development courses to keep your legal knowledge and skills up to date will maintain the high standards expected in the profession.

Good time management and file organisation will also ensure that you keep on top of your work so that you are able to meet important timescales and deadlines. Be prepared to be adaptable as the rules governing legal services can change as well as the way in which an advocate works as new technology and case management systems are introduced within firms/organisations and the courts.

## 1.3.1 Maintaining Levels of Competency and Legal Knowledge

The risks of inadvertently falling into unethical behaviour are significantly reduced if an advocate maintains their professional competency by keeping their legal knowledge up to date and responding to changes and developments in the law. This is best achieved through professional courses as well as learning from more senior colleagues. It is expected that competence will be maintained through training, supervision and feedback. Part of being a competent advocate is recognising when matters are beyond your expertise and knowledge and seeking appropriate support and guidance, for example, from experts or a supervisor. Guidance and constructive feedback are necessary to the process of becoming proficient.

# How Do I Ensure Professional and Ethical Conduct?

## 1.4  SRA Code of Conduct

Peng and Others (2020) found in their research study that an ethical culture within the workplace facilitates the development of ethical leadership by impacting the 'organisational citizenship behaviour' ('OCB') within that organisation and thus positively affecting the task performance of followers (employees). Therefore, ethical practices go beyond just individual behaviour and should extend to ethical practices within the legal practice or organisation.

In addition to the seven Principles, the SRA also prescribes codes of conduct that governs the way those in the profession are expected to work to ensure competency and ethics within the workplace. There are two codes of conduct, one for firms and one for solicitors.

The SRA Codes of Conduct for Solicitors contain the standards of 'professionalism' and these are set out across eight chapters:

- *Code 1* – Maintaining Trust and Confidence.
- *Code 2* – Dispute Resolution and Proceedings Before Courts and Tribunals.
- *Code 3* – Service and Competence.
- *Code 4* – Client Money and Assets.
- *Code 5* – Referrals, Introductions and Separate Businesses.
- *Code 6* – Conflicts of Interest.
- *Code 7* – Cooperation and Accountability.
- *Code 8* – Client Identification, Complaints Handling, Information and Publicity.

Meeting the standards set in the SRA Code of Conduct for Solicitors will also be indicative that the SRA Principles are being observed. For example, Code 2.2 states:

> You do not seek to influence the substance of evidence, including generating false evidence or persuading witnesses to change their evidence.

Adhering to this standard will also ensure that you are acting in a way that upholds the rule of law and proper administration of justice (Principle 1) and upholds public trust and confidence in the solicitors' profession (Principle 2). You will also be acting honestly (Principle 4) and with integrity (Principle 5).

It is possible for the Principles and Codes of Conduct to conflict when deciding on the correct course of action to take. This is particularly so as the Principles are not ordered in terms of importance. For example, there is a requirement to act in the best interests of the client (SRA Principle 7) as well as a duty of confidentiality to the client (e.g. SRA Code of Conduct chapter 6.3). However, observing these duties to the client could also lead to an advocate's independence being compromised which would equally breach professional rules (e.g. SRA Principle 3 – acting with independence). Equally, only observing duties to the client ignores duties owed to the court and the public at large (e.g. SRA Code of Conduct chapter 2 – dispute resolution and proceedings before courts).

The duty to the court (Code 2) is often considered to be a primary and overriding duty and it even extends to experts who also have an overriding duty to the court. They include expected behaviours such as:

- "You do not misuse or tamper with evidence or attempt to do so" (2.1).
- "You do not place yourself in contempt of court, and you comply with court orders which place obligations on you" (2.5).
- "You draw the court's attention to relevant cases and statutory provisions, or procedural irregularities of which you are aware, and which are likely to have a material effect on the outcome of proceedings" (2.7).

In Chapter 4 you will also find some helpful guidelines on what to do when you are in disagreement with your client (see 4.3.2). You will also find guidance on how to avoid misconduct or unethical behaviour when giving an undertaking to the court or other legal professionals (see 4.4.4).

Ethical behaviour therefore also extends to the way in which an advocate manages themselves and their work (see SoSC D) and how an advocate treats others (see SoSC C). An advocate will build relationships with others whether this is the client, members of the public (for example witnesses and jurors) or other professionals such as barristers or experts or the judiciary and members of court staff (see the discussion in Chapter 4). At all times an advocate must behave appropriately and maintain professionalism with the client (see SoSC C2) and with others (see SoSC C3).

## 1.4.1 Conflict between the Principles and the Code

Where two or more Principles and Codes of Conduct conflict, an advocate is expected to follow the one that best serves the public interest. If an advocate is unclear as to the correct course of action to take, then the SRA and the Law Society encourage solicitors to contact their ethics helplines (see details on their websites, which are listed at the end of this chapter).

The SRA and the Law Society have also issued practice guidance, which can be found on their websites. These include guidance on how to avoid offensive communications (SRA Warning Notice on Offensive Communications) and the Law Society Practice Note: Social Media on how to avoid making offensive comments on social media. This follows a number of disciplinary proceedings brought against lawyers as a result of their use of Twitter and other social media platforms.

Legal professionals can be sued for negligence, or they can be subject to criminal proceedings and this includes advocates. Practice decisions should therefore be taken after carefully weighing up all the available evidence and information. This should involve undertaking a risk-based assessment and choosing a course of action that is not tainted simply by motives to benefit oneself. Such decisions should stand up to scrutiny by others and be transparent, rational and objective. The expectation is that when deciding on the possible actions to take, the decision will be informed by a desire to be honest and to always act with integrity. Go to the end of this chapter to try some exercises on decision-making.

In particular, remember that:

A.   An ethical advocate is expected to resist any pressure to act unethically.
B.   An ethical advocate is expected to respect equality, diversity and inclusivity.
C.   An ethical advocate is expected to recognise when they have made mistakes and take appropriate action to put things right.

## 1.5  Working within the Limits of Competency and under Supervision

Part of acting ethically is being able to recognise when mistakes are made and how to correct them and not being afraid to ask for help. Learning from mistakes and accepting the feedback of others is an important skill in the development of competency and the professional self. Do not be afraid to admit when work is beyond your capability and knowledge as it would be worse to undertake work that you do not have the relevant experience to complete to the standards required. Using experts to help fill gaps in your own knowledge is necessary and an important part of the collaborative way of working that takes place when putting together an effective case strategy.

As indicated earlier, if you are unclear about how best to proceed, you should always seek further guidance from your professional body. There are resources and guidelines available on the websites for the Law Society and the SRA as well as practice helplines.

## Disciplinary Proceedings

### 1.5.1  Misconduct

When things go wrong, it is likely to have serious consequences for an advocate who has not behaved professionally or ethically. An incompetent or unethical advocate is likely to bring the legal profession into disrepute by causing harm or loss to members of the public. Such advocates are also likely to face disciplinary proceedings brought by the regulator of their profession. Inappropriate or unethical behaviour could lead to disciplinary proceedings and a finding of professional misconduct being made by a tribunal. Professional misconduct has been defined in *Walker v Bar Standards Board* [2013] (unreported 19 September 2013) as misconduct, which can be "properly regarded as serious" and must be "more than trivial". Allegations of professional misconduct will lead to an advocate being investigated and possibly disciplined by the Solicitors' Disciplinary Tribunal ('SDT').

Disciplinary bodies and panels such as the SRA and SDT will also be mindful of the overarching objectives set out in s. 1 of the Legal Services Act 2007 relating to (1) the protection and promotion of the public interest, (2) supporting the rule of law, (3) improving access to justice, (4) protecting and promoting the interests of consumers, (5) promoting competition in legal services, and (6) encouraging its independence, strength and diversity, (7) increasing public understanding of their rights and (8) promoting and maintaining adherence to professional principles.

Even if the lack of competence is not serious enough to merit disciplinary proceedings it could still lead to the making of a wasted costs order against the advocate under the Senior Courts Act 1981, s. 51(6) as inserted by the Courts and Legal Services Act 1990, s. 4. This section provides that the court may "order the legal or other representative concerned to meet, the whole of any wasted costs or such part of them as may be determined in accordance with rules of court".

## 1.5.2  Solicitors' Disciplinary Tribunal

The Solicitors Disciplinary Tribunal ('SDT') is the body that hears and determines allegations of professional misconduct or breaches of the SRA Standards and Regulations. Its powers derive from the Solicitors Act 1974 (as amended by the Courts and Legal Services Act 1990). The Solicitors Regulation Authority ('SRA') will investigate complaints and refer serious matters to the SDT.

The SDT functions as an independent tribunal with the power to discipline solicitors (see Solicitors Act 1974, s. 47). The SDT decides cases based on the evidence that the SRA and others have collected and presented to it. The Tribunal also has jurisdiction to determine allegations of misconduct against employees of solicitors such as 'solicitors' clerks' as well as trainee solicitors, solicitors, former solicitors, registered European lawyers, registered foreign lawyers and recognised bodies. As one of the roles of the SRA is to prosecute cases for non-compliance with its standards, the SRA will be represented at SDT hearings as well. Respondents will also be represented (if they choose). The SDT will apply the Solicitors (Disciplinary Proceedings) Rules 2019 to the Tribunal process.

Like courts, the SDT rules confirm an "overriding objective" to "deal with cases justly and at proportionate cost" (see 2019 Rules, rule 4). The standard of proof applied in the proceedings is the civil standard of proof (see rule 5). Cases are heard by a panel of two solicitors and one lay member. All SDT panel members are appointed by the Master of the Rolls. Unless the Tribunal decides otherwise, all cases are heard in public (rule 35). Costs orders can be made and will carry 8% interest in accordance with the Judgments Act 1838, s. 17.

The SDT also acts as an appellate body for licensed bodies regulated by the SRA where the SRA has issued sanctions such as a rebuke or a fine. In respect of solicitors, the appellate body is the High Court.

The decisions of the SDT are published on its website: www.solicitorstribunal.org.uk.

### 1.5.3  The Role of the SRA

The SRA will decide whether or not to refer matters to the SDT for sanctions. You will find some information on the matters it takes into account in its Guidance on Issuing Disciplinary Tribunal Proceedings (this can be found on the SRA website: www.sra .org.uk). If the SRA Principles, Code of Conduct or Solicitors Account Rules have been breached then a referral to the SDT will take place. The main test is:

1.   Whether there is a realistic prospect of the Tribunal making an order if the allegation is referred to it, and
2.   It is in the public interest to make the referral.

There must be sufficient evidence available and the alleged conduct must be regarded as sufficiently serious to warrant a referral to the SDT.

The SRA has its own investigatory powers and can impose its own sanctions. The disciplinary process is detailed in the SRA Regulatory and Disciplinary Rules. Investigations can take place based on written evidence only or after a hearing in private before an adjudication panel. However, only the SDT can impose a sanction of striking a solicitor from the Roll so that they are unable to practice again. As such if, after the SRA has conducted an investigation, it considers the evidence warrants the more serious sanction of striking off the Roll or other sanctions that only the SDT has the power to make then it must refer the matter to the SDT.

The SRA approach to its investigatory powers is set out in the SRA Enforcement Strategy.

### 1.5.4  SRA Enforcement Strategy

The SRA has a written document which sets out its approach to enforcement. It will investigate "serious breaches" that the Enforcement Strategy defines as including "serious misconduct", serious breaches of the Codes of Conduct, Principles or Solicitors Accounts Rules as well as convictions and cautions. To assess seriousness the SRA will consider aggravating factors (matters that tend to make the conduct more serious) such as taking advantage of a vulnerable client or evidence of a pattern of misconduct that has been repeated and mitigating factors (matters that lessen the seriousness of the conduct, for example, taking steps to remedy the loss or harm or showing remorse). The SRA will also consider past conduct and how this impacts the present allegations as well as the degree of harm that has resulted and the level of experience of the person involved. Certain conduct will be considered more serious than others, such as conduct that involves dishonesty, abuse of trust or violent and sexual misconduct.

## 1.5.5 Sanctions
The SRA can impose sanctions such as:

1. Suspension of practising certificate.
2. Impose conditions on practising certificate.
3. Impose a warning.
4. Impose a fine.
5. Impose a rebuke.
6. Refuse admission to the Roll.
7. Restrict non-authorised persons from being employed by a law firm.

The SDT can impose the following sanctions:

1. Reprimand.
2. Unlimited financial penalty (payable to HM Treasury).
3. Restriction order for a definite or indefinite period of time (restrictions imposed on the way/ability to practise).
4. Suspension from practice for an indefinite or definite period (application can be made to resume practice).
5. Striking off the Roll (still possible to apply to be restored to the Roll).
6. No order.
7. Costs order.

In *Fuglers and Others v Solicitors Regulation Authority* [2014] EWHC 179 Popplewell J confirmed that when deciding on the correct sanction to use the disciplinary panel should first assess the seriousness of the misconduct that is alleged, it should then as the second step consider the purpose for which the sanction is to be imposed (see overarching principles in Legal Services Act 2007, s. 1) and then the third and last stage is to choose the appropriate sanction that fulfils the purpose identified.

We will continue to work with the SRA Standards and Regulations in Part B.

# In Summary

## Being Ethical

### (SQE Advocacy Assessed skill – see www.sra.org.uk)

A competent advocate should be able to:

- Follow professional rules, principles and codes of conduct related to standards and regulation and act honestly and with integrity.
- Comply with and observe equality, diversity and inclusion in their treatment of others.
- Understand, identify and observe professional rules, principles and codes of conduct in both working life and social life (where behaviours would impact on life in practice).
- Recognise ethical issues and use effective judgment to solve ethical dilemmas.
- Be selfless, objective, transparent and rational in their decision-taking.
- Show an awareness of and apply professional rules, principles and codes of conduct to accounting and financial matters.
- Deal with unforeseen circumstances by finding appropriate and ethical solutions.
- Avoid unethical behavior that could lead to disciplinary proceedings and/or the imposition of a wasted costs order by the court by resisting pressure to condone or adopt such behaviour.
- Resist any pressures by the client to act unethically and explain the ethical framework that advocates must operate under and manage their expectations.
- Know that where professional rules and codes of conduct conflict, an advocate should follow the one that best serves the public interest.

## Being Professional and Exercising Judgment

### (SQE Advocacy Assessed skill – see www.sra.org.uk)

A competent advocate should be able to:

- Treat clients and others with courtesy and respect including observing equality, diversity and inclusivity.
- Act in the client's best interests and act to achieve the client's intended objectives by assessing, analysing, evaluating evidence and information and making effective judgments.
- Reflect on where and how improvements can be made and recognise when mistakes occur and take appropriate action.

- Recognise when to seek help from others including delegating matters beyond their expertise or seek guidance on ethical behaviours or ask for support to solve ethical dilemmas.
- Be sensitive to the individual characteristics of others and use communication that is appropriate to the situation and takes account of the recipient.
- Use appropriate language that is not offensive and also language that is clear and succinct and easy for the client or others to understand.
- Keep skills and knowledge up to date and take responsibility for professional learning and development.
- Supervise the work of others to ensure shared values about correct behaviours and to eliminate the risks of unethical behaviour by employees or those connected to the firm.
- Manage available resources efficiently and in a way that ensures the high standards in practice that society expects of the profession and be prepared to adapt to new ways of working and new technology and developments in the delivery of legal services.
- Respond promptly and appropriately to client concerns and complaints and follow internal complaints procedures.

# Managing Yourself and Your Work

### (SQE Advocacy Assessed skill – see www.sra.org.uk)

A competent advocate should be able to:

- Clarify client instructions to avoid mistakes and misunderstandings.
- Use all available resources in an efficient way so that work activities can be planned and executed.
- Control budgets and have a good grasp of resource needs and other financial matters to complete work in practice.
- Manage their time effectively by meeting deadlines and dealing with unforeseen circumstances as they arise.
- Keep the client informed of progress at regular intervals.
- Pay attention to detail so as to ensure high standards of work and eradicate errors.

## Key Practice Case

The case of *Arthur JS Hall & Co v Simons and Ansell and Others* [2000] UKHL 38 concerned conjoined appeals of three separate cases. One of the cases related to a building dispute and the other two cases related to family proceedings. Solicitors' negligence was alleged in all three cases. The question for the court was whether an advocate should continue to have immunity for prosecution in criminal proceedings or a claim being brought against them in civil proceedings for the way they handled their client's case at trial. The House of Lords recognised the difficulties of retaining the common law position in an earlier case that confirmed advocate immunity. This was because ultimately the nature and purpose of civil and criminal litigation was to protect public interests and not private interests.

The House of Lords had previously decided in a landmark case in 1967 (*Rondel v Worsley* [1969] 1 AC 191) that it was in the public interest for barristers to retain their immunity from suit in respect of the conduct of litigation. This decision did not specifically extend to solicitor advocates. However, this immunity was removed for both barristers and solicitor advocates following the decision in *Arthur JS Hall*. As a result of this decision an advocate no longer has immunity from either being sued in the civil courts or being prosecuted in the criminal courts.

The House of Lords held that an advocate's immunity in civil proceedings was no longer defensible for the following reasons:

> In civil litigation, defining the boundaries of what constitutes advocacy and would therefore qualify for the advocacy immunity is a serious problem not capable of satisfactory solution. The position has been made more difficult by the CPR. There is not a single moment of confrontation. The exercise of advocacy extends over a series of processes of which the trial is only one and the advocacy may be conducted as much in writing as orally.

In terms of criminal litigation, the court noted that the criminal advocate takes on a public duty to enforce the criminal law to see justice done in public and therefore advocates should not enjoy a different treatment to other participants:

> The prosecuting advocate has a duty to see that the prosecution case is, on behalf of the Crown, presented effectively and fairly. That of the defending advocate is to see that the defendant has a fair trial, that the prosecution case is properly probed and tested both in fact and in law and that his factual and legal defences are properly placed before the court supported by the available evidence and arguments.

The court noted advocates, like other professionals, were bound by ethical codes. In addition, they owed a duty to the court. Any advocate acting ethically and following their duty to the court would be unlikely to be prosecuted or sued and that was essentially an implicit protection that remained despite the decision. The House of Lords was of the firm view that to leave the question of immunity from suit for Parliament to decide (by passing appropriate legislation) would have "the unfortunate consequences of plunging both branches of the legal profession in England into a state of uncertainty for a prolonged period". Lord Millett took the view that a blanket policy on professional immunity would also be hard to justify in light of the European Convention on Human Rights 1950.

## Practice Tips

- Remember that advocacy is a craft that can be improved upon with experience and training and so always keep your skills and knowledge up to date.
- Ensure that you familiarise yourself with the rules and codes of conduct for your profession.
- If you are in any doubt as to how to make an ethical decision then refer to guidance from your professional body or contact their practice advice helpline (where relevant) – see information at the end of this chapter.

## Practice Risks

- Failure to acquaint yourself with professional rules and codes of conduct.
- Undue pressure from the client that could lead to unethical behaviour on your part.
- Unilaterally taking action that would be regarded as unethical.
- Failure to seek advice from your professional body when you are unclear how to proceed in terms of conflicting ethical dilemmas.
- Assuming that ethical behaviour only applies when you are at work.

## EXERCISE A

### Test Your Knowledge – Problem Scenario

Refer to the SRA Standards and Regulations and consider the following problem scenario:

You are an advocate involved in your first criminal trial. You are acting for the defendant in a theft trial. Before trial, and as part of the disclosure process, the prosecution sends a list of the defendant's previous convictions to you. The list shows that the defendant has five previous convictions (two for GBH and three for ABH). Your client however tells you that the prosecution has missed two convictions, these are both for theft and were committed in the last 12 months.

Your client says that it would not help his case if the prosecution were to be made aware of their omission.

Which rules/principles/code of conduct would you need to consider in order to decide how to proceed?

**Go to Part C for a suggested answer.**

---

**EXERCISE B**

**Test Your Knowledge – MCQs**

*Test One*

You are due to represent a claimant client at a personal injury trial in which the client seeks extensive damages for a debilitating back injury. You are waiting for the client to attend court when you see him get out of his car and run to the court building and enter the court using his crutches. What would you do? Select ONE of the following:

1. Pretend that you have not seen the client running because you have a duty of confidentiality to the client and what you have seen would prejudice his case.
2. Quickly approach the client and tell him to be careful about his movements and behaviour in court and explain that you have seen him running from the car park.
3. Immediately inform your opponent and the court about what you have seen.
4. Take your client to one side and explain that what you have seen means that you cannot present any case on his behalf that would involve presenting evidence (including calling and/or examining witnesses) that would suggest his back injury is so debilitating that it prevents him from running. You will need to stop representing him if he disagrees.
5. Tell the judge, but not your opponent, what you have seen. This is because you have a duty to the court.

*Test Two*

You are acting for a defendant client in a criminal trial for murder. The defendant has raised a defence of diminished responsibility. Your expert, who is due to give evidence in the next 30 minutes, takes you to one side and says that she has some reservations about the defendant's defence and the conclusions contained in her earlier report. The expert asks you what she should do. How would you reply?

1. Tell the expert that it is now too late for her to change her evidence and she will not be allowed to refer to her reservations during her testimony and so should keep quiet.
2. As the evidence she wishes to give is unlikely to help your client's case, tell the expert that she must give evidence that supports her previous report.
3. Accept that the expert will have to refer to her reservations when giving evidence and if she does then you can deal with this through your questioning and witness examination during the trial.
4. Tell the court and your opponent that you will no longer be calling this expert because she is ill and cannot come to court.
5. Tell the client to plead guilty, as their chance of reducing the charge of murder to one of manslaughter is now unlikely.

**Go to Part C for the suggested answers.**

## Self-Reflection Checklist

| What **three** important things have you learnt from this chapter? | 1 | 2 | 3 |
|---|---|---|---|
| Set out **three** additional steps that you need to take to learn the skills in this chapter in more detail | 1 | 2 | 3 |

# References

## Books

E Hoyle and PD John, *Professional Knowledge and Professional Practice* (Cassell, 1995).
R Pound, *The Lawyer from Antiquity to Modern Times* (West Publishing, 1953).

## Journal Articles

A Boon, J Flood and J Webb, 'Postmodern Professions? The Fragmentation of Legal Education and the Legal Profession' (2005) 32 (3) Journal of Law and Society 473.
S Lester, 'Professional Standards, Competence and Capability' (2014) 4 (1) Higher Education Skills and Work-Based Learning 31.
AC Peng and D Kim, 'A Meta-Analytical Test of the Differential Pathways Linking Ethical Leadership to Normative Conduct' (2020) Journal of Organisational Behaviour 1.

## Cases

*Arthur JS Hall & Co v Simons and Ansell and Others* [2000] UKHL 38.
*Beckwith v SRA* [2020] EWHC 3231 (Admin).

*Bolton v The Law Society* [1993] EWCA Civ 32.

*Fuglers and Others v Solicitors Regulation Authority* [2014] EWHC 179.

*Hoodless v Financial Services Authority* [2003] UKFTT 007 (FSM).

*Ivey v Genting Casinos (UK) Ltd (t/a Crockfords)* [2017] UKSC 67).

*Kaza Ltd and Another v Akcil and Others* [2019] EWCA Civ 891.

*Leigh Ravenscroft v Canal and River Trust* [2016] EWHC 2282.

*Medcalf v Weatherill and Another* [2002] UKHL 27.

*Newell-Austin v Solicitors Regulation Authority* [2017] Med LR 194.

*Scott v Solicitors Regulation Authority* [2016] EWHC 1256.

*SRA v Lewis* [2018] SDT Case No. 11856-2018.

*Walker v Bar Standards Board* (unreported 19 September 2013).

*Williams v Solicitors Regulation Authority* [2017] EWHC 1478 (Admin).

*Wingate and Evans v Solicitors Regulation Authority; Solicitors Regulation Authority v Malins* [2018] EWCA Civ 366.

## Legislation

Courts and Legal Services Act 1990.

Equality Act 2010.

European Convention on Human Rights 1950.

Legal Services Act 2007.

Senior Courts Act 1981.

Solicitors Act 1974.

## Procedure Rules

Civil Procedure Rules.

Criminal Procedure Rules.

Solicitors (Disciplinary Proceedings) Rules 2019.

## Codes of Conduct and Guidance

Bar Standards Board Handbook and Code of Conduct.

Law Society Practice Note: Social Media.

SRA Enforcement Strategy.

SRA Principles 2019.

SRA Regulatory and Disciplinary Rules.

SRA Standards and Regulations Handbook 2019.

SRA Statement of Solicitor Competence 2019.

SRA Warning Notice on Offensive Communications.

## Reports

G Hunter, J Jacobson and A Kirby, *Judicial Perceptions of the Quality of Criminal Advocacy* (2018, Institute for Criminal Policy Research and Birkbeck, University of London).

Solicitors' Regulation Authority, *Assuring Advocacy Standards: Consultation August 2019* (2019, SRA).

# Websites

www.barstandardsboard.org.uk
www.judiciary.uk
www.lawsociety.org.uk
www.sra.org.uk
www.solicitorstribunal.org.uk
www.supportthroughcourt.org
www.theadvocatesgateway.org

# 2

# Developing Skills of Case Planning and Analysis

## Effective Preparation, Research Skills and Strategy

1.  Always ensure that you have read and know the details of your case.
2.  Understand your client's goals and objectives.
3.  Obtain relevant information through effective questioning of the client.
4.  Conduct relevant legal research.
5.  Be prepared to negotiate to achieve an effective and suitable compromise.
6.  Draft documents in clear, precise and accurate language that reflect court requirements.
7.  Adhere to procedural rules and court processes.

## 2.1 Introduction

This chapter will focus on the preliminary stages of (1) fact finding, (2) legal research and (3) case planning. These align with the technical legal practice aspects of the SRA Statement of Solicitor Competence ('SoSC', Figure 2.1) included under B1 (obtaining relevant facts), B2 (undertaking legal research), B3 (developing and advising on relevant options and strategies), B6 (negotiating solutions) and B7 (planning, managing and progressing cases). We will also continue to develop these technical practice skills in Part B (criminal and civil litigation).

Case preparation is an important first step for an advocate. Even before a case reaches trial, competency is called for at the early stage of pre-trial case preparation. In this chapter we will also focus on the skills shown in Figure 2.2.

DOI: 10.4324/9781003134770-4

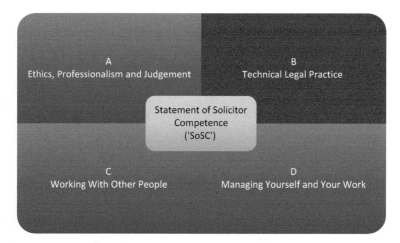

**Figure 2.1** Statement of Solicitor Competence.

**Figure 2.2** Chapter Content.

## 2.2 Fact Finding

It will be important for the advocate to know his/her case well and be able to identify and describe the issues. This will allow categorisation of the issues in terms of levels of strengths and weaknesses and simplicity and complexity as well as their importance to the client's overall goal. First the advocate must elicit facts that are relevant and this will include facts that support and strengthen a case as well as facts that weaken a case. In addition both the civil and criminal procedural rules require cases to be prepared in accordance with the overriding objective. This includes dealing with cases by considering the complexity of the issues or the gravity of the offence. We will look at the overriding objective in more detail in Chapter 4 and again in Chapters 5 (criminal) and 6 (civil). These are all parts of the so-called technical legal skills and abilities that an advocate will need to acquire.

# How to Obtain Relevant Facts from a Client

## 2.2.1 Interview Skills

Effective preparation first starts with the gathering of information from the client and this will usually be done at the first client interview. To prepare a case effectively, an advocate must first understand what the client's case is about and what the client wishes to achieve in terms of desired outcomes. Relevant information can be obtained from the client by using a combination of questioning and active listening.

Active listening means not just hearing what the client is saying but observing how they say it. This is done by observing their body language and behaviour and allows the listener to pick up on signals and clues about how the client is feeling, the impact events have had on them and whether there is something more the client would like to say but has not. This method of listening also enables the advocate to be sensitive about when they should respond and when they should remain silent or when the client may need encouragement to continue with their story.

An advocate should be able to elicit relevant information from the client by using a mix of 'open' and 'closed' questions. An 'open' question is one that allows the client to give the information freely and in their own way. An example of such a question is "can you tell me what happened on that day?" A 'closed' question is used to restrict the length of the answer that the client can give, or to elicit just a 'yes' or 'no' response from the client. For example, "when did this happen?" or "was it raining on that day?" It is useful to use closed questioning when fact-checking during the interview.

Taking notes will also help in the retention of information but reading the information back to the client at various stages in the interview also serves to ensure the accuracy of the facts recorded.

## 2.2.2 Identify the Client's Goals

Before case preparation can begin, it is important for an advocate to identify and understand the client's goal(s). These may arise from the client's personal circumstances or their commercial needs. The client may have several objectives, but these should be identified in order of priority and any constraints or limitations identified. This may mean that you need to explore more than one goal or objective with the client and prioritise these according to an agreed case strategy. For example, a commercial client who is involved in a construction dispute with a long-standing client may have other interests to serve in terms of retaining the goodwill of that client, preserving their own reputation in the industry and finding ways to ensure that the project is completed within a non-negotiable deadline. This may mean that arbitration rather than litigation is the best method forward and many construction contracts include mandatory arbitration clauses for this reason.

In civil cases, it is important to be clear as to whether the client's goals can be achieved by negotiating a settlement rather than proceeding with litigation. It will usually be necessary to consider whether alternative dispute resolution such as mediation, arbitration or conciliation would achieve the client's goals (we will discuss this further in Chapter 3). This offers an opportunity to explore the issues in a way that will find a resolution that is acceptable to both parties and reduce costs.

In civil cases, pre-action protocols and court procedural rules emphasise that parties should seek alternative means of resolution wherever possible (we will consider this in more detail below at 2.8.2). Negotiating a settlement can achieve mutual benefits for both parties in a fair, open and transparent way and might even result in better outcomes than litigation which is itself lengthy and costly. The client's goals may therefore change from one of "what do I want to win by going to court?" to "what am I prepared to settle for to avoid going to court?"

An advocate should be cautious of advising too soon, as obtaining further information may be necessary or the advocate may have to conduct further legal research. It is better to promise to get back to the client with detailed advice rather than promising that you can solve the problem on the spot!

Once the advocate has gathered information and identified the client's goals, he/she should then examine all elements of the client's case in detail to ascertain whether the client's goals are realistic and obtainable. This will mean familiarisation with the case to the point that the advocate becomes knowledgeable about all aspects, including the elements of the charge (criminal case) or claim (civil case) as well as the factual and legal issues. Case analysis and evaluation are essential to the mastery of the arguments needed to persuade the court.

## 2.2.3 Know the History of your Case

To succeed in a case, an advocate must be familiar with the case including evaluating the strengths and weaknesses of the case with reference to the facts ('factual analysis'). This means an advocate will have to be able to assimilate information and identify possible consequences for the client in taking different actions. This will involve recognising when further documentation or other forms of evidence are required, when it is necessary to conduct legal research or obtain expert advice and how to interpret legislation and case law and other sources of law. An advocate may also have to discuss alternative forms of funding or advice with a client, and it is therefore important that an advocate always has an eye on costs.

The factual background of a case will contain key dates and events. It is necessary to first understand how the main events unfolded. It is helpful to prepare a Chronology of Key Dates and Events to help with the assimilation of the facts. A version of this can also be included in trial bundles to assist the court.

For an example of how to prepare a Chronology of Key Dates and Events, consider the following set of facts in a civil case:

## Case Example 1

Summary of Facts – Civil Case

*You act for the defendants (Mr and Mrs Trelorn). On 12 September last year, the claimant (River Interior Designs) agreed to carry out landscaping work at the home of the defendants. River Interior Designs is owned by Jack River who is also a neighbour of the defendants. The defendants allege that during a dinner party at their house on 12 September, the claimant offered to help 'improve' their garden through a redesign. This was to be a gift for the defendants' wedding anniversary. On 16 September, it is alleged that the claimant visited the defendants' home in order to draw up preliminary plans for the redesign of the garden. Both parties agree that during those discussions, the claimant informed the defendants' that the work would involve a cost of £10,000. It is disputed that the claimant made it clear to the defendants that this would be the price they would be expected to actually pay for the work to be carried out. The claimant wrote to the defendants on 23 September enclosing receipts for a total of £2,000 representing materials that had been purchased for the garden. On 28 September the claimant and his wife attended the defendants' wedding anniversary celebrations. The claimant did not arrive with any gifts on that day and so the defendants say that they continued to believe that the landscaping of their garden was to be the claimant's gift to them. On 9 October the claimant began work at the defendants' premises. On 11 October, work had to be halted after it was discovered that the roots from an oak tree situated in the defendants' garden was causing problems for the groundwork. The defendants allege that they offered to pay the claimant the sum of £1,500 for the removal of the tree, as they did not want the claimant to undergo any additional expense. The defendants emphatically deny that this offer constituted any acceptance of responsibility for the overall cost of the landscaping project. The landscaping project was completed on 18 October. On 21 October, the claimant sent the defendants an invoice for £11,500. To this date, the invoice remains unpaid.*

There is a large amount of information contained in the narrative above. Part of the role of the advocate is to separate the relevant issues from the irrelevant issues and identify the facts that are agreed and the facts that are in dispute. Ordering the narrative by key dates and events helps to highlight the facts in issue.

The events and key dates might be put in chronological order as follows:

| Event | Key Date |
|---|---|
| Oral agreement between the parties (disputed) | 12 September [year] |
| Discussion of contract terms and price (disputed) | 16 September [year] |
| First invoice with receipts (disputed) | 23 September [year] |
| Defendants' wedding anniversary party | 28 September [year] |
| Landscaping work begins | 9 October [year] |
| Interruption to works and defendants' acceptance of cost of £1,500 for additional work | 11 October [year] |
| Completion of landscaping works | 18 October [year] |
| Final invoice of £11,500 sent | 21 October [year] |

Preparing a table of this nature will help to identify the so-called 'known knowns' (Snowden and Boone, 2007). In the context of case preparation, these so-called 'known knowns' in an advocacy situation can be thought of as essentially the undisputed facts of the case that are discernible and easy to prove.

The table will also help you to identify the issues that are in dispute and in particular, what additional information you require (the 'unknown knowns') in order to be able to plan and prepare your case strategy and this may involve obtaining additional information and investigating a number of different options.

## 2.2.4 Identify the Issues

Identifying the factual and legal issues that are relevant to the case will then help you to separate out the disputed and undisputed facts and to identify relevant authorities (e.g. cases, legislation, books of authority) that you will need to use to help you to prove your client's case.

The factual issues can often be identified by using a very simple questioning structure of, 'What', 'How' and 'Why'. For each issue identified, you should then highlight a corresponding legal issue that may arise.

For example, if we turn back to **Case Example 1**, a relevant legal issue relates to whether the contract can be said to be a valid one given that it was an oral agreement with unclear terms. This might give rise to a legal issue arising from principles in cases such as *Felthouse v Bindley* [1862] EWHC CP J35 where it was held that a contract cannot be imposed on a person through their silence and silence does not necessarily constitute acceptance.

Similarly, if we take a tort action such as medical negligence, your 'What' 'How' and 'Why' analysis might look like Figure 2.3.

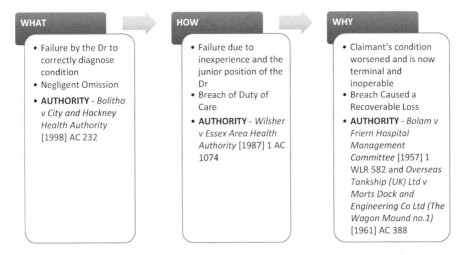

**Figure 2.3** What, How and Why Analysis.

Sometimes the issue may be neither a factual nor a legal one but instead an expert one that requires evidence from an expert. It is important to recognise when the determination of an issue is outside of your expertise and where it is necessary to seek additional help in progressing the case. An expert might, for example, include a medical expert, a surveyor or a forensic accountant. This will also require you to undertake further legal research as to the most suitable expert and the nature of the opinion required from them.

## How to Recognise when Additional Information Is Needed

## 2.3 Obtaining Additional Documents and Materials

During preparation for trial, the parties will disclose to each other the documents that they wish to rely upon in support of their case. In criminal proceedings disclosure is governed by the Criminal Procedure and Investigations Act 1996, s. 3, the Criminal Procedure and Investigations Act (Code of Practice) Order 2015 and the CrimPR Part 15. In civil proceedings disclosure is governed by CPR Part 31 and PD 31A–31C. The duty of disclosure is a continuing duty until proceedings are concluded. The disclosure rules essentially provide for transparency and fairness. In advance of the trial, parties are expected to disclose the documents that they will rely upon.

In criminal proceedings, the prosecution must also disclose any previously undisclosed material that they believe might undermine the case for the prosecution. Non-disclosure of relevant information might lead to the jury being misled and result in a wrongful conviction. In addition, the accused and his/her representatives do not have the same time and resources available to them to investigate a case in the way that the prosecution has. However, in the Crown Court, the defendant must give disclosure through a 'defence statement' (see CrimPR Part 15.4) whereas in a Magistrates' Court the provision of a defence statement is optional.

In civil proceedings, a party must make 'standard disclosure' (see CPR PD 31A para 1.1–1.4). This is restricted to documents on which they rely in support of their case and any documents which adversely affect their case or another party's case (see CPR Part 31.6). Disclosure is through the provision of a 'list of documents' that are to be disclosed (see CPR Part 31.10 and PD 31A para 3.1–4.7). The other party then has a right to inspect the documents (see CPR 31.3).

Whilst the process of disclosure is prescribed by the rules, the exact documents to be disclosed are not. Therefore, when an advocate receives prosecution disclosure (criminal cases) or a list of documents for disclosure (civil cases) they should consider the documents very carefully and decide whether further documents are needed because, for example, there are gaps in the sequence of the documents provided or a particular document throws some light on the existence of other important documents. An application can be made for what is known as 'specific disclosure'. The process for making such an application in criminal cases is set out in CrimPR Part 15.5 and in civil cases under CPR Part 31.12. In all cases, the party making the application must describe the material or document sought and explain why they believe it is in the other party's possession.

It is important to ensure that the client brings in all relevant documents at your first meeting with them and at subsequent meetings. If documents or other materials are held by third parties, e.g. employers or a GP then make sure you obtain copies from those third parties directly by getting the client to sign an authorisation form. Some pre-action protocols will specify what documents you should send to your opponent and what they should send to you.

It is also possible to make an application for pre-action disclosure in civil proceedings (see CPR 31.16). This is disclosure of documents or information before proceedings start, and this may be necessary to help clarify the correct defendant to sue or even if there is a cause of action. When making such an application, the court must be satisfied that the parties would be parties to subsequent proceedings and the documents sought would normally form part of standard disclosure. Remember it may be necessary to prove the authenticity of documents before they can be admitted so always request originals.

Privileged documents (on which a claim of confidentiality is made) or documents on which a claim for public interest immunity is made are excluded from disclosure and we will discuss this further in Chapter 4.

In civil proceedings, another method of obtaining further information about a statement of case is to ask the court to order that the other party answer a series of questions to clarify their case and provide further information. This can be done in a formal way as a Further Information document under CPR Part 18 and must contain a statement of truth (see CPR Part 22). We will discuss this requirement again in Chapter 6.

## 2.3.1 Obtaining Expert Evidence

Often, consideration of the material facts of a case may require an understanding of non-legal matters, for example, scientific, actuarial, or IT knowledge that is beyond the expertise of a lawyer. Alternatively, the area of law may be one with which the lawyer is unfamiliar. In those circumstances, research alone may not produce the necessary level of detailed knowledge needed to prepare a good case. As such, advocates should know when to seek assistance from an expert. As part of trial preparation, expert evidence may be crucial to establishing proof. Such evidence will need to be independent, objective and unbiased. The court will only allow expert evidence to be called on matters that go beyond the expertise of the judge or jury. When an expert is used in court proceedings, their duty will be to the court and not to the party instructing them. They will also be required to prepare a written report for the court.

---

### Case Example 2

Consider the following set of facts in a criminal case:

Summary of Facts – Criminal Case

*You act for the defendant. The defendant (D) has been charged with murder. It is alleged that he fatally stabbed the victim (V), a complete stranger, who had asked for directions to a nearby street. D says in evidence that at the time of the stabbing, he was suffering a psychotic episode having previously drunk a whole bottle of whisky and consumed cocaine. When police officers arrived at the scene, they found D staring at the knife in his hands, shaking his head and saying, "how did this happen?" He was arrested and charged with murder. D says that he did not have the necessary intent to kill as he was acting with diminished responsibility. Whilst on remand in prison, D was assessed by a forensic psychiatrist, Dr Keefer who carried out a psychiatric evaluation on the instructions of D's defence team. Dr Keefer noted that prior to the stabbing, D had been prescribed a well-known antipsychotic medication for treating mood disorders. Dr Keefer recorded in his report that D had a history of drug abuse and had previously mixed drugs and alcohol with his medication and that whilst he had a clinical pattern of paranoid psychosis, there was no known history of violence. However, prior to the incident D had been put on a new brand of medication that he had not taken before. Dr Keefer did not consider that D was medically or legally insane.*

---

In the above scenario the client's goal is to avoid a charge of murder and to establish a partial defence of diminished responsibility. The defence of diminished responsibility (if accepted by the jury) would reduce the offence of murder to manslaughter. The client does not deny the act itself (the unlawful killing causing death) but maintains that he did not have the necessary mental element (the *mens rea*) for murder, namely intention.

Below is one example of a table that an advocate might prepare to identify and categorise the issues relating to the defence of diminished responsibility:

| Issues | Strengths | Weaknesses | Evidential Simplicity | Evidential Complexity | Method of proof |
|---|---|---|---|---|---|
| 1. What caused the paranoid psychosis? (**expert and legal issue**) | An underlying illness or the combined effect of all these triggers would more likely support a defence of diminished responsibility | Voluntary intoxication with drink and drugs may weaken a defence of diminished intoxication | Existence of expert evidence confirming paranoid psychosis | Expert evidence is vague on actual causal link and so may need to explore this through questioning at trial but cannot control the answers given | Expert's report/oral testimony |
| 2. What were D's levels of awareness about having a knife in his hands? (**factual and legal issue**) | Reduced levels of awareness would support impaired ability for the test of diminished responsibility. D's words at the scene of the crime may suggest low awareness | High levels of awareness would not tend to show that there was impaired ability. D may have been aware of the knife immediately prior to the stabbing | Defendant's evidence could be dealt with in examination-in-chief | Defendant may exercise right of silence at trial or make a poor witness if he gives evidence. The police officer may not be able to recall events and the police officer's testimony and notebook are arguably admissible hearsay | Defendant's oral testimony/police officer's oral testimony/police officer's notebook as admissible hearsay (see Chapter 5) |
| 3. Is there any suggestion that violence is a consequence of the medication and/or intoxication? (**factual and expert issue**) | D had been placed on new medication which might have produced as yet unknown effects including violence | No previous history of violence when on previous medication | Violence might be easily explained as out of character and caused by an external element and negate intention | Further evidence needed about the side effects of the new drug and these may not yet be known or recorded as it is a new drug | Expert's report/oral testimony |

The above scenario raises legal issues in relation to whether the requirements for a defence of diminished responsibility under s. 2 of the Homicide Act 1957 (as amended by the Coroners and Justice Act 2009, s. 52) have been met. There is a reverse burden of proof that is placed on the defendant under this Act.

This requires the defendant to prove that there was an abnormality of mental functioning that was caused by a recognised medical condition that caused substantial impairment in the defendant's ability to either (1) understand the nature of the conduct, or (2) form a rational judgment or (3) exercise self-control. This must in turn provide an explanation for the defendant's actions. Medical evidence is needed to prove this defence, as established in cases such as *R v Dix* [1982] 74 Crim LR. Voluntary and temporary acute intoxication may remove the ability to rely on this defence as seen in cases such as *R v Dowds* [2012] EWCA Crim 281.

Using the above method is one way to help you to identify any risks to your client in pursuing this defence as well as highlighting where information is missing or inconsistent or where further legal research is needed.

## 2.3.2 Evidence Gathering

It is important at an early stage to identify the nature and type of evidence that will be necessary to support the client's case. Evidence must be relevant to the issues in dispute between the parties and also capable of settling the issue by proving it ('probative') to the correct standard. In civil proceedings, evidence must prove the issues to the standard of 'on a balance of probabilities'. This is commonly stated as being at least 51% proof or 'more probable than not' as stated by Lord Denning in *Miller v Minister of Pensions* [1947] 2 All ER 372. In the criminal cases the standard of proof is 'beyond reasonable doubt' and this is taken to mean to the point where the judge or jury are 'satisfied so that they are sure' – see the 'sure test' as set out in *R v Summers* (1952) Cr App R 14.

In criminal proceedings the prosecution bears the burden of proving the case and disproving any defences put forward by a defendant – see the remarks of Viscount Sankey LC in *Woolmington v DPP* [1935] AC 462. However, in certain limited circumstances, a defendant will also have a burden of proof for example, certain defences such as diminished responsibility and insanity place the burden of proof on a defendant. If a co-defendant wants to use the confession evidence of another co-defendant they will have to prove it was not obtained in breach of the Police and Criminal Evidence Act ('PACE') 1984 and we will discuss this further in chapter five. Where the burden of proof is reversed onto a defendant in this way then the standard of proof becomes 'on a balance of probabilities'. This was stated in the case of *R v Carr-Briant* [1943] 1 KB 607. An advocate should always be clear as to if and when their client has a burden of proof.

Similarly in civil proceedings the burden of proof rests on the claimant in line with the 'he who asserts must prove' *dictum* – see *Joseph Constantine Steamship Line v Imperial Smelting Corporation* [1942] AC 154. A defendant will have a reverse burden of proof in certain situations such as when asserting contributory negligence by a claimant or relying on an exemption clause in a contract. The standard of proof will however remain 'on a balance of probabilities' for a defendant. The standard of proof in civil proceedings is capable however of changing to the criminal standard. This is because some civil proceedings have a quasi-criminal aspect to them such as confiscation proceedings – see *R v Briggs-Price* [2009] UKHL 19.

Part of the evidence gathering process involves (1) finding documents and then (2) analysing their contents to ascertain their importance to the issues in the case and then (3) evaluating how and if the evidence should be used. It may also be necessary to inspect the '*locus in quo*' (the place where events happened). This is particularly relevant in road traffic accidents in personal injury cases. Photographs should be taken especially if there is a risk that the layout might change. Going back to the scene may also help to jog the client's memory.

It is important to collect evidence at an early stage when events are still fresh in the memories of key witnesses. Evidence must however be both relevant and admissible before it can be used at trial. Evidence is relevant if it is capable of either proving or disproving a disputed fact. In both the civil and criminal courts there are certain rules about the admissibility of specific types of evidence. For example, in criminal proceedings hearsay evidence (out of court statements used to prove the truth of the matter stated within the statement) is inadmissible unless it falls into one of the exceptions found in ss. 116–120 Criminal Justice Act 2003. Another example is that in civil proceedings a witness who is not an expert can only give opinion evidence if it is based on facts perceived by them (Civil Evidence Act 1972, s. 3(2)).

Disproportionate cost or delays may also be reasons for ruling evidence inadmissible. The court retains a judicial discretion to exclude any irrelevant or inadmissible evidence. For example, see s. 78 and s. 82(3) of the Police and Criminal Proceedings Act 1984 in the case of criminal proceedings. The former allows evidence to be excluded if the evidence would have an adverse effect on the fairness of the proceedings and the latter if its prejudicial effect outweighs its probative value (see *R v Sang* [1979] 3 WLR 263 for a full discussion of the general judicial discretion now found under s. 82(3)). In criminal proceedings the admissibility of evidence is decided at a voir dire' (a trial within a trial) or during a preliminary hearing. In civil proceedings the court has wide powers to make orders or exclude evidence as part of its case management powers (see CPR Part 3 and CPR Part 32.1 (2)).

Even if a piece of evidence is relevant and admissible, it may do little more than simply duplicate other evidence that is available in which case an advocate should decide whether it is really necessary to produce the piece of evidence in question at the trial.

If we return to **Case Example 1,** we can consider the relevant and admissible evidence that might be gathered in order to support a case on behalf of the defendants (Mr and Mrs Trelorn). As the claim is a contractual one based on an oral rather than a written contract then the evidence of Mr and Mrs Trelorn becomes important. Witness statements should be obtained from them. These statements should set out in detail their recollection about what exactly was agreed with the claimant on the key dates of 12 September and 16 September. However, other evidence may also be important.

## Confidence Exercise

Re-read Case Example 1. What other types of evidence would you collect from the following categories below?

1. Oral evidence (e.g. through witness statements and/or testimony at court).
2. Documentary evidence (including e.g. photographs and sketches).
3. Expert evidence (reasoned opinion from a person with expertise in the field).
4. Real evidence (physical evidence).

Once you have collected evidence, you must next consider how best to present that evidence at trial. The court appreciates brevity and where possible prefers that the parties agree on the use of evidence.

In civil proceedings, the court relies on written evidence at interim hearings (see CPR Part 32.2(b) but oral evidence at a trial (see CPR Part 32.2(a)). In criminal cases, the court is required to ensure as part of its case management function that the evidence (both disputed and undisputed) is "presented in the shortest and clearest way" (see CrimPR Part 3.2(e)). In civil proceedings, the court can give directions about the issues for which evidence should be presented, the nature of the evidence that should be placed before the court and the way that this should be done (see CPR Part 32.1).

Carrying out a case analysis involves identifying all possible courses of action and the consequences of pursuing each as well as considering the weight of the available evidence and whether this will help the client achieve their goal. The analysis may reveal some constraints in terms of what the client would like to achieve, and these constraints must be identified and discussed with the client. This may require the advocate to manage the client's expectations or prioritise the steps that will be taken to achieve the client's goals.

# Finding and Analysing Material

## 2.4 Legal Research

An advocate will ordinarily use their existing legal knowledge to identify the legal issues involved as the client begins to tell their story. However, an advocate should always check that their understanding of the law is up to date and research any areas of law that they are unfamiliar with. Recognising when legal research is needed is essential to good preparation. The purpose of using sources of authority is to enable an advocate to present a reasoned case with solutions that have previously been accepted by the court as sound and rational.

An advocate should be able to identify the correct resources to use to undertake the research. This may be in the form of court procedural rules, cases, legislation, or other sources of law such as books of authority.

When referring to procedural rules, an advocate must always identify the specific rule (and where applicable) the subsection of the rule that they are relying on in making or opposing the application.

Sometimes the paragraphs or sub-paragraphs must be read in conjunction with another in order to fully understand what is required. It is important to pay attention to whether sub-sections use the words 'or' or 'and' to connect other sub-sections. Let us take the example of the Civil Procedure Rules ('CPR') Part 24.2. This rule provides that:

The court may give summary judgment against a claimant or a defendant on the whole of the claim or on a particular issue if:

(a)  It considers that
    (i)  that claimant has no real prospects of succeeding on the claim or issue; or
    (ii)  that defendant has no real prospect of successfully defending the claim or issue; and
(b)  there is no compelling reason why the case or issue should be disposed of at trial.

An application under CPR 24.2 can therefore rely on either ground 24.2(a)(i) or 24.2(a)(ii) but both grounds must also establish (b) that there is no compelling reason why the case or issue should be disposed of at trial.

We will look at this particular procedural rule in more detail in Part B.

# Using Cases as Precedent

## 2.4.1 Researching Cases

Legal research will involve an advocate finding appropriate cases (often referred to as 'common law') to support the factual and legal arguments that they wish to make. Once they have found the names of useful cases, they will then read the full case in the relevant law report. The reason why it is vital that law reports are read in full is that only a portion of a court's decision is binding:

*ratio decidendi* – This is the reason for deciding the case and is where the legal principle arising from the case is to be found. It is essentially the statement of law that has been applied in deciding the legal problem raised by the facts of the case.

*obiter dicta* – This can be loosely defined as 'things said by the way'. These are additional legal statements made by judges in the case but do not form part of the final decision. Such statements are not binding and are simply the opinion of the judge, though they may be persuasive in arguing a different point of view to show a different approach could or should be taken.

Judgments do not always distinguish between what is the *ratio* and the parts that form obiter only. It requires skill in ascertaining this from reading the cases. This is because a panel of judges can each give different reasons for the decision of the court.

If we take the example of theft in criminal law, we find the *ratio decidendi* in the case of *R v Morris* [1984 AC 320 [332] in the judgment of Lord Roskill. The ratio decidendi provides an interpretation of the meaning of 'appropriation' in s. 3 of the Theft Act 1968. The meaning is taken to include the usurpation or interference of the 'right' (singular) or 'rights' (plural) of the owner. Therefore, any of the rights of an owner could be appropriated.

However, Lord Roskill also included further commentary, which for some time was believed to be part of the *ratio decidendi* and this was that usurpation or interference of those rights could only occur in the absence of the consent of the owner. This part of the decision however conflicted with a previous House of Lords decision in *R v Lawrence* [1972] AC 626 which stated that appropriation could occur even with the consent of the owner.

It took another House of Lords decision in *R v Gomez* [1993] AC 442 to add clarity to the law by stating that Lord Roskill's comment about consent in *R v Morris* was *obiter dicta* whilst the decision about the meaning of appropriation remained the *ratio decidendi*.

However, an advocate who is arguing an appeal can make use of *obiter dicta* comments in previous decisions to try to persuade the judges that the time has come to consider a point of law afresh.

Cases may also be important in setting out a test that needs to be applied to for example, establish criminal liability or obtain a civil remedy. For example, in the case of *American Cyanamid Co (No 1) v Ethicon Ltd* [1975] UKHL 1 the court set out a guideline test to be met before the granting of an injunction which has become known as the 'American Cyanamid Principles'. This requires the court to consider whether:

1. the claimant has a strong or arguable case (this means there must be a serious issue to be determined),
2. whether damages would be an adequate remedy,
3. whether the so-called 'balance of convenience' has been met (this involves weighing the inconvenience or loss to each party of the injunction either being granted or refused) and,
4. whether or not the status quo should be maintained instead.

An advocate's reading of the law can be greatly assisted by the use of what we can term a 'synopsis case'. This can be defined as a case that surveys and summarises the different previous court decisions affecting an area of law and then either clarifies the importance of certain decisions or adds a new principle. An example of a 'synopsis' case would be *R v Jogee* [2016] UKSC 8, which clarified the criminal law in the area of accomplices. The decision in *Jogee* corrected previous case law which had wrongly concluded that foresight was proof of intent rather than merely evidence towards the proof of intent. You will find a helpful list of 'synopsis cases' in Table B in Chapter 5.

## 2.4.2  Research Trail

Legal research often starts with one case leading to the reading of another in order to establish how a legal principle has developed. If we return to **Case Example 2** for example, conducting further legal research about the use of medical evidence to prove diminished responsibility would, as stated, take us to cases such as *R v Dix*. This case tells us that medical evidence is necessary to establish a defence of diminished responsibility. Further research might lead us to cases such as *R v Brennan* [2014] EWCA Crim 2387. This case establishes that an expert who is a forensic psychiatrist might be able to go further and give evidence on the ultimate issue of guilt and that unchallenged medical evidence that supports the defence should be accepted.

In terms of deciding the evidence that might be needed to establish substantial impairment, researching cases such as *R v Golds* [2016] UKSC 61 would help to clarify the extent of the direction that a judge can give to the jury on this issue. The word 'substantial' is a matter of degree but should be regarded as 'weighty' or 'important' and there is no need to define it for the jury beyond what is commonly understood.

There are also resources available that will highlight cases that have placed a particular interpretation on a procedural rule. For example, in civil cases you can find cases that relate to the relevant civil rule that you are searching by using the *White Book* (Sweet & Maxwell), *The Civil Court Practice: The Green Book* (LexisNexis). In criminal cases you can find cases that relate to the relevant rule that you are searching by using books such as *Stone's Justices' Manual for Magistrates' Court* (Butterworths) or *Blackstone's Criminal Practice* (Oxford University Press). The court rules themselves can also be accessed online (www.gov.uk). The Supreme Court has its own set of rules known as the Supreme Court Rules and these can be found on the Supreme Court website (www.supremecourt.uk).[1]

## 2.4.3 Citing Cases

As stated earlier, it is important to note that the court appreciates brevity, therefore, when using cases it is important to use cases that establish a legal principle rather than merely being illustrative of that principle or merely restating it. This is set out in court practice directions – see, for example, the Criminal Practice Direction 2015 (as amended).

However, it may be relevant to also cite cases that follow a similar fact pattern as the facts in your own case.

When citing cases in a skeleton argument, an advocate should always provide the neutral citation followed by the law report reference. A neutral citation is the unique number that HM Courts and Tribunals Service has given to a case and this will first appear when the judgment is first published by the court.

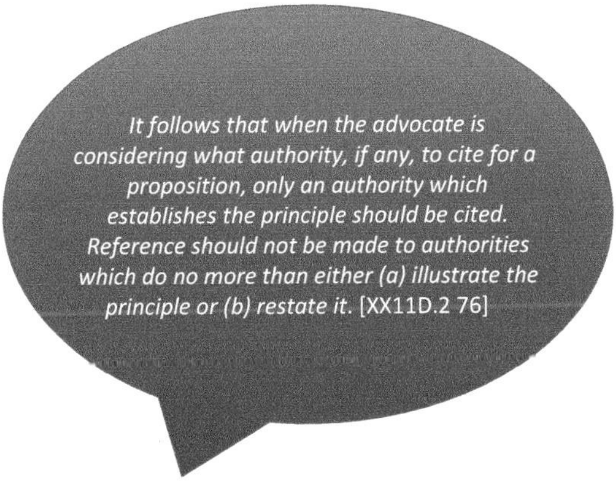

*It follows that when the advocate is considering what authority, if any, to cite for a proposition, only an authority which establishes the principle should be cited. Reference should not be made to authorities which do no more than either (a) illustrate the principle or (b) restate it. [XX11D.2 76]*

**Figure 2.4** Citing Authorities.

---

1 From April 2022 the National Archives will be the main repository for finding all court judgments in England and Wales including judicial review rulings and Tribunal judgments – see www.national-archives.gov.uk.

If, for example, we take the case of *R v Dowds* from **Scenario 2**, the neutral citation given is *R v Dowds* [2012] EWCA Crim 281. 'EW' is an abbreviation for England and Wales and 'CA' is an abbreviation for the Court of Appeal. 'Crim 281' tells us that it is criminal case number 281 for the year 2012.

This neutral citation should then be followed by whatever law report is being used by the advocate (assuming the case has been reported in a law report). For example, the same case can be found reported in the All England Law Reports at [2012] 3 All ER 154. The full case citation required would therefore be *R v Dowds* [2012] EWCA Crim 28, [2012] 3 All ER 154.

The Practice Direction: Citation of Authorities 2012 states that where a case is reported in the official law reports of the Incorporated Council of Law Reporting (AC, QB, ch, fam) then those reports *must* be cited as they are regarded as the most authoritative reports.

Neutral citations were introduced in 2001 by the Practice Directions (Judgments: Form and Citation). Therefore, not all cases will have a neutral citation, although some older cases have been given neutral citations. If a case does not have a neutral citation then in those circumstances you should simply cite the law report reference using the official law reports first (AC, QB, ch, fam).

For details of a full list of law reports and their abbreviations you can use resources from websites such as BAILII, Incorporated Council of Law Reporting or Cardiff Index to Legal Abbreviations.

Some examples of law report abbreviations can be found in the table below:

| | |
|---|---|
| **All ER** | All England Law Reports |
| **WLR** | Weekly Law Reports |
| **AC** | Law Reports: Appeal Cases |
| **QB** | Law Reports: Queen's Bench Division |
| **ECR** | European Court Reports |
| **EHRR** | European Human Rights Report |
| **Cr App R** | Criminal Appeal Reports |
| **UKSC** | Law Reports: Supreme Court |
| **CA** | Court of Appeal |
| **M & W** | Meeson and Welsby's Exchequer Reports |
| **Exch** | Exchequer Reports |
| **Ll LR** | Lloyd's Law Reports |

# Assessing the Relevance of Sources of Law

## 2.5 Researching Legislation

Cases are not the only legal authorities that can be used to support arguments. There are other sources of law that an advocate can draw upon. These include legislation and conventions (such as the European Convention on Human Rights 1950).

Legislation represents the laws that govern the behaviour of society. Its function is to identify wrongdoing and then to punish or offer remedies or guidance to offer protections to citizens and ensure the proper functioning of justice.

Legislation will also help an advocate to determine the legal basis for their arguments. Legislation broadly comprises statute (primary legislation), statutory instruments, regulations, orders and rules (secondary legislation) and codes of practice, e.g. codes of practice to the Police and Criminal Evidence Act 1984, the sentencing code to the Sentencing Act 2020 or the codes of practice to the Mental Capacity Act 2005 (quasi-legislation). It is always important to read the legislation in conjunction with any existing codes of practice. It is also important to read legislation in conjunction with court procedural rules.

The role of an advocate will involve reading, analysing, and evaluating legislation in the context of how it applies to their case. However, legislation is not always easy to read, particularly if it is capable of having alternative meanings applied to certain sections.

### 2.5.1 Statutory Interpretation

Even if legislation represents the existing law, it may be possible to argue that the legislation is incompatible with changing values and behaviour of society. An example might be found in legislation that accords certain rights to individuals based on an assumption of gender without recognising that gender can be reassigned.

Statutes/Acts of Parliament will have a commencement date after they have received Royal Assent and passed through both Houses of Parliament (House of Commons and House of Lords). After going through a rigorous process of 'First Reading' (formal presentation of the Bill of Parliament) the Bill progresses to 'Second Reading' (the debate stage where the purpose of the legislation is expressed and tested) and then the 'Committee Stage' (where a committee considers each clause of the Bill), followed by the 'Report Stage' (where the amendments of the Bill by the committee are formally considered by the House).

Finally, the Bill reaches the 'Third Reading' (review of amendments and decision as to whether the Bill should proceed). The Parliament Act 1949 allows a Bill that has been

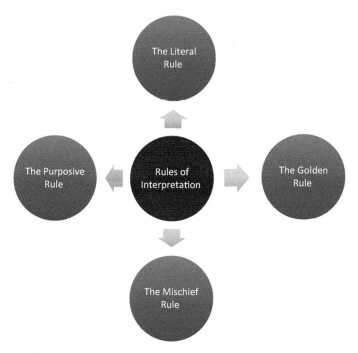

**Figure 2.5** Rules of Interpretation.

passed in the House of Commons (but not in the House of Lords), to still become law, in some circumstances after a one-year delay.

An advocate can therefore learn a lot about the original intention and purpose of a statute by referring to the reported parliamentary debates in Hansard (official report of the proceedings in the House of Commons and House of Lords). This is a helpful starting point when seeking to interpret the main purpose of a piece of an Act of Parliament.

The court uses a number of established rules to help them to interpret legislation. These are shown in Figure 2.5.

## 2.5.2 The Literal Rule

This is where the judges give the words of the statute its ordinary, literal and plain meaning. As stated by Lord Diplock in *Duport Steel v Sirs* [1980] 1 WLR 142 "where the meaning of a statute is plain and unambiguous it is not for the judges to invent fancied ambiguities for failing to give effect to its plain meaning because they consider the consequences of doing so would be inexpedient, or even unjust or immoral". Such an approach arguably promotes certainty in the law and avoids usurping parliamentary sovereignty.

### 2.5.3 The Golden Rule

This is where the courts look at whole sentences or the statute as a whole in order to construe the true meaning of the words in order to avoid what might otherwise lead to an absurd result. As Lord Blackburn stated in the case of *River Wear Commissioners v Adamson* (1876–77) 2 App Cas 743:

> [W]e take the whole statute together and construe it all together, giving the words their ordinary signification unless when so applied they produce an inconsistency, or an absurdity or inconvenience so great as to convince the court that the intention could not have been to use them in their ordinary signification.

This is an approach that is effectively an extension of the literal rule and therefore only operates if to give the words of the statute its ordinary meaning would produce absurdity. The words are modified to remove the absurdity or the risk of absurdity but not beyond this. The advantage of this approach is that it allows the courts to take into account public policy considerations that Parliament themselves might have taken into account if the legislation went before Parliament again.

### 2.5.4 The Mischief Rule

This approach involves looking behind the words of the statute to ascertain the true purpose and intention of Parliament in passing the Act and what remedy Parliament had intended to provide in order to deal with that mischief (wrongdoing). The case of *Pepper v Hart* [1992] UKHL 3 held that the previous rule preventing the use of parliamentary materials to interpret statute could be departed from if it would help clarify ambiguous or obscure sections of a statute or prevent the interpretation of the words of the statute leading to an absurd result. The mischief rule was intended to be used where neither the literal rule nor golden rule were appropriate. Extrinsic material such as Hansard can be used to assist the court in the interpretation of the statute. The case of *Three Rivers District Council v Bank of England (No 2)* (1996) 2 All ER 363 extended the use of Hansard to not just ambiguous legislation but also where the legislation might be considered to be ineffective in its intention to give effect to a particular European Directive where the issue is about the object of the statute.

### 2.5.5 The Purposive Rule

This is the approach most commonly associated with the Court of the European Union (also commonly referred to as the ECJ) and is used when interpreting EU law. Like the mischief rule it looks at the purpose behind the legislation. However, unlike the mischief rule it is not constrained by only being used if the literal and golden rules have first been ruled out as inappropriate to use. The courts in England and Wales have also used the purposive approach to interpret EU law. An example can be seen in *R v Secretary of State for Health ex parte Quintavalle* [2003] UKHL 13 where the court took the view that the use of this method of statutory interpretation was not necessarily restricted to interpreting EU law. In this case the issue was the interpretation of the national law relating to cell nuclear replacement (s. 1(1) of the Human Fertilisation and Embryology Act 1990). The court held that the use of the purposive approach might be necessary for the construction of statutes generally depending on the context. In this case, the courts were asked to look at a new scientific development, which had not been in place at the time of the 1990 Act.

Sales (2017) argues that the courts now take a very modern approach to statutory interpretation that is based on a mixture of legal values and expectations from statute, established local value systems and judicial reasoning.

In 1969 the Law Commission and the Scottish Law Commission carried out a review of the efficacy of the established rules on the interpretation of statute, namely the Literal Rule, the Golden Rule and the Mischief Rule. They concluded that the starting point should always be to give a statute the meaning it was intended to have in the context of the background to which it was enacted by drawing on the setting, the language used and the assumptions of the legislator. The Law Commissions were however reluctant to lay down any legislative requirements about how statutory interpretation should take place and felt that this should be left flexible enough for the courts to be able to clarify or relax some aspects of statute to, for example, comply with international obligations. They also recommended the revision of the Interpretation Act 1889, which was eventually replaced by the Interpretation Act 1978.

The Interpretation Act 1978 is a useful starting point when interpreting words and expressions in statute as it provides some basic definitions. For example, the Act tells us that the use of the word "writing" should be defined as including typing, printing, lithography, photography and any modes capable of representing or reproducing words.

The Act also confirms that words importing the masculine gender will also include the female gender and that words in the singular will include the plural. The Act also reminds us that where an Act that has repealed a previous Act is itself repealed, this will not revive the original Act repealed unless this is expressly stated. The Interpretation Act 1978 therefore provides some helpful presumptions for the interpretation of statute.

An advocate need not therefore be constrained by the literal meaning of statute and can argue new interpretations if these are based on rational and logical arguments using rules of interpretation.

It is also worth noting that the Human Rights Act 1998 requires legislation to be interpreted in conformity with rights under the European Convention on Human Rights 1950 (s. 3 of the 1998 Act) and the courts are also expected to decide cases in a way that is compatible with the Convention (s. 2 of the 1998 Act). The Convention rights are set out in section one of the 1998 Act and include the right to a fair trial (Article 6). A court may make a 'declaration of incompatibility' on the basis that legislation is incompatible with Convention rights. This can result in changes to the law. For example, in *R (on the application of Anderson) v Secretary of State for the Home Department* [2002] UKHL 46, the House of Lords held that s. 29 of the Crime (Sentences) Act 1997 which allowed the Home Office to set the minimum period that had to be served under a mandatory life sentence was incompatible with Article 6 of the 1950 Convention. This was because it denied a defendant the right to have his/her sentence imposed by an independent and impartial tribunal. As a result, s. 29 of the 1997 Act was repealed by the Criminal Justice Act 2003.[2]

# How to Develop Strategies and Solutions

## 2.6 Strategy and Planning

As we have discussed earlier, it is important to understand the client's goals. However, this must be done in the context of their needs and this may be in terms of their personal, economic or commercial circumstances. Devising a strategy that best meets those needs will ensure that you can plan towards achieving successful outcomes for the client. Part of the early planning is to identify the correct court procedure. For example, in civil proceedings a claim will usually be brought using the Part 7 Procedure (see CPR Part 7). However, there are some instances when it would be appropriate to use the Part 8 Alternative Procedure, for example, where the issues are relatively simple such as a claim that has settled and the only issue between the parties is the question of costs (see CPR Part 8.1). In criminal cases it will be necessary to determine whether the offence is to be categorised as 'summary only' (minor in nature and heard in the Magistrates' Court only) or an either-way offence of medium seriousness that is capable of being heard in the Magistrates' or Crown Court or whether it is a serious case and therefore will be regarded as an 'indictable offence' triable only in the Crown Court. If the client is a child there may be additional procedures that apply such as the use of special 'Youth Courts' in criminal proceedings or the appointment of a 'Litigation Friend' in civil proceedings. The Client's financial situation will also impact how the case is funded and also whether the client is able to pay any fines, compensation or costs as a result of the action.

### 2.6.1 Using a Focused Strategy

Advocacy is a craft that uses knowledge, skills and judgment to achieve a focused strategy with the aim of successfully resolving a case. Success is not necessarily measured by winning the case. Sometimes, the course of action that best serves the

---

2 Although the UK has left the European Union, some legislation, such as the Human Rights Act 1998 continues to be governed by EU law until such time as the national legislation in question is repealed by Parliament.

client's interests will be reaching a compromise or bringing the dispute to an early resolution. An effective advocate will know when it is appropriate to negotiate to bring the case to a conclusion and to avoid further litigation. It would be wrong to think that all cases are there to be won. In law, compromise is often needed, and outcomes may not always be the same as the stated goal from the outset. An advocate needs to explore all possible outcomes in the client's case and map out how each outcome might arise as well as how to avoid unfavourable outcomes. There are various methods that can be used to strategise but one of these is the 'SWOT' method of identifying 'strengths', 'weaknesses', 'opportunities' and 'threats'. Any identified outcomes must be specific and achievable.

## 2.6.2 Identify the Elements of the Charge/Claim

In order to advise the client effectively and conduct a successful case, it is first necessary to consider all the possible causes of action and the legal consequence of pursuing each. This will also involve a consideration of costs as well as a risk-benefit analysis.

In a civil case the claim will usually be a contractual or tortious one. In a criminal case the offence will be set out either in statute or the common law. If we take a criminal case as our example, it will first be necessary to identify from the charge sheet what the elements of the offence are in terms of identifying the *actus reus* (the guilty act) and the *mens rea* (the required mental element) and any defences that might apply.

Let's take the following example: a defendant is charged under s. 16 of the Offences Against the Person Act 1861 with the offence of making threats to kill. The elements of the charge will first have to be established from the statute.

### Section 16
*A person who without lawful excuse makes to another a threat, intending that that other would fear that it would be carried out, to kill that other or a third person shall be guilty of an offence and liable to conviction on indictment to imprisonment for a term not exceeding ten years.*

The *actus reus* (the guilty act) can be identified as follows:

**Makes a threat to another...to kill that other or a third person.**

The *mens rea* (the mental element) can be identified as follows:

**Intending that the other person would fear that it** (the threat) **would be carried out.**

The defence can be found in the words:

**Without lawful excuse.**

A defendant who has a lawful excuse to make a threat to kill (for example a police officer involved in a hostage situation) might have an arguable defence.

The strategy here would be to convince a jury that the defendant is not guilty of the offence by producing evidence showing the *actus reus* and/or the *mens rea* elements of the offence were not present. Another strategy would be to accept that the *actus reus* and *mens rea* elements were present but that the defendant had a defence that can act as a complete defence leading to an acquittal. We will consider different types of criminal offences in Part B.

In a civil claim, it will be necessary to identify the type of claim that might arise. This might, for example, be a contractual or tortious claim. The available remedies that should be sought and any defences that might apply will also have to be identified.

Let's take another example:

> You act for a claimant in a civil claim who has purchased a painting, which has been described as having been painted by a particular artist. The claimant intends to give the painting as a gift to her husband who collects works of art from the artist in question. She later discovers that the painting was in fact the work of another (less well known) artist.

The Consumer Rights Act 2015 provides statutory rights to consumers in certain specified situations. Such rights include the right to expect that goods will be of satisfactory quality, fit for a particular purpose and match their description. The Act makes provisions for remedies such as the right to reject goods or request a replacement or repair of goods.

In addition to any remedies found in statute, it is possible to make an application for general interim remedies (temporary orders until the case reaches final trial). The court's power to grant such remedies is found in the Civil Procedure Rules Part 25 and include injunctions, interim payments, inspection, detention, custody or preservation of property and an order restraining a party from removing their assets from the court's jurisdiction.

The strategy here might be to produce evidence to suggest the goods in question have not met the quality, purpose or description expected. However, instead of requesting a replacement good, the client may be asking to exercise their right to reject the goods. Alternatively, you may decide to pursue a strategy that involves applying for an interim remedy under Part 25 of the Civil Procedure Rules. For example, if the seller asked the claimant to return the painting but then refused to issue a refund, it might be necessary to apply for an injunction seeking the return of the painting if that becomes the client's stated goal. We will consider different types of civil claims in Part B.

### 2.6.3 Identifying Risks

Deciding on a particular strategy might depend on whether there is an element of risk involved in that strategy. For example, are the prospects of success dependent purely on whether the jury believes the version of events of your witnesses? Are there excessive costs involved in the case and what are the prospects of recovering those costs from the opposing party?

Conducting a risk-benefit analysis at an early stage will help to identify the risk and decide whether it is one worth taking. A risk-benefit analysis involves considering the risks of taking a particular course of action as against the potential benefits that taking that action might bring. For example, a decision as to whether to pursue a case to trial might involve a risk-benefit analysis where an increase in costs is the known risk but obtaining a particular remedy for your client would be the potential benefit. However, if, for example, the remedy in question is compensation but the costs of pursuing the matter to trial are likely to outstrip any compensation that the court might award, then the risk of going to trial is not a risk worth taking.

How the case will be funded and whether the opponent is worth suing are all relevant considerations for a risk-analysis in civil proceedings. In a civil case, there may be time-limits imposed on bringing a claim and the strategy may then depend on whether these time limits have been missed and what this will mean to the client's case. In a criminal case there may be risks in a defendant exercising their right to silence at trial rather than giving evidence or failing to plead guilty at an early stage. Risks must always be noted and prepared for.

In criminal cases decisions may have to be made about whether particular evidence is admissible or might risk prejudicing a trial (for example if the evidence has been obtained illegally through covert surveillance). As we will see in Part B, a court has a discretion to admit evidence regardless of the means in which it was obtained.

A defence advocate in criminal proceedings may also need to assess whether to advise a client to give a 'no comment' interview at a police station, although the jury may be able to draw an adverse inference from the defendant's decision to remain silent at the police station. We will discuss this in more detail in Part B when considering confession evidence.

Another important assessment that has to be made in criminal proceedings is whether a defendant should enter an early plea of guilty in order to obtain a 'discount' in relation to the final sentence that they will receive. Section 73 of the Sentencing Act 2020 requires a court to consider:

(a) The stage in the proceedings for the offence at which the offender indicated the intention to plead guilty, and
(b) The circumstances in which the indication was given.

The focus is on when an unequivocal intention to plead guilty is indicated rather than when the plea itself is actually entered at court – see *Plaku and Others v The Queen, The Queen v Benjamin Smith* [2021] EWCA Crim 568 and the Sentencing Act 2020, s. 73.

In addition, the Sentencing Council have produced guidelines on the factors that the court should take into consideration when deciding whether to reduce a sentence due to an early plea of guilty being entered by a defendant. These guidelines are known as "Reduction in Sentence for a Guilty Plea" – see www.sentencingcouncil.org.uk.

The principle behind allowing discounted sentences in this way is that it saves public time and money that would otherwise be spent on a full trial and saves victims and witnesses from going through what could be distressing testimony. It is also thought to reduce the impact of the crime on victims if they do not have to face the offender in court but can be certain the offender will still be sentenced.

A defendant can receive as much as a one-third discount on their sentence depending on when they plead guilty. The Sentencing Act 2020, s. 73 and the Sentencing Code 'Reduction in Sentence for a Guilty Plea' (section D) provides that a discount of one-third is the maximum level of reduction and applies if a defendant indicates he/she intends to plead guilty at the first stage of the proceedings. This will normally be at the first hearing where a plea is requested and can be entered by the court. In the case of 'summary only' offences this would usually be at the first hearing in the Magistrates' Court (see CrimPR 3.16(3)) or at the plea before venue procedure for either-way offences (see s. 17A(5) Magistrates' Courts Act 1980) or following allocation to the crown court in the case of indictable offences (see Criminal Procedure Rule Part 9.7(5)). An indication of plea can also be recorded in the 'Better Case Management ('BCM') form in the Magistrates' Court.

Thereafter the reduction is on a sliding scale with a reduction of one quarter if the indication of a guilty plea is given after the first stage of the proceedings and one tenth reduction if the indication of a plea of guilty is made at the first day of the trial. This can be reduced to zero if the guilty plea is indicated or made later during the trial.

If a defendant needs further advice or assistance before entering a plea the court has a discretion to disapply the start points of the reduction and can still grant a one-third reduction (see section F1 of the Sentencing Code).

The defence advocate should therefore assess, based on the weight of the prosecution evidence, whether a defendant is likely to be found guilty by a jury and therefore whether a defendant should consider pleading guilty at an early stage. For example, the defendant may want to initially plead 'not guilty' to test the weight of the prosecution evidence, knowing that they will change their plea if the evidence proves to be strong. It will be necessary to advice the defendant client of the risks in taking this course of action if the defendant is expecting a discount in sentence.

Discounts in sentencing are different to mitigating factors that might be put forward on behalf of a defendant to reduce the severity of possible sentences. For example, where the defendant cooperated with police investigations or has shown remorse for their actions – see the decision in *R v Price* [2018] EWCA Crim 1784 and s. 74 of the Sentencing Act 2020. We will consider sentencing in greater detail in Part B.

# How to Negotiate Solutions

## 2.7  Negotiation Skills

An advocate should always have in mind, as part of their strategy, how they will bring the case to a conclusion. For example, when would it be appropriate to settle a civil case? Should a defendant in a criminal case change their plea to guilty to obtain the benefit of a discount to their sentence?

### 2.7.1  Negotiated Settlements

To achieve the possible outcome for the client and to reduce costs, an advocate should always consider whether a negotiated settlement would be preferable to a trial. The aim of negotiation is to explore and find solutions that are acceptable to both parties; this usually means a compromise will be necessary.

The civil courts are keen to encourage alternative means of resolution wherever possible and encourage the use of Alternative Dispute Resolution ('ADR') at an early stage in pre-action protocols. In addition, in civil cases once proceedings have been issued a party can make an offer to settle at any point and this is known as a 'Part 36 offer'. Failure to accept such an offer may have cost consequences for the other party. We will explore both pre-action protocols and Part 36 offers later in this section at 2.7.2.

A good negotiator will aim to maintain good relationships between the parties whilst seeking solutions that mutually benefit both parties. Avoiding conflict and argument by coming to the negotiating table to explore solutions, will inevitably mean that the client's case can be resolved much quicker and at a reduced cost. It will also ensure that it removes future barriers to communication between the parties.

What is always required is to do the best for the client working with the available evidence and within the confines of the court procedural rules, particularly the overriding objective. An advocate must ensure that litigation never becomes personalised between the lawyers whilst at the same time matching courtesy with firmness.

When entering any negotiation, an advocate should be mindful of the 'position' adopted by the opposing party and explore what is behind their position, this can be termed their 'interests'. For example, Let's take the following case:

> *You act for Office Magic Ltd who have signed a £20 million contract to have Build-as-u-like Ltd build a new office complex for them. The work on Phase I has started and completion is due in eight months' time.*

*The contract has an arbitration clause that requires any dispute to be settled through arbitration. The contract also includes a penalty clause of £5000 for each day of delay to the build. It is estimated that the build will not now be completed until ten months at the earliest. This is because Build-as-u-like Ltd use timber imported from a warehouse in Indonesia. The warehouse has recently caught fire leading to the loss of a substantial amount of timber. This has affected all timber imports from the country.*

Position of Office Magic Ltd
*The contract terms are clear, Build-as-u-like Ltd must pay the penalty or the matter will be referred for arbitration.*

Position of Build-as-u-like Ltd
*The delays were not foreseeable and are beyond their control and there should be some flexibility given in the contract terms.*

Interests of Office Magic Ltd
*They have already entered a contract to lease the first office block in eight months' time, and this contract is worth £80,000 in the first year.*

Interests of Build-as-u-like Ltd
*They have already begun enquiries to source timber from an alternative destination and although this will cost them an extra £50,000 they think they will be able to complete the contract in nine months' time.*

By getting each party to reveal the interests that are impacting the positions that they have adopted, a negotiator can start to see some possible solutions and compromises. One solution might be for Office Magic to reduce the total penalty due by £50,000 as a gesture of goodwill to enable Build-as-u-like to source alternative timber and complete the project one month earlier than currently estimated. Another solution might be found in limiting the penalty to be paid by Build-as-u-like to £80,000 plus any legal costs to reflect any lost revenue if Office Magic are unable to honour the lease contract. Yet another solution might be to allow a one-month penalty free period to allow Build-as-u-like time to source timber from an alternative location and then place the burden on Build-as-u-like to reduce any future penalty payments themselves by accelerating the build time.

A negotiator will always have more than one possible offer on the table but will start with the lowest offer and then be prepared to negotiate upwards to come closer to the opponent's position.

However, the best outcome for a client might not be a negotiated settlement or deal and so a good negotiator must also know when to stand their ground but also when to walk away. Fisher and Ury (1981) argue that a negotiator should always be aware of their 'Best Alternative to a Negotiated Agreement' ('BATNA'). This is essentially the 'litmus test' as to whether any negotiated agreement is a good one. If the agreement is less advantageous than the expected outcome (for example, if the matter were to proceed to arbitration) then it should not be accepted and the negotiator should be prepared to either reopen the negotiations, or if this is not possible, to walk away. A BATNA is therefore a known alternative to the current settlement and will have been identified by the negotiator in advance.

We will continue to work with the skills of preparation, legal research and case planning in the detailed case studies in Parts B and C of this textbook.

## 2.7.2  Making Offers and Concessions

Most cases in the criminal and civil courts settle before reaching trial and therefore knowing when to concede or reach a compromise is an important part of a case strategy.

In civil proceedings, a party can make an offer to settle a claim by making what is known as a 'Part 36 offer' (see CPR Part 36). These offers will have cost consequences if refused and the other party fails to better the offer in terms of what they receive in a final court judgment. Part 36 offers can relate to a payment of a sum of money or settling an issue in the trial. The offers can be made by either a claimant or a defendant at any point before or during trial (including before proceedings are commenced).

However, to attract cost consequences, a Part 36 offer must follow the requirements of Part 36.5. The requirements are that the Part 36 offer is:

1.  Made in writing.
2.  States that it is made under Part 36 (which is regarded as a self-contained procedural rule).
3.  Specify a period of time (not less than 21 days) when the offer can be accepted after which the party (if they are the defendant) will be liable for the claimant's costs.
4.  State whether the Part 36 offer relates to the whole claim or part of a claim or to a particular issue in the case.
5.  State whether it takes account of any counterclaim.

Certain claims require the Part 36 offer to contain additional information. For example, see the additional requirements for personal injury claims for future pecuniary loss (CPR Part 36.18).

If the offer relates to only part of the claim, then that part of the claim will be 'stayed' if the offer is accepted and only the remaining parts of the claim will proceed to trial. This may therefore be a useful way to narrow issues and achieve a compromise on areas where the evidence is weaker and the risks of losing are greater.

If the Part 36 offer relates to an issue, it must be clear what that issue is. As indicated in the civil case of *Seabrook and Adam* [2021] EWCA 382 it cannot necessarily be assumed that liability and causation will be regarded as separate issues or even the same issue. This will depend on the facts of each case and so it is important that the Part 36 offer clarifies which aspect is to be settled, for example, is breach of duty to be admitted or does the offer require admission of particular damage or loss?

A defendant who wishes to make a Part 36 offer to settle the claim must offer payment of a single sum to be paid within 14 days of the claimant accepting the Part 36 offer (see CPR Part 36.6).

The costs consequences are dealt with under CPR Parts 36.13, 36.17 and 36.20 and relate to both accepting and rejecting an offer. For example, if a claimant rejects the defendant's Part 36 offer and at trial the claimant receives judgment against the defendant which is 'at least as advantageous' as the offer that was made in the defendant's Part 36 offer, then the claimant will be entitled to interest on the whole sum claimed at a rate not exceeding 10% above the base rate from the date the defendant would have been liable to pay the claimant's costs if they had accepted the offer ('the relevant period'). In addition, the claimant is entitled to costs on an 'indemnity basis' (see discussion below) from the date of the 'relevant period' as well as interest on those costs not exceeding 10% above base rate (see CPR Part 36.17(4)).

Where a claimant fails to obtain a judgment more advantageous than a defendant's Part 36 offer the defendant will be entitled to their costs and interest on those costs (see CPR Part 36.17(3)).

An advocate will need to consider when and if a Part 36 offer should be made in civil proceedings to obtain the available costs consequences or whether negotiating without formal offers would be a better strategy.

## How to Plan, Manage and Progress Cases

## 2.8 Progressing the Case

The strength of a good performance at court lies in a good case plan. Managing the case before it reaches court will ensure that you are able to present the best possible version of your client's story. This will enable you to draw on the 'factual strengths' so that you can advance arguments more likely to persuade the court to grant the order sought or decide in your client's favour.

Familiarity with all aspects of your case will also enable you to deal with any unexpected issues as they arise. By drawing on the strong factual elements of your case you will find that you are able to improvise and provide 'on the spot' responses or arguments. The nature of the allegations may change, or new facts emerge in which case it is important to review existing court documents that have been drafted or filed and consider whether amendments are needed. In civil proceedings it is possible to amend statements of case (all the documents setting out the issues in a case) at any time before they are served on the other party after which an amendment can only occur with consent of the other party or permission of the court (see CPR Part 17).

It is also important in civil proceedings to ensure that the correct defendant has been joined to the proceedings. It is always possible to add additional defendants later (see CPR 20.7) by applying for permission from the court to add an additional claim and amend existing statements of case.

## 2.8.1  The Jurisdiction of the Court

Before starting a case in court, an advocate will need to consider which court the case should be started in and why. Determining the jurisdiction of the court is an important first step for an advocate. This will help an advocate to understand which court their client's case should be started in and therefore the correct procedure the advocate will need to follow and any additional special rules that they will be bound by. In addition, certain types of cases can only be heard by judges at a particular level of seniority. For example, in civil cases, a Master, District Judge or Deputy District Judge cannot hear cases where a claim has been made under the Human Rights Act 1998 (see Civil Procedure Rules Practice Direction 2B para 7A). In criminal proceedings, for example, a District Judge sitting in the Magistrates' Court has jurisdiction to sit alone and try summary offences (see s. 26 of the Courts Act 2003).

For civil cases, the starting point is to consider the type and value of the claim as this will determine the most suitable court to issue proceedings. For example, CPR PD 2C para 1.1 provides that any civil claim can be started in a County Court unless a particular rule, practice direction or statute provides otherwise. Judicial review applications must be made in the High Court (s. 31 of the Senior Courts Act 1981, CPR PD 54A and Schedule 1 of the Senior Courts Act 1981). Personal injury claims must be worth a minimum value to be issued in the High Court (£50,000 – see CPR 16.3(5)(c)). For money claims generally, the High Court minimum value is £100,000 (see CPR PD 7A para 2.1).

In addition, cases will be placed on specific 'tracks' in the civil courts according to the amount of money claimed or the complexity of the issues in the case. The small claims track is reserved for claims of £10,000 or less or where a claim is made under the Pre-action Protocol for Personal Injury Claim Below the Small Claims Limit in Road Traffic Accident Cases (see CPR PD 27B). For housing disrepair cases the small claims track value is reduced to £1,000 (see CPR Part 27.1). For personal injury cases that arise from a road traffic accident the limit is not more than £5,000. This is reduced to £1,000 if the accident took place before 31st May 2021 and involved a child or a protected party. In any other types of personal injury cases the small claims limit is not more than £1,000 (see CPR Part 26.6 and 26.6A). Fast track cases usually apply to cases where the value is over £10,000 but not more than £25,000 and can include cases where the value is less than this sum, but the case is complex because, for example, it raises complex evidential issues or the number of witnesses to be called means that the trial is likely to last more than a day. Claims for injunctions may also be suitable for this track. Multi-track cases are more suitable for complex cases or cases that are likely to take more than one day and require more case management. Provisions are made in the rules for case management conferences and pre-trial reviews to be held (see CPR Part 29).

## 2.8.2 Pre-Action Protocols

In civil proceedings there is a further requirement on advocates to ensure that the case preparation has first followed a relevant pre-action protocol or the Practice Direction on Pre-action Conduct. These prescribe steps that should be taken before proceedings are started. There are different pre-action protocols for different types of civil proceedings. For example, pre-action protocols exist for personal injury claims, clinical dispute claims, professional negligence claims, housing disrepair cases, resolution of package travel claims and judicial review actions to name but a few. Details of all the pre-action protocols that are in existence can be found on the government website www.gov.uk.

The protocols are designed to help narrow the areas of dispute between the parties and also allow the party to consider alternative means of settlement through Alternative Dispute Resolution ('ADR'). They require a proposed claimant to first send a 'letter of claim' to the defendant outlining the nature of their claim (often with a copy to be sent to the defendant's insurers) and giving sufficient detail to enable a defendant to assess their potential liability. The defendant is then given a period of time to respond to the letter. This period varies between the different protocols but can be between three and four months on average. This is to enable the defendant sufficient time to investigate the allegations without fear of proceedings being issued. After the investigation period has expired the defendant will then serve a 'letter of response' stating whether they admit or deny the allegations. There are also provisions within the protocols for the parties to agree on instructing experts to help clarify the issues before proceedings are started.

The civil courts will expect all parties to comply with the relevant protocol and can make costs orders where a party has failed to follow the protocol.

## 2.8.3 Drafting Witness Statements and Defence Statements

In civil proceedings some applications must be supported by a sworn affidavit (see CPR PD 32 para 2-16), but most interim applications are supported with a witness statement as the parties do not give oral evidence at interim hearings. Witness statements will usually be used at the trial itself. In civil proceedings the format and content of witness statements is prescribed (see CPR Part 32 and PD 32 para 19.1).

In criminal cases the prosecution will be responsible for drafting witness statements from prosecution witnesses and these must comply with the Magistrates' Court Act 1980, s. 9 (known as 'section 9 statements'). However, the defence will set out their case in a defence statement. This is a written statement that sets out the nature of the defence, the facts that are disputed, any alibi details and any relevant law. A defence statement is optional in the Magistrates' Court but compulsory in the crown court (see the Criminal Procedure and Investigation Act 1996, ss. 5 and 6).

## 2.8.4 Meeting Time Limits

As part of the overriding objective to deal with cases justly and proportionate to costs, the court expects all parties' legal representatives to adhere to the strict time limits imposed by the procedural rules. The court will enforce compliance with the rules and practice directions as part of the overriding objective in CPR Part 1 and CrimPR Part 1 as well as the courts' general case management powers. For example, in civil proceedings, claim forms and accompanying documentation must be served on the other party within specified time periods. A claim form must be served within England and Wales within four months of the claim form being issued by the court (CPR 7.5(1)) and within six months if the claim form is served outside England or Wales (CPR 7.5(2)). A particulars of claim is usually served at the same times as a claim form but if it is served after, this must be no later than 14 days after the claim form was served and before the expiry of the time for service of a claim form (see CPR 7.4(1)(a) and CPR 7.4(2). We will discuss the obligation to meet time limits in more detail in Chapter 4. Go to Chapter 4, Section 4.4.5 for a full discussion of the 'overriding objective'.

## 2.8.5 Damages and Interest

In civil proceedings, part of the case planning will involve deciding on the type and nature of the remedy that is suitable for a case. For example, should the claim include solely a claim for monies or is there another issue to be resolved such as forcing a defendant to take a particular course of action or refrain from a particular course of action? If so, an injunction might be more suitable or should be combined with a claim for monies (see for example Senior Courts Act 1981, s. 50). The CPR Part 25 sets out the different types of remedies that can be applied for such as a 'mandatory injunction' (to force a party to act) or a 'prohibitory injunction' (to prevent a party from acting in a certain way) or a 'freezing injunction' (to temporarily prevent a party accessing a particular financial source) or 'stop and search' to permit entry and search of a property where evidence may be concealed.

However, it is also possible to apply for damages as a remedy and this would also bring an entitlement to claim interest on the damages in the county court (see the County Court Act 1984, s. 69) and the High Court (see the Senior Courts Act 1981, s. 35A).

Compensatory damages put the claimant back in the position as if the loss, injury or damage had never happened whereas aggravated damages are additional to compensatory damages and are intended to compensate for injury to the claimant's pride and dignity, e.g. claims of malicious falsehood in civil proceedings.

Exemplary (punitive) damages are awarded to punish the defendant for his/her conduct and are in addition to compensatory damages. If the claimant has not suffered damage or loss then exemplary damages cannot be awarded.

Contemptuous damages however occur where the claimant wins the case, but damages are small. These are awarded to indicate the court's displeasure at the way the claimant has behaved. An advocate will need to consider the type of damages or other remedy that they wish the court to make.

In personal injury cases in the civil courts, there are also special categories of damages to consider. For example, the court can make an award for provisional damages'. This is an exception to the usual rule that damages are decided once and only for a particular case. If evidence in a personal injuries case suggests the claimant may go on to develop a disease or that there may be a deterioration in the claimant's condition at a later date post trial, the court can assess damages but make an order that if the specified disease or deterioration does occur then the claimant can come back to court for an assessment of further damages (see CPR Part 41).

In personal injury cases, damages are also divided between special damages (those losses that occur pre-trial and can be quantified) and 'general damages' (post-trial future damages that can only be estimated based on actuarial evaluations).

## 2.8.6 Costs

An advocate will need to have in mind how and whether the costs of the case can be recovered from the other party. In criminal proceedings the court has power to award costs by virtue of various statutes including the Prosecution of Offences Act 1985 (ss. 16–19B) and the Legal Aid, Sentencing and Punishment of Offenders Act 2012. An order for costs can be made in favour of a defendant and defence costs can be paid out of Central Funds (see Prosecution of Offences Act 1985, ss. 16 and 16A). Equally a convicted defendant or an appellant who has been unsuccessful in an appeal can be ordered to pay costs (see s. 18 of the 1985 Act). The court can also make wasted costs orders against legal professionals and their firms.

In civil proceedings, in addition to wasted costs orders against legal professionals, the courts can order summary assessment of costs after each interim hearing or a one-day fast track trial (see CPR Parts 44.6 and 47). Fixed costs are also recoverable for some steps taken in proceedings such as steps to enforce a judgment that has been made against a defendant (see CPR Part 45.8). Fixed costs also apply in low value road traffic accident cases (see CPR 45.9–CPR 45.15). A completed Schedule of Costs form should be filed with the court prior to any interim hearing where costs ares sought. All court forms including Schedule of Costs can be obtained from the government website at www.gov.uk.

Civil costs are also awarded at the end of a trial (see CPR Part 47 and PD 47). However, costs do not necessarily follow a successful outcome. As we have discussed above, a Part 36 offer can decrease or increase the costs a party might otherwise have received at the end of a trial. The court also has powers under s. 51 of the Senior Courts Act 1981 to impose 'cost capping' to limit the amount that a party can claim from an opponent. This can be done at the court's discretion or on an application being made by a party (see CPR 3.19–21). In certain courts (multi-track) the court can also order that the parties file and exchange a 'costs budget' to help the court manage costs as part of the overriding objective. Only costs which are proportionate and reasonable are recoverable. If there is any doubt as to whether an item of costs is 'proportionate' then this is usually decided in favour of the party paying the costs (known as 'the standard basis' – see CPR 44.3(2)). If however the court feels a party has behaved in a way that the court regards as unacceptable then they can resolve any question of proportionality in the receiving party's favour (this is known as 'the indemnity basis' – see CPR 44.3(3)).

# In Summary

## Fact Finding

**(SQE Advocacy Assessed skill - see www.sra.org.uk)**

A competent advocate will be able to:

- Obtain clear instructions from the client.
- Be prepared to assess whether the client's goals are realistic and achievable.
- Learn the facts of the case and know them well.
- Assess what they know about a case by putting the key issues and dates in order of when events unfolded.
- Identify what they do not know and list these and then obtain the further information that they need to progress the case.
- Analyse the 'What', 'How' and Why' of the case from the facts.
- Be clear about which issues are in dispute and which are not.
- Collect relevant and admissible evidence as soon as possible.
- Know when it is appropriate to seek expert evidence to support the client's case.

### Legal Research

A competent advocate will be able to:

- Find a corresponding legal issue or principle for each factual issue.
- Support the legal issues identified with relevant authorities using sources of law such as case law, legislation, Conventions etc.

- Identify the correct resource that will help to support the legal points that are to be made in argument.
- Cite cases in the format required by the Practice Direction: Citation of Authorities 2012.
- Be clear about the legal principle (*ratio decidendi*) that arises from all cases used to support an argument.
- Always be clear as to the original intention and purpose of the legislation that is used to support the case presentation.
- Use statutory interpretation to argue different possible meanings to legislation, where it is relevant and appropriate to do so.

## Case Planning

A competent advocate will be able to:

- Be clear about all elements of the charge/claim.
- Identify the correct court and jurisdiction for the case.
- Explore possible defences or remedies.
- Explore alternative dispute resolution with the client in a civil case.
- Carry out a risk-benefit analysis before taking a course of action.
- Assess how they will bring the case to a conclusion.

### Key Practice Case

### *Mitchell v News Group Newspapers Ltd* [2013] EWCA Civ 1537

This is an important case as it was the first time the Court of Appeal was called upon to consider the question of enforcement for lack of compliance with court procedural rules. The rule in question in this particular case was the Civil Procedure rule CPR 3.9. The court had to consider whether the practice should remain that non-compliance of a court rule might be excused if it could be remedied by alternative means, for example, by the court issuing an appropriate direction about future preparation of the case or by a wasted costs order.

The facts of the case concerned the claimant, a former Chief Whip of the Conservative Party who had brought libel proceedings against the Sun Newspaper who in turn had published allegations that the claimant had berated police officers at the entrance to Downing Street and had used foul language to do so.

The judgement itself arose from a dispute relating to a decision made in a costs budget hearing at the conclusion of the main libel action. It was alleged that the claimant had failed to provide a costs budget within the required timeframe and was therefore in breach of Practice Direction 51D. The Practice Direction stated that a breach would lead to a sanction but did not stipulate the nature of the sanction. The Master in the High Court costs hearing imposed a sanction limiting the claimant's claim for costs to the amount of court fees only. This was done by using CPR 3.14 as an analogy (although it did not cover the type of application in question in this case). The claimants appealed.

The Court of Appeal, in dismissing the appeal, took the opportunity to offer guidance as to when and to what extent sanctions should be imposed for non-compliance of a procedural rule:

1. The court should first consider the nature of the non-compliance.
2. If the non-compliance is 'trivial' (e.g. failure of form rather than substance, narrowly missing a deadline) then the court can grant some form of relief from sanctions.
3. If the non-compliance is not 'trivial' then relief from sanctions will not be automatic and the burden will shift to the party responsible for non-compliance to persuade the court, why sanctions should not be imposed.
4. In considering whether or not to impose sanctions the court will consider relevant issues such as (a) why the non-compliance occurred, (b) whether there are good reasons for the non-compliance, (c) whether those 'good reasons' were outside the control of the party in default, (d) whether the contemplated sanction complies with the overriding objective under CPR 1.
5. Missing a deadline due to pressures of work is unlikely to be regarded as a good reason.

## Practice Tips

- Familiarise yourself with the facts and key events of your case so that you become an expert rather than a novice who merely has the background facts.
- To help you to identify at an early stage what evidence you will need to gather, prepare standard checklists for each type of case, e.g. civil, criminal, family, etc so that you do not forget to ask for key information from the client
- Take the time to plan the strategy of your case by considering possible and alternative courses of action by drawing a 'risks' table for each case.
- Identify any weaknesses in your client's case and be prepared to deal with these in your case presentation by minimising those weaknesses.
- Boost the impact of your case presentation through evidence collection and document preparation – always take early drafts of witness statements ('proofs').
- Familiarise yourself with the pre-trial requirements of court procedural rules.

**Practice Risks**

- A lack of preparation or understanding of the case that leads to a detrimental outcome for the client.
- Failure to anticipate alternative outcomes, solutions or actions in the case that leads to an improperly prepared case where the opponent has the benefit of surprising you.
- A misunderstanding of court rules and procedures that impacts on the preparation of the case causing delays or poor outcomes for the client.
- Misjudging the strengths of your case and ignoring or failing to deal with the weaknesses.
- Failure to seek expert advice or accept that certain matters are beyond your expertise – this could lead to a poor outcome for the client.

**EXERCISE A**

**Test Your Knowledge – Problem Scenario**

You have been instructed to act on behalf of 'IMA', which stands for Internet Meme Artists. This is a group of social media users who have formed a collective with the common purpose of exposing what they consider to be ridiculous elements of humankind. They do this by using satire expressed through the use of memes. Memes are videos, images or text which have been modified to produce a humorous response in the viewer. IMA are crowd funded (raising finance from voluntary online contributions) and have produced a series of 'memes' which are now available as an App. They would like to advertise the App with a radio advert. The App contains 50 memes with the intention that more will be added in the future. The current version of the App contains one meme aimed at voting systems generally. The meme is called 'Coat My Vote'. The clearance centre for broadcast advertisement has refused to clear the advert for radio. The centre states that the advert "is wholly or mainly of a political nature and contravenes ss. 319(2)(g) and 321(2)(a) and (b) of the Communications Act 2003 when read together." In particular, it is stated that the 'Coat My Vote' meme included in the App shows IMA's true objects are political and fall under s. 321(3)(a) and (f) of the 2003 Act.

Read the relevant sections of the 2003 Act. Using statutory interpretation, set out **three** arguments that would support a case that s. 321 should be read in a way that would support IMA's case.

**Go to Part C for a suggested answer.**

**EXERCISE B**

## Test Your Knowledge – Multiple-Choice Tests

### Test One

You are acting for the parents of a child patient who is seriously ill in hospital and is in a 'minimally conscious state'. The hospital would like to withdraw treatment and allow the child to die as they believe that continuing treatment and prolonging the child's life is merely causing the child unnecessary pain. You have researched the case of *Briggs v Briggs and Others* that you wish to use the case in your skeleton arguments. The case has the following citations: [2016] EWCOP 53 and [2017] All ER (D) 02 (Jan). Which would you use? Choose **ONE** of the following:

1. [2016] EWCOP 53 only because this is the neutral citation and only neutral citations should be given in court documents.
2. [2016] EWCOP 53 only because this is the first year in which the judgment was reported.
3. [2016] EWCOP 53 followed by [2017] All ER (D) 02 (Jan) because where a law report exists, the neutral citation should be given first but then followed by the law report citation.
4. [2017] All ER (D) 02 (Jan) followed by [2016] EWCOP 53 because where a law report exists, the law report citation should be given first but then followed by the neutral citation.
5. [2017] All ER (D) 02 (Jan) because only the law report citation is needed.

### Test Two

You are acting for a client in civil proceedings. A fact in dispute is whether your client hid any of his financial assets. You wish to instruct a forensic accountant to establish that your client has not moved any of his assets out of the country or placed them into offshore trusts. You are thinking of using your client's current accountants to prepare an expert forensic accountants' report. Which of the following is *false*? You can select more than one answer:

1. Forensic accountancy is a matter likely to be beyond the expertise of the trial judge and therefore it would be appropriate to use expert evidence.
2. Using the client's own accountant will save time and cost and therefore it is unlikely the court or the opposing party will object to their use as an expert.
3. An expert's opinion must be independent, objective and unbiased.
4. An expert's duty is to the party instructing them.
5. An expert will usually provide a written report for the court.

**Go to Part C for the suggested answers.**

# Self-Reflection Checklist

| What **three** important things have you learnt from this chapter? | 1 | 2 | 3 |
|---|---|---|---|
| Set out **three** additional steps that you need to take to learn the skills in this chapter in more detail | 1 | 2 | 3 |

# References

## Books

D Ormero and D Perry (ed), *Criminal Practice* (Oxford University Press, 2022).

AJ Turner, AJ Kelly, NJ Wattam and SE Jones, *Stone's Justice Manual* (Butterworths, 2022).

P Coulson, IR Scott, B Fontaine and J Sorabji (ed), *The White Book* (Sweet and Maxwell, 2022).

Anon, *The Civil Court Practice: The Green Book* (Jordan Publishing, 2022).

R Fisher and W Ury, *Getting to Yes: Negotiating an Agreement Without Giving in* (Random House Business, 2012).

## Journal Articles

P Sales, 'Modern Statutory Interpretation' (2017) 38 (2) Statute Law Review 125.

DJ Snowden and ME Boone, 'A Leader's Framework for Decision-Making' (2007) 85 Harvard Business Review 68.

## Cases

*American Cyanamid Co (No 1) v Ethicon Ltd* [1975] UKHL 1.

*Black-Clawson International Ltd v Papierwerke Waldhof Aschaffenburg Aktiengesellschaft* [1975] AC 591.

*Bolam v Friern Hospital Management Committee* [1957] 1 WLR 582.

*Bolitho v City and Hackney Health Authority* [1998] AC 232.

*Duport Steel v Sirs* [1980] 1 WLR 142.

*Felthouse v Bindley* [1862] EWHC CP J35.

*Joseph Constantine Steamship Line v Imperial Smelting Corporation* [1942] AC 154.

*Miller v Minister of Pensions* [1947] 2 All ER 372.

*Mitchell v News Group Newspapers Ltd* [2013] EWCA Civ 1537.

*Overseas Tankship (UK) Ltd v Morts Dock and Engineering Co Ltd (The Wagon Mound no 1)* [1961] AC 388.

*Pepper v Hart* [1992] 3 WLR 1032.

*Plaku and Others v The Queen; The Queen v Benjamin Smith* [2021] EWCA Crim 568.

*R (on the application of Anderson) v Secretary of State for the Home Department* [2002] UKHL 46.
*R v Briggs-Price* [2009] UKHL 19.
*R v Carr-Briant* (1943) 1 KB 607.
*R v Dix* [1982] 74 Crim LR.
*R v Dowds* [2012] EWCA Crim 281.
*R v Golds* [2016] UKSC 61, 4 All ER 64.
*R v Gomez* [1993] AC 442.
*R v Jogee* [2016] UKSC 8.
*R v Lawrence* [1972] AC 626.
*R v Mitchell* [1995] Crim LR 506.
*R v Morris* [1984 AC 320 [332].
*R v Price* [2018] EWCA Crim 1784.
*R v Sang* [1979] 3 WLR 263.
*R v Saunders* [1991] Crim LR 781.
*R v Secretary of State for Health ex parte Quintavalle* [2003] UKHL 13.
*River Wear Commissioners v Adamson* (1876–77) 2 App Cas 743.
*Seabrook and Adam* [2021] EWCA 382.
*Three Rivers District Council v Bank of England (No 2)* (1996) 2 All ER 363.
*Wilsher v Essex Area Health Authority* [1987] 1 AC 1074.
*Woolmington v DPP* [1935] AC 462.

## Legislation
Consumer Rights Act 2015.
Coroners and Justice Act 2009.
County Courts Act 1984, s. 69.
Criminal Justice Act 2003, ss. 116–120.
Criminal Procedure and Investigations Act 1996, s. 3, s. 5 & s. 6.
European Convention on Human Rights 1950, Article 6.
Homicide Act 1957.
Human Rights Act 1998, s. 2, s. 3.
Interpretation Act 1978.
Legal Aid, Sentencing and Punishment of Offenders Act 2012.
Parliament Act 1949.
Prosecution of Offences Act 1985.
Senior Courts Act 1981, s. 35A, s. 50.
Sentencing Act 2020, s. 73.

## Procedure Rules
Civil Procedure Rules, Parts 1, 2, 7,17, 20, 25, 31, 32, 36.
Criminal Procedure Rules, Parts 15.

## Practice Directions

Criminal Practice Direction 2015 (as amended by amendment no.11 in 2020) [2015] EWCA Crim 1567.

Practice Direction: Citation of Authorities [2012] 1 WLR 780.

Practice Directions (Judgments: Form and Citation) [2001] 1 W.L.R. 194.

## Reports

The Law Commission and the Scottish Law Commission, 'The Interpretation of Statute' Law Com No.21 (HMSO, 1969).

## Websites

http://www.bailii.org/bailii/citation.html

www.gov.uk

www.legalabbrevs.cardiff.ac.uk

www.legislation.gov.uk

www.legalsolutions.thomsonreuters.com

www.lawtel.com

www.practicallaw.thomsonreuters.com

www.sentencingcouncil.org.uk

# 3 Communicating with Others
## Effective Communication and Written Skills

| Key Chapter Points |
| --- |

- In order to share information effectively, an advocate requires both written and verbal communication skills.
- Good writing skills will result in documents that are drafted in clear, precise and accurate language that reflects court requirements and achieve the client's objectives.
- Always tailor your oral presentation to your audience (e.g. client, expert, judge).
- Ensure that your presentation has a clear structure and that you deliver your speech with passion, enthusiasm and conviction.
- Adhere to procedural rules and court processes relating to communication but be ready to adapt as court processes change.
- Special evidential rules apply to the questioning and treatment of witnesses that impact on the competency of witnesses, the type and manner of questions that can be asked and the right to silence of defendant witnesses.

## 3.1 Introduction

In this chapter we will continue our focus on Technical Legal Practice but this time we will consider the key skills of drafting documents (B4), effective speaking as an advocate and effective written advocacy through written argument (B5) as well as communicating effectively with others (C1) (Figure 3.1).

Speaking to clients, work colleagues, judges, and other professionals, means adapting the way we express ourselves, to the particular context. This includes both our written and spoken communication. However, communication only becomes effective if we can test the information through conversation. Imparting information through writing, talking and asking questions are all part of the skills of communication. Listening is also a key aspect as it allows us to send the correct messages through our conversation.

DOI: 10.4324/9781003134770-5

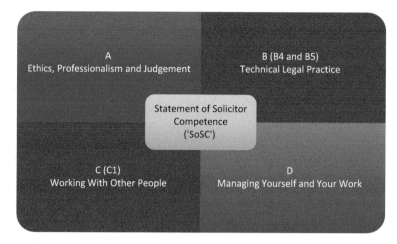

**Figure 3.1** Statement of Solictor Competence.

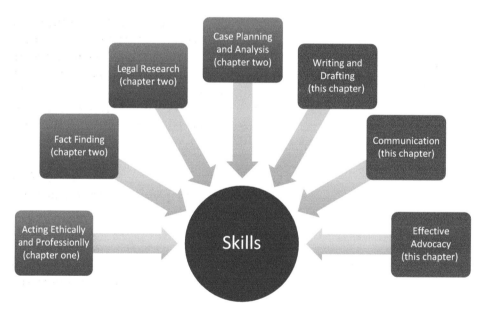

**Figure 3.2** Chapter Content.

In the previous chapter we considered skills relating to case preparation. In this chapter we will consider skills relating to communication (oral and written) and writing skills (drafting).

## 3.2 Effective Writing and Drafting

An advocate will need to communicate with the client as well as communicating the client's case to other legal professionals and the court. Writing in an organised and logical manner will ensure that important information is presented in a way that is easy for others to read and digest. This means that the information that you have previously gathered must be recorded and presented accurately and clearly. In addition, following procedural rules will ensure that documents are drafted in a way that will avoid errors or render a document legally invalid. When drafting legal documents for the court it is acceptable to use legal terms and include references to cases. However, the court encourages the use of simple and concise language when drafting documents. Just as your planned arguments will need to identify the main issues and disputed facts, your court documentation will also need to clearly set out your client's case in a concise and logical way.

# How to Draft Legally Effective Documents to Achieve Objectives

## 3.2.1 Drafting Case Documents ('Statements of Case')

Drafting is a preparatory skill that all advocates will need to become proficient in, particularly when drafting skeleton arguments and consent orders. One of the most common documents that an advocate will draft is a skeleton argument. The court provides guidance on how skeleton arguments and other written submissions should be submitted to the court. For example, the guidance covers font size, paper size, line spacing, length and content (see, for example, Criminal Practice Direction Division XII D.17 for criminal proceedings). You will find an example of skeleton arguments in a civil case in Part B of this guide.

Drafting documents from scratch or using precedents in the form of pre-drafted documents will help to ensure that you set out your arguments clearly and in a way that reflects your client's goals.

It is important to use precedents with care as the precedents may not precisely reflect the nature of the case that you need to argue. Do not copy precedents verbatim but instead use them as an aid to create your own arguments. Precedents can be found on legal databases such as Westlaw, Lawtel and Practical Law.

Court *pro forma* documents are different from a precedent in that they are templates for court forms and determine the layout, look, and to some degree, the content of the documents to be used in court proceedings. These should be followed as required by the form itself. An example can be found in form N244. This is the application notice, a form used to commence most interim hearings in the civil court. Another example is the claim form (form N1) in which the claimant sets out particulars of their claim. These forms, and others, can be found on the government website (www.gov.uk).

In civil proceedings, the court usually prescribes the content of documents and how documents should be formatted and bound. Advocates should familiarise themselves with the requirements under the Civil Procedure Rules ('CPR') Practice Direction 5A para 2.2 which includes the requirement that all documents are legible, and pages numbered consecutively.

In civil proceedings, all documents setting out the nature of the case and the nature of the defence (known collectively as statements of case) are to be drafted following the requirements set out in CPR Part 16. For example, one of the documents that will set out the claimant's case is known as the particulars of claim. Part 16 and its accompanying practice direction states that this document must contain certain information and headings such as the name of the court, the claim number, the title of the proceedings and the claimant's address for service. The document must also contain a statement to the effect that the facts mentioned in the particulars of claim are true (this is required by Part 22).

It is important for an advocate to understand how statements of case and other court documentation should be drafted as it may be possible to argue at an interim hearing that the opponent's application should fail because of procedural errors in the drafting of documentation or the failure to follow other procedural rules.

## Drafting Example 1

Below you will find an example of a particulars of claim document relating to a personal injury road traffic accident claim in the civil courts. This document is matched with the procedural requirements (see footnotes) under the Civil Procedure Rules.

**IN THE HIGH COURT OF JUSTICE**                                   Claim No. QB2389A
**QUEEN'S BENCH DIVISION**[1]
**BETWEEN**

**TYSON DAWKINS**          Claimant

**AND**

**RAY CREEK**          Defendant[2]

**PARTICULARS OF CLAIM**

1.  On the 14th August [year] the Claimant was driving his Mini Electric motor vehicle registration number RE75RDT 765R along Crescent Road, Anytown, Landshire when a BMW Roadster motorcycle registration number BM56XED driven by the

---

1  The name of the court and the claim number are required under CPR PD 16 para 3.8 (1)).
2  The name of the parties forms part of the title of the proceedings and is required under CPR 16 PD para 3.8 (3)). See CPR PD 7A para 4.1 for the full details of the headings for a statement of case such as a particulars of claim.

Defendant emerged from a side road known as Pheasant Walk and collided with the motorcycle.
2. The above accident was caused by the negligence of the Defendant.

### Detailed Allegations of Negligence of the Defendant

a) Driving too fast
b) Failing to stop at a stop sign
c) Failing to give priority to the Claimant
d) Emerging from the junction when it was not safe to do so
e) Ignoring or inadequately observing the signs, markings and layout of the junction
f) Failing to exercise sufficient care and attention by giving consideration to other traffic on the road
g) Failing to adequately observe or notice the claimant and/or the claimant's motor vehicle at all or in time
h) Having emerged from the junction, failing to slow down, swerve or avoid the claimant's motor vehicle
i) Carelessly managing or controlling his motorcycle so as to cause the accident.[3]

Further on the 30th September [year] at the Landshire Magistrates Court the Defendant was convicted of the offence of careless and inconsiderate driving under section 3 Road Traffic Act 1988.[4] This conviction is relevant to the issue of negligence in this matter and the Claimant intends to rely upon it as evidence in this action.

As a result of the Defendant's negligence, the Claimant has suffered injury in the form of a broken hip and bruising to his face, legs and arms as well as loss and damage.[5]

### Details of Consequential Loss

See attached Schedule of Loss. Further the Claimant claims interest upon such damages pursuant to section 35A of the Senior Courts Act 1981.[6]

---

3 As the claim is based on allegations of wrongful conduct by the defendant, the particulars of claim must clearly specify the conduct and when it took place – see CPR PD 16 para 7.5.
4 A claimant can rely on the previous conviction of the defendant in a criminal court for the same incident as proof of their liability in the pending civil trial. This is permitted by the Civil Evidence Act 1968, s. 11. However, the claimant must include the type of conviction, details of the court and the date of the court's decision – see CPR PD 16 para 8.1.
5 In a personal injury action the particulars of claim must also contain brief details of the claimant's injuries – see CPR PD 16 para 4.1(2).
6 In a personal injury action the particulars of claim will be sent with a separate document setting out the calculation of past and future expenses and losses – this is known as the schedule of loss and is required under CPR PD 16 para 4.2.

## Details of Injury

The Claimant whose date of birth is 11th April 2000 [7]was caused pain, suffering and loss of amenity. Further information is contained in the attached medical report.

## Details of the Basis of the Claim for Interest

Interest is claimed under section 35A of the Senior Courts Act 1981.[8]

Special Damages

Interest is claimed on each and every item of quantifiable and consequential loss incurred from the date the loss occurred and to be assessed under the provisions of the Court Fund Rules 2011 (as amended) at half the prescribed full special account rate.[9]

General Damages

The Claimant claims interest on general damages at the rate of 2% from the date of service of the claim form in this case until the date of judgment.

AND the Claimant claims:

1.  Damages exceeding £50,000[10]
2.  Interest pursuant to section 35A of the Senior Courts Act 1981
3.  STATEMENT OF TRUTH

The claimant believes that the facts stated in this particulars of claim are true. The claimant understands that proceedings for contempt of court may be brought against anyone who makes, or causes to be made, a false statement in a document verified by a statement of truth without an honest belief in its truth.[11]

Signed...**Tyson Dawkins**...................

7  In a personal injury action the particulars of claim must also contain the claimant's date of birth – see CPR PD 16 4.1(1).
8  Any claim for interest on damages must be separately stated in the document and this is required by CPR Part 16 3.7
9  In personal injury cases it is possible to link the interest claimed on quantifiable losses (known as 'special damages') to the Court Fund Office's special account interest rate which is currently set at 0.1% as at 1 June 2020.
10  This indicates to the court that as a personal injury claim it is within the relevant damages threshold to be started in the High Court – see Civil Procedure Rules 16.3(5)(c) and Practice Direction 7A para 2.2.
11  The particulars of claim document must contain a statement of truth at the end of the document, and this is required by CPR PD 16 3.4 and is also in accordance with the set wording found in CPR Part 22.1(a) and PD 22 para 2.1.

Dated this 30th day of October [year]

> FairLaw LLP
> 30 Market Square
> Any Town
> Landshire
> Solicitors for the Claimants who will
> accept service of proceedings at the
> above address.[12]

Note the wording for the Statement of Truth in the sample document above. A statement of Truth must also be incorporated into other case documents, including av expert's report (although the wording differs slightly). See the list below for examples of documents that should contain a Statement of Truth:

1.  Particulars of Claim
2.  Acknowledgement of Service (Part 8 Claims only)
3.  Certificate of Service
4.  Defence
5.  Defence and Counterclaim
6.  Reply
7.  Request for Further Information
8.  Witness Statements
9.  Expert's Report

It is important to ensure that all documents that you draft comply with court requirements. In the case of *Gould and Others v R* [2021] EWCA Crim 447 technical errors occurred in the drafting of charges in four conjoined appeal cases, Edis LJ noted that "it is the duty of the prosecution to stop making basic procedural errors" [3]. The errors included typographical errors resulting in the wrong dates being used on indictments, failure to properly particularise multiple charges in terms of identifying the victims and failure to note that the date the offence was committed meant it did not come under new provisions for sentencing made by a change in the law. The court noted that such errors could, in certain circumstances, lead to the proceedings being rendered null and void where the procedure to correct the errors was in itself defective and led to convictions being quashed in the case of the defendant Gould.

Accuracy, conciseness, preciseness and quality are therefore all to be regarded as important drafting skills needed by a competent advocate.

---

12 The address where documents can be served on the claimant is also required under CPR PD 16 para 3.8(4). This will usually be the claimant's solicitors' address.

## How to Draft Effective Letters, Emails and Notes to Achieve Objectives

# 3.3 Writing Skills

An advocate will also be expected to enter into written communications with the client as well as third parties such as experts and the court. Communication may take place in the form of letters, emails or telephone calls or telephone hearings. It is important that all forms of communication are conducted in a professional and courteous manner.

## 3.3.1 Letter Writing Skills

A professional letter, whilst containing information about the case, may also need to contain additional information that meets the requirements of professional bodies. For example, the SRA Standards and Regulations (8.6 and 8.7) require you to give information to clients in a way that they can understand, including information about your costs. You are also expected to give clients information about how the services that you provide are regulated (8.10) and information about complaints handling (8.2–8.5).

When writing to a client you may need to convey important information and you may decide to use sub-headings throughout your letter to help signpost important information.

It is important that you summarise the nature of the client's case and any advice that you have given to the client so that there is a written record that both you and the client can refer to. If you are a trainee solicitor, you should also give the client details of your supervising solicitor.

When writing to the client you should also use language that is simple to understand and avoid using legal terminology or Latin expressions (for example, *res ipsa loquitur*) as 'legalese' will be meaningless to the client. Instead, you should use concise and precise words and phrases in plain English. You should aim to describe events or your advice using a simple 'what', 'why', 'when', how' structure. You may occasionally include 'who' when discussing the role of other parties.

You should also avoid referring to reported cases when writing to the client as this is unlikely to be meaningful to the client. However, if you have had a previous discussion with the client about an important court decision that is awaited that may strengthen or change the advice that you have given to them, then it would be appropriate to include the details of the case for context. Ordinarily, you would simply summarise the legal principles that arise from case law and do so in a way that puts the client's legal problem, aims and objectives at the forefront.

Keeping your sentences short will also help the client to read with speed and accuracy. You can achieve this by cutting out any unnecessary words from your sentences; this will enable you to be concise. It is also important to adopt an appropriate tone (friendly rather than too formal) and to ensure that you use correct grammar and punctuation.

Always write using the firm's headed notepaper when writing to clients and those connected with your cases. Follow the rules for letter writing, so as a general rule, the recipient's name and address will appear at the top left-hand side of the letter and your firm's address will appear on the top right-hand side. If you start your letter with the more formal salutation, 'Dear Sir/Madam', then you should end with 'yours faithfully'. However, if you have referred to the client by name, for example, 'Dear Mrs Portland' or 'Dear Harriet' then you should end with 'yours sincerely'. When writing to a new client that you have not met before, it is better to maintain formality and address the client either using their surname, for example, 'Dear Mrs Portland' or 'Dear Madam'.

The letter should always be dated with the current date.

Try to write using an 'active' voice rather than a 'passive' voice. You should, make your verbs active. Here are some examples of passive sentences (to be avoided) and active sentences (to be encouraged):

"Your file has been passed to me" (*passive*).
"I have taken over your file" (*active*).
"Further advice can be obtained from me as your case progresses" (*passive*).
"I will give you further advice as your case progresses" (*active*).

### Drafting Exercise 2

Consider the following extract from the letter below and *highlight where you think this letter could be improved*:

**Confidence Exercise**

Dear Mrs Portland,

Thank you for coming to see me yesterday to discuss your case. As you know, the senior partner has passed your case on to me.

I note that you are currently awaiting trial on a charge of fraud under section 2 and 3 of the Fraud Act 2006. This is in relation to your failure to disclose to Mr

Forshall important information about the painting that he purchased from you. Mr Forshall alleges that you knew that the painting that he purchased from you was a reproduction but that you led him to believe that it was in fact an original painting by a well-known artist. It is alleged that you therefore made a false representation to him and that he relied on this to his detriment.

We discussed the fact that you were concerned that the prosecution has not disclosed all the available evidence. You state that a letter exists that you wrote to Mr Forshall after he had purchased the painting in which you told him that as a result of receiving further information you now had doubts about the authenticity of the painting that you had sold to him. This letter is of course important to the question of whether or not you have been dishonest, but you do not have a copy of this letter.

I promised to write to you with some further advice about this. The law in this area states that the original information you gave must have been deliberately untrue or misleading. You must also have been under either a legal or moral duty to disclose the information about the true origins of the painting. Whilst the 2006 Act does not define what is meant by a legal or a moral duty, some guidance on this can be found in the Law Commission Report (Law Com No 276) paragraphs 7.28–7.34.

My advice is that we should ask the prosecution to disclose the letter that you wrote to Mr Forshall and that we should do this through the process of 'specific disclosure'. The prosecution have an obligation to provide us with what is called 'unused material' which is effectively any evidence collected during the investigation which is either capable of undermining the prosecution case or capable of assisting our case and this is what we mean by the term 'disclosure'.

I believe therefore that the letter is important and forms part of what would be regarded as 'unused material'. The prosecution has an initial duty to disclose such material according to section 3 of the Criminal Investigation and Procedure Act ('CPIA') 1996. They also have a continuing duty under section 7A of the same Act.

In the case of *R v DPP, ex parte Lee* (1999) 2 Cr App R 304, the Court of Appeal emphasised the need for prosecutors to act responsibly and always consider the need for early disclosure of any information that might assist the defendant at an early stage, for example, when applying for bail or for a stay of proceedings. I would have expected the prosecution to have behaved more professionally and to be aware of their obligations under the Code of Practice set out in Part II section 23 of the CPIA 1996.

We can apply to the court by using the Criminal Procedure Rules to force the defendant to reveal the letter by making an application for specific disclosure under Part 15.5.

I hope this advice is helpful. Please do not hesitate to contact me if you have any questions arising from this letter.

Yours faithfully

A Laws

**How much of this letter do you think the client is likely to have understood?**

Whilst knowledge of the law is important, communication of that knowledge must be carried out in language that can be easily understood. For example, the same advice could have been given to Mrs Portland without the need to make reference to the primary sources. The letter also does not adhere to the formalities that we have previously discussed in terms of style and format.

## 3.3.2  Writing Emails

Emails are a quick way of communicating but should be reserved for short messages that require some action on the readers' part. This is because lengthy emails are less likely to be read in detail, especially in a busy work environment where the recipient may be receiving a large number of emails throughout the day. Emails (like letters) should also be proofread as it is easy to make mistakes when writing quick messages.

Business emails still require a degree of formality especially if writing to the client or the court and so it may still be appropriate to use 'Dear' as the salutation. However, if you know the person well, such as a colleague or another legal professional, then you might use a courteous greeting such as 'Hello'. Depending on the degree of familiarity you might also replace the more formal ending of 'yours faithfully' or 'yours sincerely' with 'Best wishes'.

It is important to include a subject line in your email and to also indicate if the matter is urgent. Keep the body of the email relatively short. If you need to write a long email, ensure that you use sub-headings to divide the content.

Ensure that you end your email with a 'signature' – this is a standard footer that is essentially your brand. It helps to identify you by your name, your position, your work address, and other contact information. It will usually contain details of your firm's website and be followed by an email disclaimer notice. This is a warning notice added to outgoing emails that warns the recipient that the email is intended solely for the recipient and that confidential information should be treated as confidential and private, and unauthorised use, disclosure or copying is not permitted. In some circumstances such information may also be protected by legal privilege (treated as confidential and exempt from disclosure in court). Such a disclaimer also protects your firm as it will usually stipulate that the views and opinions in the email belong to you and not the firm.

There are many formalities to observe when contacting and communicating with the court by email. For example, in civil proceedings, the Civil Procedure Rules Practice Direction 5B states that emails to the court must contain the name, address and contact telephone number of the sender and be in plain or rich text format (para 3.1). If proceedings have been started then the email must also contain the case number, the parties' names, and the dates of any forthcoming hearings (see para 3.6). A hard copy of the email must also be sent separately to the court (see para 4.1).

### 3.3.3  Note-Taking for Record Purposes

It is a feature of open justice that court proceedings should be transparent. There is a convention (understood practice) that anyone attending court (including members of the public) are permitted to take notes without the judge's permission as long as it is not done for a wrongful purpose and does not interfere with the proper administration of justice (see, for example, guidance contained in the Criminal Practice Direction 2015 (as amended) Division I 6D). This was confirmed in *Ewing v Crown Court Sitting at Cardiff and Newport and DPP* [2016] EWHC 183 (Admin). In addition, court transcripts are available for the public to purchase at a fee.

Brice (2007) argues that even where proceedings are recorded, and a transcript is available, personal notes of advocates are useful where findings of fact are questioned on appeal. An advocate will be expected to take notes during most hearings. As such, note-taking is an important skill, yet it is not a skill that is routinely taught within law courses. Notes are also a useful reference point for the advocate during the hearing or trial so that they can keep track of the evidence or query any discrepancy in the evidence or indeed in the transcript itself. Writing down information also helps to ensure that the information is assimilated and processed by the brain. This also helps to aid concentration and keeps the advocate's mind focused on the evidence and issues heard in court.

An advocate is free to develop their own note-taking style using shorthand, as long as they are able to decipher their own notes at a later date. Try to keep any shortening of words logical, for example, you might use 'C' for claimant and 'D' for defendant and 'J' for judge. However, where you have more than one legal representative or counsel then abbreviations might be based on names or status, for example, 'EofD' to represent the expert acting for the defendant. When taking a note of evidence, do not attempt to write down everything that the witness says, instead paraphrase the nature of the evidence; remember a transcript will be available. However, where a witness's reply or response is crucial to your client's case then try to get the exact wording of what the witness has said. This requires you to remain alert and focused throughout the hearing.

If the hearing or trial is taking place across more than one day, then be sure to make clear in your notes the date of the evidence. It might also be helpful to indicate if the evidence took place in the morning or afternoon in case a copy of the full transcript is needed at a later date.

# Becoming a Good Communicator

## 3.4 Effective Communication Skills

A good communicator will command respect through their 'presence' (the ability to present oneself as a person of authority who deserves to be heard). Judgments are made by others about a person early on based on both their speech and appearance. Following court etiquette on appearance and order of speech will ensure that an advocate holds the attention of the court.

### 3.4.1 Court Communication Etiquette

You should observe both oral and written communication etiquette when working with others such as judges and court officials. For example, CPR Part 39.8 provides that any communication between a party and the court must be disclosed to the other party unless there is a compelling reason not to do so. Such communication must explicitly state it is being copied to the other party with details of their identity and capacity in the proceedings.

When appearing before a judge in a civil case, the claimant will usually start speaking first. In a criminal case, the prosecution will make the opening speech. However, where the hearing involves an interim application then the party that made the application will speak first.

It is also important to address judges and opponents with their correct titles when writing or speaking to them. In court, barristers will usually address each other as 'my learned friend' and address a solicitor as 'my friend' (although solicitor-advocates may be called 'my learned friend'). Avoid referring to your client as 'my client' in court and instead use their litigation status, e.g. 'claimant' or 'defendant', or simply the client's name.

Always ensure that you check the court list to find out which level of judge will be hearing your case so that you can address them by their correct title when you are in court. If in doubt, always check with the court clerk before entering the courtroom. See Figures 3.3 and 3.4 for examples.

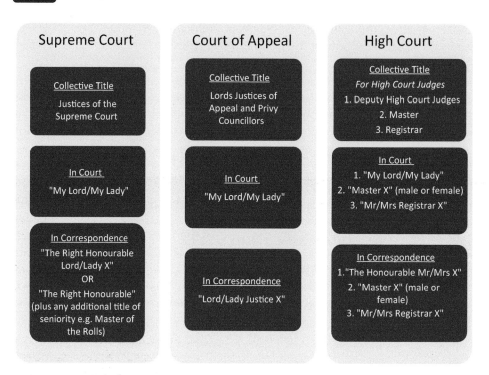

**Figure 3.3** How to Address a Judge in the Higher Courts. Source: The Criminal Practice Directions 2015 XII B and www.judiciary.uk

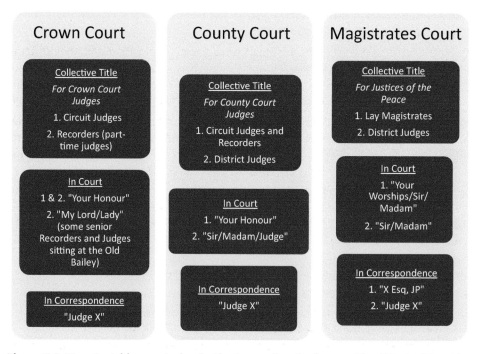

**Figure 3.4** How to Address a Judge in the Lower Courts. Source: The Criminal Practice Directions 2015 XII B and www.judiciary.uk

Judges sitting in tribunals (e.g. employment tribunals) are referred to as 'Sir' or 'Madam' and are referred to as 'Judge' in correspondence.

## 3.4.2 Communication Through Appearance

Appearance can affect the way that others respond to you and whether you are perceived as having authority and commanding respect. An advocate will be expected to observe certain traditions relating to the operation of the court and legal process. One of these is to appear in 'court dress'. This involves wearing a suit in dark colours ('business attire'). These colours are normally black, navy and grey to reflect the sombre occasion of the business at hand. For some proceedings and courts an advocate will also need to wear a wig and gown ('court dress') depending on the level of their rights of audience. The Criminal Practice Directions 2015 XII A sets out guidance on court dress. For example, the practice direction states that advocates do not need to wear robes or wigs in the Magistrates' Court (including youth courts) but are expected to do so in all other criminal courts (except for bail applications heard in chambers). Court robes will differ depending on whether an advocate is Queen's Counsel ('QC'), junior counsel or a solicitor advocate.

In the civil courts court dress is required in the High Court (except commercial, admiralty and technology courts) and in the Family Division. Business attire is sufficient for interim applications in the County Court, but court dress is usually expected at a trial or an appeal from a trial.

## 3.4.3 Communicating with Vulnerable Clients and Witnesses

An advocate should be mindful of the need to adapt the method and style of their communication when dealing with clients and witnesses. A person may be vulnerable due to lacking mental capacity or due to age. In Chapter 4 we will consider in more detail the court processes surrounding vulnerable parties. It is useful for an advocate to acquaint themselves with court terminology relating to vulnerable parties. For example, when dealing with children varying terminology is used for child defendants. Those under 14 are termed 'children', those between 14 and 18 are termed 'young persons' and collectively all those under 18 are referred to as 'juveniles'. This includes those who are 17 when arrested or appear to be under 18 (see *R (C) v Secretary of State for the Home Department and Another* [2013] EWHC 982 (Admin) and the Criminal Justice and Courts Act 2015, s. 42). In addition, the courts tend to avoid referring to 'sentence' or 'convictions' of a child but instead refer to 'findings of guilt' or 'orders'.

## 3.4.4 Video Conferencing

Courts are increasingly using video conferencing for communication and this increased substantially during the Covid-19 pandemic. For example, the Coronavirus Act 2020 modified court practice and procedure to allow for remote working and virtual attendance at hearings and to extend the broadcast of public hearings as well as the use of electronic bundles of court documents. These changes also included a new temporary Civil Procedure Practice Direction 51Y on 'Video or Audio Hearings During Coronavirus Pandemic.' However, only the court, rather than the parties or members of the public, can record the hearings.

The use of cameras in the courtroom is not new and the use of cameras was extended by ss. 31 and 32 of the Crime and Courts Act 2013. Stephen Mason (2012) argues that the introduction of cameras in courtrooms can increase transparency and need not necessarily lead to human rights breaches if the broadcast itself is controlled by the courts. Cameras and live transmissions would also act to counter the way in which the media report events in court as the public would be able to judge the proceedings for themselves. Paul Lambert (2011), however, argues that social media has permeated the courtroom to the extent that everyone is now a journalist and that the rise of social media has the potential to change the traditional method of court reporting.

An advocate should be flexible and adaptable as court practices are constantly evolving with new ways of working. This includes familiarisation with software platforms that enable live group chat and collaboration or the use of audio or live streaming. This places new demands on how an advocate communicates using body language, deals with interruptions resulting from technology failures (rather than questions from the judge), and pays attention not just to their own physical appearance but also to the physical appearance of the room that they are in.

When attending a virtual hearing it might be helpful to run through a simple checklist of 'remote-ready' actions. Whilst the judge will be responsible for directing any virtual proceedings, it is helpful to check that you know how to carry out the following tasks:

1. Have you blurred/changed/tidied your background to maintain privacy?
2. Have you muted your microphone when you are not speaking (this will prevent 'feedback' noise)?
3. Have you remembered to unmute your microphone when you are speaking?
4. Do you know how to use the 'raised hand icon' when you want to speak so that you do not interrupt other speakers?
5. Do you know how to lower the 'raised hand icon' when you have finished speaking so that others know that you have finished your contribution?
6. Do you know how to share your screen so that you can display documents to your audience when needed?
7. Have you cleared other non-relevant documents from your desktop to maintain privacy when sharing your screen and avoid sharing content unintentionally?
8. If your internet connection is weak, do you know what to do if your screen 'freezes' or if the connection is lost or do you have IT support?
9. Do you need to appear on screen in 'court dress' (gown/wig) or has the court dispensed with this?

Ensuring that you have an ethernet cable connected to your device and your internet portal will ensure that you have a stronger connection. Turning off incoming video and muting your microphone will also ensure that the connection remains more stable than otherwise.

# How to Conduct Effective Spoken Advocacy

## 3.5 Effective Advocacy

Most people would argue that central to an advocate's role is their ability to construct arguments. However, as we have seen, an advocate's skill set is diverse and argument construction is only one part of this. An advocate will take a focused, measured and analytical approach to case preparation to lay down the foundations for their eventual appearance at court. Being able to effectively communicate that case strategy is imperative. Keeping an audience's attention allows an advocate to impart information in a way that is understood by an audience and ensures key messages are picked up by that audience. A listener can be easily distracted and so keeping people engaged requires personable skills as well as adhering to certain formalities. In the next section we will consider some tips on how to communicate effectively with an audience in a court setting.

### 3.5.1 Know Your Audience

It is important to adjust your presentation skills according to your audience. For example, the client will want information presented in a simple and clear way and for complex ideas or legal terms to be explained. A judge will expect legal arguments to be presented with reference to case law and other forms of legal authority. Whilst you can assume some prior understanding of the case by a judge you should always check whether the judge would like a summary of the facts or to be reminded of the facts of cases.

You may employ different questioning techniques when questioning witnesses to elicit important facts, acknowledgements and concessions that are important for your audience (judge/jury) to hear. Your style may depend on the issues in the case and the category of your witness. For example, are you questioning your own client, an opponent or a witness? Each may require a different approach.

As a general rule, questioning usually involves mixing 'open questions' (where the subject is allowed to tell their story freely) with 'closed questions' (designed to elicit a 'yes' or 'no' response). See below for examples:

*Open Question* – "can you tell me what happened on the night of the alleged rape?"
*Closed Question* – "was the defendant there on that day?"

During a trial you will usually use a mix of open and closed questioning during your examination of witnesses.

You may, however, communicate through arguments rather than questioning and you will need to adjust your style as the emphasis is then on logical structure and content.

Let's compare the different approach that you might take when communicating with a judge, client and general witness in court:

### 3.5.1.1 Judge

If you are leading on the presentation before a judge in court (because, for example, you have made the application) then your presentation would usually follow the seven steps shown in Figure 3.5.

The judge is your audience and the communication is direct rather than observed (as in the case of a jury). Your communications with a judge will always be respectful and formal, for example "if it may please your Honour...", or "may I have permission to move to my next submission, Madam?". We will explore the direct communication structure in more detail in Chapter 4.

### 3.5.1.2 Client

At trial, you will use a mix of open and closed questioning for a client who is also a witness and the main questioning will take place as 'examination-in-chief' and allow

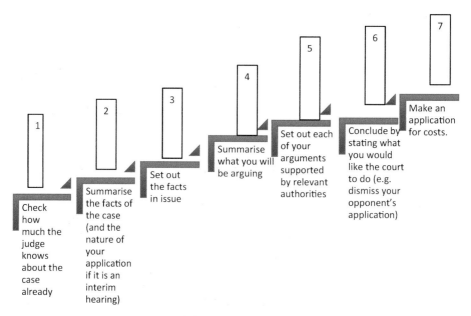

**Figure 3.5** Steps to a Good Presentation.

the witness to tell their own story (see discussion in 3.6.1 ). You should ensure that your questioning helps you to elicit the relevant information. This is information that you will need to know in order to progress the client's case in court. For example, in a criminal case, your questions should elicit sufficient information to enable you to assess the following:

| Areas for Questioning | Reason |
|---|---|
| Plea | If the defendant pleads not guilty there will be a trial, if the defendant pleads guilty then matters can move swiftly to sentencing. |
| Severity of offence | This will determine the venue for trial. 'Summary' offences (minor nature) will be heard in the Magistrates' Court. 'Either way offences' (medium severity) can be heard in either the Magistrates' or Crown Court. 'Indictable offences' (serious cases) are heard only in the Crown Court. |
| Evidence | This will help you to determine what case management directions you will need from the court, e.g. use of expert evidence, specific disclosure of evidence from the prosecution, etc. |
| Personal circumstances | This information will be needed for sentencing, particularly when dealing with a 'plea in mitigation' to try to reduce the possible sentence. We will look at this in more detail in Part B, Chapter 7. |

## 3.5.1.3 Witness

Your approaches to questioning a non-client witness will differ. This is because you are focused on the disputed facts and the evidence that is needed to prove or disprove those facts to the relevant standard of proof.

| Areas for Questioning | Reason |
|---|---|
| Undisputed facts | This enables you to set the scene and to relax the witness into the story and introduce uncontentious points to the judge/jury. |
| Disputed facts | These facts require proof to the necessary standard (beyond reasonable doubt in criminal proceedings or on a balance of probabilities in civil proceedings or 'reverse burden' criminal situations). Through cross-examination you can give credence to your client's version of events by challenging the truthfulness, accuracy or credibility of the opponent's version of events. |
| Evidence | These are your tools of proof and help to support or challenge the disputed facts. As discussed in Chapter 2, evidence may come in the form of oral, documentary or real evidence. |
| Personal circumstances | This information may help with some of the rules of evidence, for example, is the witness to be regarded as competent or do their age or physical characteristics impact on their competence? Perhaps the witness requires a 'special measures' order to be made because they are a vulnerable witness. We will discuss this in more detail in Chapter 4. |

### 3.5.2 Oral Presentation

As stated earlier, effective speaking is an important part of communication. Becoming a good oral communicator is not just about the choice of words or how these are expressed. Communication is a combination of verbal and physical signals. To command the attention of others you need to be heard not just by using your voice but also through the display of positive body language that reinforces your message. Think about the content needed in your speech to get your message across. You will need to adjust the style of your language and the level of formality used depending on your audience. Here are some aspects of oral presentation that an advocate will need to consider:

### 3.5.3 Use of Voice

Language is important so you should choose your words carefully and avoid using slang or uncommon terms. Using short sentences and avoiding irrelevant information will ensure that your audience (the judge/jury/your opponent) can concentrate on what the essence of your arguments is and how the evidence supports your case.

It is important to keep your voice loud enough so that it can be heard by others. It is also important to speak with intonation (the rise and fall of your voice). This allows a listener to follow your messages and remain engaged with what you are saying rather than become distracted or bored. You may have to adjust the volume of your voice depending on room size and the number of people in a room. Build in pauses in between sentences as this will help to emphasise the information that you want to get across.

### 3.5.4 Content

Always tailor the content of your speech to your audience. Ask yourself how much your audience knows about the subject already and what information you need to get across and why. In particular, pay attention to the tone that you will use. Will it be friendly, formal, informal or empathetic? If you are explaining difficult concepts to a non-specialist audience then be careful to use short sentences and repeat key information to reinforce its importance. Build in pauses to give your audience time to assimilate the information. Sometimes difficult factual or legal content can be best explained by using diagrams and other pictorial representations.

### 3.5.5 Body Language

Your appearance and the way you behave can also have a bearing on how other people perceive you. How you deliver your message will ensure that your oral presentation skills are effective and enable you to obtain the respect and trust of your audience. You should always appear confident and hide any nerves. This can often be achieved by placing one hand over the other so that you remain still when sitting and avoid fidgeting. If you are standing, then you may find it easier to place one hand behind your back to control nerves and avoid gesticulating with your hands which can be distracting. Holding your hands either in front of you or behind you will also prevent fidgeting or shuffling of papers.

Using visual cues such as hand gestures can be helpful if kept under control as it will also allow you to emphasise your points. You should be careful however not to over-use the body language, as this risks your audience watching but not listening. Good eye contact with the judge is essential to communication as it will establish a 'communication intimacy' which you will need to take the judge through the importance of what you are saying.

Using your body as a way to make positive affirmations (e.g. nodding your head, facial expressions) also shows that you are listening and that you are hearing and understanding what is said to you. Being able to empathise by seeing things from another person's point of view is also an important part of good communication. Ensure that you maintain good eye contact during a conversation or a presentation as this helps to create a bond of trust between you and the listener or between you and other speakers.

Try to use the following positive body language rather than the negative body language outlined in Figure 3.6.

Court etiquette also requires that an advocate is smartly dressed as appearance also acts as positive body language by suggesting a degree of authority.

## 3.5.6 Persuasion

This is the art of leading others towards your point of view. This can involve a form of storytelling or 'rhetoric' (eloquent speaking) whereby you gain trust by giving credible information and aligning your purpose with that of your audience (to see justice done).

Aristotle in his work 'Rhetoric', divided the methods of persuasion into three categories, shown in Figure 3.7.

As an advocate you should therefore bring 'presence', 'emotion' and 'proof' to your performances in court.

Good presentation is also linked to being assertive and standing up for what you believe in. This will enable you to be more persuasive. However, as a rule, advocates should avoid giving their own opinion. You should therefore work simply with the facts and the law. You should also avoid repetition. You can instead emphasise important points by building pauses into your speech to allow the point you have made to be heard and assimilated by the judge.

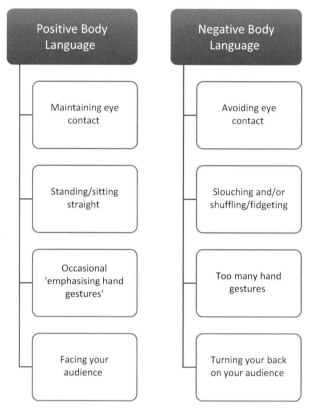

**Figure 3.6** The Essentials of Body Language.

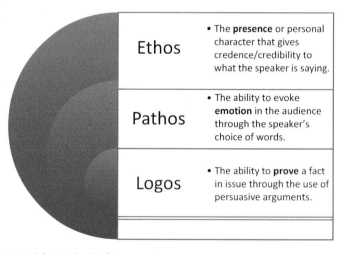

**Figure 3.7** Aristotle's Method of Persuasion.

### 3.5.7 How to Formulate Legal Arguments

Whilst presentation is important, the quality of the content is essential because it ensures leadership and dominance in the courtroom to achieve what can be regarded as 'courtroom hegemony'. Marcus Fabius Quintilianus, another famous rhetorician, argued that the art of persuasion lies in the content of the speech, not merely the structure. He argued that the speech should contain three elements:

**Invention** – finding the relevant arguments and evidence.
**Disposition** – arranging the arguments and evidence.
**Style** – choosing the words and method of verbal delivery to express the arguments and evidence.

The Quintillian approach would remove the character or behaviours of the advocate from the equation and instead focus on the active choices made by the advocate in terms of their case preparation. Content can only be successfully assimilated if it is presented in a logical structure.

Therefore, you should carefully select the points that you want to argue. Important facts should be included and emphasised, and your arguments should be capable of undermining the arguments of your opponent. This means that you will also need to pre-empt your opponent's arguments.

You should familiarise yourself with all the key arguments that you wish to present in court so that you can avoid reading from a pre-prepared script. However, you should make use of any bundles or documents that the court has before it. You can do this by referring to those documents during the course of your arguments and pointing the judge to any important passages from the documents.

If you think of your presentation as a story, you will be able to organise facts into a logical order. Structuring your speech will enable you to ensure that you present information in a way that can be readily understood and assimilated by others. Like a story, you need an introduction, middle and conclusion. Aristotle argued that speech was an important part of what he called 'judicial rhetoric'. He recognised that a speech had two parts; firstly, to state the thing in issue and secondly, to demonstrate it. As a result, each speech follows a particular structure in terms of an introduction, a statement addressing the thing in issue, the persuasive arguments and then ends with an epilogue.

Here is an example of how a speech in court might follow (1) an introduction, (2) a statement addressing the issue, (3) a persuasive argument and (4) an epilogue/conclusion. We will use the facts from **Drafting Example 1**:

- Any speech should start with an introduction. This will usually involve the advocate introducing themselves and their opponent. For example:

*Your Honour, I am Frieda Lauderdale and I appear on behalf of the claimant. My learned friend Mr Patel appears on behalf of the defendant in these proceedings.*

- Any arguments should first identify the issues and the nature of the application (or evidence in the case of a trial) and the remedy sought. For example:

  *Your Honour, this case concerns a personal injury action arising from a road traffic accident that occurred on 14 August (year). The claimant has made an application to enter summary judgment under Part 24 of the Civil Procedure Rules on the basis that the defendant has no real prospects of successfully defending the action and that there is no compelling reason why the case should be disposed of at trial.*

- You should present each persuasive argument separately with clear signposting as to when you are moving on to your next argument. This can be achieved if you present your arguments as a series of submissions. This will enable you to build in pauses and to also emphasise important points – this is a helpful style to adopt when trying to persuade. For example:
  *Your Honour my first submission is this...*

- For each point of law ensure that you cite the relevant authority and point the judge to the relevant facts and evidence. This might, for example, be a case, legislation or procedural rules or a combination of these. This is a further way to ensure that your arguments can persuade. For example:

  *When deciding whether the defendant has any real prospects of successfully defending the action, as emphasised in the case of* Royal Brompton Hospital National Health Service v Hammond and Others *[2001] EWCA Civ 550, the focus of this application should be on the statement of case as opposed to the evidence.*

- Ensure that your speech has a clear epilogue – this is the final section of your speech that serves as a conclusion by bringing together the important points that you have made into one commentary. For example:

  *For the reasons I have outlined, namely the defendant's failure to plead a proper and valid defence, the strength of the undisputed facts and the defendant's own admissions of mechanical failings of his vehicle, the defendant's defence is unlikely to succeed at trial. As such, it would not be in the interests of justice to allow the matter to proceed to a costly trial bearing in mind the overriding objective to ensure cases are dealt with expeditiously and fairly and saving expense.*

We will continue to work with both content and structure of arguments in Part B.

# Understanding the Evidential Rules on Questioning

## 3.6 Trial Questioning

In the average trial the prosecution or claimant will begin and call their witnesses first. Once they have completed their evidence the defence/defendant will then produce their witnesses and after the half-way stage the defence call their witnesses. In a criminal trial a defendant may give evidence and will usually be called before the other defence witnesses.

Each witness will be subject to questioning in three stages (1) evidence in chief (2) cross-examination and (3) re-examination. It is the duty of the judge to ensure witnesses are treated properly and the judge may disallow particular questions to be asked if they amount to bullying or disrespectful treatment of a witness or breach established rules on the questioning of witnesses. If the witness breaks down in the witness box the judge can decide whether to adjourn the trial. As indicated in *R v Lubemba; R v JP* [2014] EWCA Crim 2064 "a trial judge is not only entitled, he is duty bound to control the questioning of a witness. He is not obliged to allow a defence advocate to put their case. He is entitled to and should set reasonable time limits and to interrupt where he considers questioning is inappropriate" [51].

As discussed in Chapter 3, an advocate will have to be mindful of their relationship and the approach that they take in dealing with vulnerable witnesses and clients and this extends to questioning at trial. When dealing with a vulnerable witness, advocates should adapt their normal questioning structure. Short questions that are simple to understand and words that have clear meanings are preferable. An advocate should also avoid any words with double meanings. Failing to adapt the style of questioning could result in 'tag' questions being asked. This is where confrontational questions are put to the witness in the style of making an assertion and then asking for confirmation. An example would be, "you never take responsibility, do you?" A vulnerable witness may find it harder to unravel such a question by noting that it already includes an assumption, or they may be reluctant to challenge the statement in the question because of a fear of someone in authority such as an advocate. Tag type questions are more suited to questioning adult witnesses who are able to challenge them. As *Lubemba* reminds us "If Justice is to be done to the vulnerable witness and also to the accused, a radical departure from the traditional style of advocacy will be necessary. Advocates must adapt to the witness, not the other way round"[45].

Advocates can find useful resources and toolkits to help them with questioning style by visiting the Advocates Gateway website listed at the end of this chapter.

We will start by looking at some of the rules of questioning.

### 3.6.1 Examination-in-Chief

This is the process by which the party calling the witness elicits their testimony. It is a process to allow a party's own witness to tell their story. The main purpose is to obtain answers which support the party's case and raise matters which the advocate anticipates will be brought up by the opposing party on cross-examination. It is also an opportunity to showcase the witness's credibility to the judge or jury.

During examination-in-chief 'leading questions' are not usually permitted. A leading question is one which already has an answer implicit within it. An example would be "is it correct to say that at that stage you lost your temper?" By asking this question an advocate has led the witness down the route of suggesting that they lost their temper without first establishing that this was indeed the witness's emotion at the time. A better question would be "how did that make you feel at that point?"

### 3.6.2 Cross-Examination

This is the questioning of one party's witness by the opposing party and the purpose is to test the truthfulness of the evidence that has just been given by the witness in their evidence-in-chief and/or undermine the witness's credibility. Cross-examination therefore performs four main functions: (1) to test the witness's veracity, (2) to test the accuracy of the witness's account of events, (3) to undermine the witness's previous testimony and (4) to cast doubt on the witness's credibility.

During cross-examination an advocate can ask 'leading questions'; this is because at this point the witness's account has been given and is known and leading questions may be useful in progressing the questioning and speeding up the trial. However, such questions should be relevant and the witness should not be harangued, bullied or misled by this form of questioning. The judge may intervene to prevent abuse, irrelevance or repetition.

During cross-examination an advocate must put the opposite party's version of events to the witness so they can comment on it. They should not be taken to have accepted it. In addition, where the witness's evidence has been challenged, they should be given an opportunity to respond to that challenge.

Questions asked in cross-examination to undermine a witness's general credibility are generally subject to the 'rule of collateral finality' (this is a matter of convenience to avoid slowing down trials). This means that usually evidence cannot be called to rebut a witness's first answer – even if the advocate does not accept the answer given by the witness. This is because the witness's credibility is regarded as a collateral or secondary issue to the important central issue at trial which is whether the defendant is innocent or guilty.

It is recognised, however, that the 'rule of collateral finality' could impede the ability to uncover the truth and so cases have recognised that in certain situations, it may be appropriate to continue to question a witness about matters which are not central to the issues in the trial but are important to, for example, uncovering a hidden bias of the witness, uncovering that the witness has a reputation for lying or has relevant previous convictions or that the witness has a physical or mental condition that might impact on their competency as a witness.

### 3.6.3 Re-examination
This allows the party who originally called the witness to ask them questions again but only on matters arising from cross-examination. If a party forgets to ask a witness a question during examination-in-chief and remembers at a later stage, he/she will need to ask the judge for permission to cross-examine on this point. The general rule however is that questions on re-examination are restricted to those matters arising during cross-examination.

---

**Confidence Exercise**

Try this One on Your Own!

Consider the following excerpt from a fictional examination-in-chief of a child witness aged 13. Consider what might be wrong with the style of the questions that have been highlighted in bold by considering the rules of trial questioning discussed in this section. Rewrite the questions in a way that you consider would be a more acceptable style and wording:

*Advocate:* Can you tell the court what you were doing on that day?
*Witness:* I was walking on Latimer Street with my friend minding my own business when it happened.
*Advocate:* **Is that when the defendant started the fight with you?**
*Witness:* Hmmm, what do you mean?
*Advocate:* **Would it be fair to say that by "minding my own business" you mean that you were not looking to get into any trouble because you don't like to challenge people, do you?**
*Witness:* I suppose so.
*Advocate:* What did the defendant do then?
*Witness:* He started punching me and my friend.
*Advocate:* **In your experience, why might he have done this?**
*Witness:* Because he is not right in the head is he?
*Advocate:* **And what did your friend say and do next after the defendant had punched him in the head?**

### 3.6.4 Questioning Special Groups
A witness is under a legal obligation to answer questions, or they will be in contempt of court. However, there are some groups who are exempt from this requirement. An

advocate must identify at an early stage whether a witness falls into one of these special groups and if so, what limitations will be placed on the ability to call the witness or to put certain questions to them. The category of special groups includes the defendant, spouses, children, hostile witnesses and protected witnesses.

### 3.6.4.1 *Defendant in Criminal Proceedings*

The Criminal Evidence Act 1898, s. 1 made the defendant competent to give evidence for the defence in all criminal proceedings but not compellable to do so. This means a defendant can choose to exercise their 'right of silence'. However, a defendant cannot give evidence against himself and for the prosecution (see s. 53(4) of the Youth Justice and Criminal Evidence Act 1999) as he will not be considered either competent or compellable in those circumstances.

A defendant is competent but not compellable as a witness for a co-accused and therefore cannot be forced to testify in support of somebody charged with them. A defendant is, however, neither competent nor compellable to give evidence for the prosecution against a co-defendant for the obvious reason that a defendant may have a motive to serve in playing down their own role to decrease their sentence or pass on the full blame to another (this is confirmed in s. 53(4) of the Youth Justice and Criminal Evidence Act 1999).

If a defendant decides to testify, he/she must be called before any other defence witnesses take the witness box. This is to prevent a defendant tailoring their evidence to fit what they have heard in court. A defendant can choose not to enter the witness box and exercise the right of silence under Criminal Justice and Public Order Act 1994, s. 35 (although adverse inferences might be drawn by the jury – see Chapter 5, 5.5–5.6).

### 3.6.4.2 *Spouses*

In civil proceedings a spouse (those who have gone through a formal marriage ceremony including civil partnerships and same sex marriages) is a competent witness under the Evidence (Further Amendment) Act 1853 but is not a compellable witness and so cannot be made to testify. It remains arguable that under the principle in *Monroe v Twistleton* (1802) Peake Add Cas 219 if the event in question occurred during the marriage/civil partnership, then even if the couple has since divorced, the spouse can rely on a claim of non-compellability to give evidence for the opposing party.

In criminal proceedings a spouse is a competent witness and can also be compelled to give evidence for the defendant. However, in most cases the spouse (excluding former spouses) cannot be compelled by the prosecution to give evidence against the defendant although they are still competent as a witness and so can choose to give evidence for the prosecution voluntarily (see s. 80 of the Police and Criminal Evidence Act 1984).

There are limited situations, however, when a spouse can be compelled by the prosecution and so forced to testify against the defendant. Under the Police and Criminal Evidence Act 1984, s. 80(2A) a spouse is compellable if:

1. the defendant is charged with an offence of violence or attempted violence, or the threat of violence towards the spouse or any child under 16, *or*
2. the defendant is charged with a sexual offence or attempted sexual offence against any child under 16 or any attempt to commit this offence.

Where the spouse (or civil partner) has the choice whether to testify or not, any failure to testify cannot be made the subject of comment by the prosecution (see s. 80(8) of the Police and Criminal Evidence Act 1984) – however this restriction applies to the prosecution and not to the judge or the co-defendant.

### 3.6.4.3 Children
Children are competent to give evidence if they meet the competency test under s. 53(3) of the Youth Justice and Criminal Evidence Act 1999. An advocate who wishes to call a witness whose competency is in dispute must prove on a balance of probabilities that they have sufficient understanding and meet the test under s. 53. However, under s. 55(2) of this Act only children who have attained the age of 14 can give sworn evidence, children under 14 must give unsworn evidence. Children are treated as vulnerable witnesses and so entitled to special measures as discussed above.

### 3.6.4.4 Hostile Witnesses
An advocate may wish to call their own witness but find that the witness is reluctant to repeat the same version of events that they have previously given, for example, in a witness statement. A witness who deliberately refuses to repeat their original testimony may be regarded as a 'hostile witness'. A hostile witness does not necessarily need to have malicious intent in refusing to answer questions or give the same version of an earlier account. It may be that the witness is simply frightened of repercussions from the defendant or his/her associates. It is for the judge to decide whether a witness is a hostile witness. This is because treating a witness as a hostile witness will involve questioning that witness as if they were a witness for the opponent.

An 'unfavourable witness', however, is someone who may potentially damage a party's case simply because they do not 'come up to proof' and relay their oral testimony as expected, e.g. because they cannot recall some facts. An advocate must simply try to undo any damage that an 'unfavourable witness' has done by giving weak or inconsistent evidence by calling other witnesses to help support the defendant's case.

An advocate who faces a hostile witness may, with the permission of the judge, cross-examine that witness by asking leading questions.

Section 3 of the Criminal Procedure Act 1865 permits the advocate to ask his own witness whether he has made an earlier statement which is inconsistent with his present testimony. The previous inconsistent statement can be admitted as an exception to the hearsay rule under s. 119 of the Criminal Justice Act 2003 (see Chapter 5).

The admissibility of previous inconsistent statements is governed by ss. 4 and 5 of the Criminal Procedure Act 1865 (which applies to civil as well as criminal proceedings) and s. 119 of the Criminal Justice Act 2003 (which applies to criminal proceedings only).

## 3.6.4.5 Protected Witnesses

There are certain witnesses who are regarded as 'protected witnesses' rather than vulnerable witnesses but who may receive the same limitations or adaptation of the rules of questioning. For example, under ss. 34 – 39 of the Youth Justice and Criminal Evidence Act 1999 protected witnesses are child witnesses and complainants in sexual offences. A protected witness cannot be questioned by a defendant acting in person at a trial – see ss. 34 and 35 of the 1999 Act. Either the accused will be asked by the judge to appoint their own legal representative in order to cross-examine the witness or if the defendant fails to do so then the court can appoint a legal representative for them – see s. 38

The court can of its own motion or after hearing representations make a direction that any witness should be protected from cross-examination by the defendant if the quality of the evidence is likely to be diminished by that cross-examination or even if it would improve the quality of the evidence of the witness by giving the direction – see s. 36 of the 1999 Act.

The judge must give a warning to the jury to ensure that the defendant is not prejudiced by any inferences to be drawn from the fact that he has been refused permission to cross-examine the witness.

Where the defendant is charged with a sexual offence (rape, burglary with intent to rape, indecent assault and unlawful sexual intercourse) s. 41(1) of the 1999 Act provides that in the absence of leave, the accused and his advocate are prevented from adducing or seeking to elicit in cross-examination 'any sexual behaviour of the complainant'.

The judge may give leave if the evidence or question would enable the accused to explain or rebut any evidence adduced by the prosecution about any sexual behaviour of the complainant or the evidence relates to an issue and the purpose is not to impugn the complainant's credibility and a refusal of leave might have the result of rendering unsafe a conclusion on any relevant issue in the case.

### 3.6.5 Challenging a Witness's Credibility

It is possible to introduce the bad character of a witness or third party. As we will see in Chapter 5 for a defendant in criminal proceedings, evidence of previous convictions or reprehensible behaviour is, in limited circumstances, admissible to challenge the credibility of a witness or a third party.

The limitations on the use of bad character evidence are there to protect witnesses and other persons participating in court proceedings from suffering unnecessary embarrassment or being asked irrelevant questions. As such, the bad character evidence must be evidence that would severely damage the credibility of the witness or third party and the witness's or third party's evidence must play a prominent role in the case itself so that it is important to challenge the credibility of the person.

In the case of a witnesses' bad character the relevant statutory provisions are found in s. 100 of the Criminal Justice Act 2003. Such evidence can be introduced by either party if the evidence is bad character evidence within the meaning of s. 98 of the 2003 Act. There are three gateways available under s. 100. In addition, admissibility is only automatic for one of the gateways (s. 100(1)(c)), in all other instances permission of the court is required (see s. 100(4)). The three gateways are:

1.  It is important explanatory evidence – s. 100(1)(a). 'Explanatory evidence' means that the evidence itself must be used to explain important information without which the judge or jury could not understand other important evidence.
2.  It has substantial probative value in relation to (1) a matter in issue and (2) is of substantial importance.
3.  All the parties agree – see s. 100(1)(c). This gateway does not require the permission of the court unlike (a) and (b).

We will continue working with aspects of the evidential rules on character in Part B.

## In Summary

# Writing and Drafting

A competent advocate will be able to:

1.  Adapt their writing skills according to the type of document and the intended audience.
2.  Comply with any formalities or requirements imposed by court procedural rules or Codes of Conduct of professional bodies.
3.  Comply with any confidentiality or privacy requirements in terms of the documentation.

4.  Use simple, clear, precise and concise language, particularly in court documents and letters to the client and avoid 'legalese'.
5.  Select appropriate precedents or form templates to assist with drafting court documents.
6.  Draft documents from scratch where precedents and form templates are not available or appropriate to use.
7.  Observe court etiquette.

# Effective Advocacy

**(SQE Advocacy Assessed skill – see www.sra.org.uk)**

A competent advocate will be able to:

*   Adopt a confident demeanour and use positive body language to reinforce verbal communication during a court presentation.
*   Master their case or application through a thorough understanding of the factual issues that require proof and the applicable legal principles that should make up the content of their arguments.
*   Use reasoned and carefully researched arguments that are presented in a logical structure.
*   Identify, pre-empt and respond to an opponent's arguments and/or questions.
*   Adapt the structure of the presentation to any interruptions made, for example by questions from the judge.
*   Understand the principles underpinning how to persuade an audience and use these effectively to ensure successful outcomes.

# Communication

**(SQE Advocacy Assessed skill – see www.sra.org.uk)**

A competent advocate will be able to:

*   Tailor communications according to the audience to be addressed (judge/client/witness/expert/other legal professional).
*   Ensure their communication is effective at achieving its intended goal.
*   Ensure that communication is sensitive to the situation at hand and that any unwelcome news is imparted empathetically.
*   Comply with court procedural rules and formalities on communication.

## Key Practice Case

*Inplayer Limited and Others v Thorogood* [2014] EWCA Civ 1511 – this case concerned a number of procedural irregularities relating to the drafting of court documentation. It is a helpful reminder of how good drafting is essential to a good outcome at trial. In this case the court allowed an appeal against findings of contempt of court that were made against the appellant in earlier proceedings. This was based on alleged breaches of an interim injunction order.

The committal proceedings and the trial took place at the same time. The Court of Appeal noted that this was in itself a procedural error. In addition, at the trial the claimants sought to question the appellant about the allegations contained in the court documents, as well as new allegations of contempt that they had not included in the court documents. The trial judge dismissed the allegations of contempt that had originally been pleaded in the court document (the application notice) but went on to uphold two further allegations of contempt that had not been pleaded. The Court of Appeal held that this was a breach of Article 6.3(a) of the European Convention on Human Rights 1950 (the right of a defendant to be informed of the nature of the charges/allegations made against him). It was held that the trial judge was wrong to accept the allegations that had not been included in the court documents.

The Court of Appeal also went on to criticise the drafting of the appellant's skeleton arguments and stated that the document drafted by counsel did not comply with the requirements of the Civil Procedure Rules Practice Direction 52A.

The court made the following observation:

As anyone who has drafted skeleton arguments knows, the task is not rocket science. It just requires a few minutes clear thought and planning before you start. A good skeleton (of which we receive many) is a real help to judges when they are re-reading (the usually voluminous) bundles. A bad skeleton simply adds to the paper jungle through which judges must hack their way in an effort to identify the issues and the competing arguments. A good skeleton argument is a real aid to the court during and after the hearing. A bad skeleton argument may be so unhelpful that the court simply proceeds on the basis of the grounds of appeal and whatever counsel says on the day.

[55]

## Practice Tips

- Check the court list prior to attendance at court to ensure you know the status of the judge that you will be appearing before.
- Always follow court etiquette and address the judge using their correct title.
- Adapt your writing style to suit your audience.
- Ensure that you maintain a professional writing style when writing emails to clients and legal professionals, including the court and judges.
- Read and become familiar with the SRA Standards and Regulations and any other Code of Conduct and Practice governing your profession.
- Always read the relevant court procedural rules relating to drafting of documents or the use of template court forms before you begin drafting court documents.
- Be adaptable to both future change and 'on the spot' change!

## Practice Risks

- Poor written or oral communication that leads to misunderstandings or a lack of sufficient information for a client, judge or opponent.
- Weak structure and lack of content to your arguments that lead to an inability to persuade the judge.
- Poorly drafted documents that fail to properly set out your client's case.
- An inability to support arguments with legal authority.
- Failure to include information to a client that is required as part of rules or regulation of your professional body.
- Ignoring your obligations and responsibilities under the court procedure rules in terms of writing and drafting.

## EXERCISE A

### Test Your Knowledge – Problem Scenario

You are instructed by your supervising solicitor to attend a debt hearing before a District Judge in the County Court. You are defending an interim application that has been brought by your opponent. Your opponent is represented by a barrister, Mr Lawman. The application is to dismiss your client's case because your firm did not serve the particulars of claim within the period of time required by the court rules. When the judge appears in the courtroom you immediately start to address the judge and to present your arguments. You refer to the judge as 'Your Honour' throughout the hearing. You argue that even though CPR 6.1 of the civil procedure rules stipulates that the particulars of claim must be served on the opponent within 14 days of service of the claim form, this is an unreasonable period of time for busy solicitors to meet. You tell the judge that 'my client believes that Mr Lawman has made the application in haste and that the application should be dismissed'.

Identify at least three communication errors that might have been made by you during this hearing.

**Go to Section C for a suggested answer.**

---

### EXERCISE B

### Test Your Knowledge – Multiple-Choice Tests

*Test One*

You are a trainee solicitor and have just seen a new client (Mr Herbert Merryman) who would like to instruct you to act for him in a housing matter. Mr Merryman has not instructed your firm before. Following the meeting, you write a letter to the client. Which of the following would you include in this first letter to the client?

1.  A salutation that addresses the client as 'Dear Herbert'.
2.  Information about the estimated cost of their case.
3.  Information about your firm's complaints procedure.
4.  A summary of the nature of their case and the advice that you have given to them.
5.  The name of your supervising solicitor.

*Test Two*

You have been instructed to act for a defendant who has been accused of theft of the sum of £25,000 from his employer. The case has been designated to be of medium severity. The matter has been listed for trial. Which of the following statement(s) is/are **false**?

1.  The matter can be tried in either the Magistrates' or Crown Court
2.  Your arguments will need to prove a fact in issue. Aristotle called the ability to prove, 'Ethos'.
3.  You will need to be aware of your client's personal circumstances just as much as understanding the factual issues in the case.
4.  You will need to pre-empt your opponent's possible arguments.
5.  You will use a mixture of open and closed questioning during the trial.

**Go to Part C for the suggested answers.**

# Self-Reflection Checklist

| What **three** important things have you learnt from this chapter? | 1 | 2 | 3 |
|---|---|---|---|
| Set out **three** additional steps that you need to take to learn the skills in this chapter in more detail | 1 | 2 | 3 |

# References

## Books

Aristotle, *The Art of Rhetoric* (Rh. III 13 1414a31–b13). RC Bartlett (ed) (University of Chicago Press, 2019).

P Lambert, *Courting Publicity: Twitter and Television Cameras in Court* (Bloomsbury Professional, 2011).

MF Quintilian, *The Orator's Education*, Volume III: Books 6–8, DA Russell (ed) (Harvard University Press, 2002).

## Journal Articles

S Mason, 'Cameras in the Courts: Why the Prohibition Occurred in the UK', (2012) 91 Amicus Curiae the Journal of the Society for Advanced Legal Studies 22.

## Cases

*Ewing v Crown Court Sitting at Cardiff and Newport and DPP* [2016] EWHC 183 (Admin).

*Gould and Others v R* [2021] EWCA Crim 447.

*Inplayer Limited and Others v Thorogood* [2014] EWCA Civ 1511.

*R (C) v Secretary of State for the Home Department and Another* [2013] EWHC 982 (Admin).

*R v DPP, ex parte Lee* (1999) 2 Cr App R 304.

*Samuels v Birmingham City Council* [2019] UKSC 28.

*The Royal Brompton Hospital National Health Service v Hammond and Others* [2001] EWCA Civ 550.

## Legislation

Coronavirus Act 2020.

European Convention on Human Rights 1950, Art. 6 (3) (a).

Fraud Act 2006.

## Procedure Rules
Civil Procedure Rules Part 6.
Civil Procedure Rules Part 7A.
Civil Procedure Rules Part 16.
Civil Procedure Rules Part 22.
Civil Procedure Rules Part 24.

## Practice Directions
Civil Procedure Rules Practice Direction 3.
Civil Procedure Rules Practice Direction 5A, para 2.2.
Civil Procedure Rules Practice Direction 7A.
Civil Procedure Rules Practice Direction 51Y.
Civil Procedure Rules Practice Direction 52A.
Criminal Practice Directions 2015 (as amended), I 6D, XIIA.

## Websites
www.judiciary.gov.uk
www.theadvocatesgateway.org

## Other
Judicial College Guidance, N Brice, *Principles in Practice* (2007): 'Take Note: They May be Needed' https://www.judiciary.uk/wp-content/uploads/2016/01/brice_taking-notes-autumn2007.pdf.
SRA Standards and Regulations.

# 4  Building Relationships
## Working with Others in a Professional Capacity

- Always treat the people you come across in your professional life with respect and courtesy and act in a professional and ethical manner with a commitment to furthering equality, diversity and inclusivity.
- You will need 'rights of audience' to present and argue cases at court and your professional body limits the right of audience depending on your status and professional accreditation.
- Partner with others to obtain the relevant expertise needed to assist your client's case and assist experts in fulfilling their duties to the court.
- Offer assistance and ensure the correct environment is provided for witnesses to give evidence.
- Observe court traditions, etiquette and procedure
- Adhere to time limits.

## 4.1 Introduction

In the previous chapters we have looked at how to research, prepare, communicate and present a case. In this chapter we will focus on how to ensure that your presentation meets court procedural rules and processes so that you can work effectively not just with your client but also the court, court staff, experts and other lawyers. We will focus on the competency of working with other people as found under the Statement of Solicitor Competence C.

Establishing and maintaining professional relationships with clients (C2) and others (C3) are key to developing competencies. This also includes effective communication that is tailored for each type of audience (C1). We have already considered aspects of C1 and C2 in Chapter 3. We will build upon the knowledge gained in the previous chapters and consider the various ways in which legal professional relationships are built and sustained.

DOI: 10.4324/9781003134770-6

**Figure 4.1** Statement of Solicitor Competence.

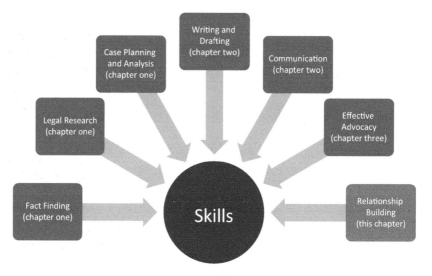

**Figure 4.2** Chapter Content.

An advocate must build a relationship of trust with the client. As we have discussed in Chapter 2, this includes responding sensitively to the client's needs and addressing their concerns and mapping out ways to achieve their goals. If the advocate is acting for the prosecution, the client will be the Crown Prosecution Service rather than an individual. If acting for a company or other organisation in civil proceedings the client will be the company/organisation although instructions will be received from directors or other senior managers.

## Maintaining Effective and Professional Relationships with Clients

# 4.2 Treating Clients with Courtesy and Respect

Code 3 of the SRA Regulations and Standards specifies that legal representatives must ensure that instructions come only from the client or somebody the client has authorised to give instructions on their behalf (3.1). In addition, there is also a duty to ensure that legal professionals who deal with clients provide a competent service that is delivered in a timely manner (3.2) and remain accountable for the work carried out (3.5) and keep their professional skills and knowledge up to date so that they remain competent to conduct work on behalf of clients (3.6). There are, however, other aspects to consider when building professional relationships with clients.

## 4.2.1 Promote Equality, Diversity and Inclusion

Advocates should ensure that at all times they act in a way to encourage equality, diversity and inclusion and compliance with the Equality Act 2010. This means an advocate should not discriminate in their treatment of clients, staff and third parties based on their age, sex, disability, race, religious beliefs, sexual orientation, gender reassignment, marital or civil partnership status and pregnancy and maternity (these are known as 'protected characteristics').

As we have seen in Chapter 1, equality, diversity and inclusion are part of the ethical behaviours that are expected from a legal professional under the mandatory SRA Principals (Principal 6). The SRA Statement of Solicitor Competence also requires that solicitors should respect diversity and act "fairly and inclusively" (A1e). It is also important to remember that a client may have an unseen disability such as a learning difficulty or may be 'neurodiverse'·(variations in the brain leading to different social responses).

Discrimination based on race or ethnicity must also be avoided. Statistical evidence such as the Equalities and Human Rights Commission Review (2018) and the Lammy Review (2017) suggests that those from an ethnic minority background can experience discrimination both within the workplace and within the criminal justice system. Judges are therefore expected to carry out their role by demonstrating an awareness and sensitivity to the different communities that they serve and to treat all individuals equally – this expectation is reinforced in the Judicial College Equal Treatment Bench Book for Judges. The Magistrates' Court Adult Bench Book also includes useful information on religious practices, traditions and customs.

An advocate can ensure inclusive practices by providing access to justice for all the clients that they represent as well as providing a non-discriminatory service to all including groups who may be at risk of marginalisation (recognised as those from the list of protected characteristics under the 2010 Act). It is important not to be judgmental or biased when dealing with clients. Any preconceived ideas or beliefs about the client, for example, their characteristics, religious beliefs or life choices, must be put to one side. An advocate will instead view the situation from the client's perspective whilst also examining any possible positions that might be adopted by an opponent.

The Law Society also has a Diversity and Inclusion Charter and legal practices are invited to sign up to the Charter to recognise the value of diversity and to promote equality, diversity and inclusion throughout their business in order to help improve social mobility for those from less disadvantaged backgrounds.

Advocates have an important leadership role to play in ensuring that justice is served regardless of disability, race or ethnic background of clients, witnesses and other professionals that an advocate comes into contact with as part of their practice.

## 4.2.2 Building Trust and Empathy

In Chapter 2, we looked at how to obtain relevant facts from a client during an initial interview. One way to ensure that you can ascertain the client's goals and objectives is to use a combination of questioning methods (both open and closed questioning) and active listening. However, questioning and listening is only one part of the communication process. You will need to respond to what the client is telling you. How you respond can determine the level of trust you are able to establish with the client. Responding in a manner that is respectful, sensitive and empathetic is an important part of relationship building.

A client will need reassurance at each stage of the legal process as litigation can be long and costly. You need to ensure that you maintain regular contact with the client and periodically check that you are on track to meet their aims and objectives. If you consider that it is necessary for the client to re-think their goals, then it is important that you involve the client in these discussions and you provide reasoned and supported arguments as to why a change is necessary. However, ultimately it is for the client, and not you, to make the final decision about outcomes.

Trust comes from your treatment of the client and how well you manage their case. It may be that the client's case involves urgent work such as applying for bail in the criminal courts (to allow a defendant to be released from prison pending trial) or applying for an emergency injunction in the civil courts. Emergency work should still be carried out with the same degree of care and consultation with the client.

### 4.2.3  Handling Sensitive Situations

Sometimes, the client's story may be a hard one to hear because it involves, for example, testimony about violence.

Where a client is upset or emotional, any responses should be carefully thought through, consider the message you want to convey and how this is likely to be heard or interpreted by a distressed client. You can diffuse tense, emotional or awkward moments by, for example, asking the client if they would like a break, pausing to allow the client to compose themselves, offering the client tea or coffee or offering a distressed client a box of tissues. Alternatively moving your questioning on to a new topic and only returning to the earlier topic once the client has indicated they are ready to continue with the discussions may also help to alleviate a client's distress or discomfort.

You may need to be mindful of differences in culture or attitudes or any unseen disabilities (e.g. learning difficulties) that your client may have. However, you must also aim to treat clients as equals and show them respect and avoid patronising them. You can check at each stage that the client has understood your advice or the information that you are giving and simplify your explanations if you need to, for example, because the client states that they have not understood your earlier explanations.

## Providing a Competent Service

## 4.3  Progressing the Client's Case

We discussed in Chapter 2 how an advocate can ensure that they identify the client's goals and objectives and map out a case strategy that includes identifying risks and possible alternative outcomes. Again, these are all important to competency of service. However, even before the work begins for a client, it is important to ensure that they have a clear understanding of the level of service that you will provide and the possible costs.

The SRA Standards and Regulations state that clients should be given information about how the work on their case will be calculated and the estimated overall cost on completion (8.7). This information will usually be provided to the client in what is known as a 'retainer letter' in which the client's instructions are summarised with details of the agreed actions that you will be taking and including estimated or actual costs and complaint procedures. If costs change, for example because an expert has to be instructed and paid, the client must be kept informed of these additional costs and agree to them before they are incurred.

A prosecution advocate will want to ensure that the Crown Prosecution Service has met the 'charging standards' in relation to decisions made to charge and progress offences (see Police and Criminal Evidence Act 1984, s. 37A and the 'Charging (The Director's Guidance)' issued by the Director of Public Prosecutions together with the 'Code for Prosecutors'). These standards include making an objective assessment of the evidence to be satisfied that there is sufficient evidence to ensure a realistic prospect of the prosecution succeeding and that the evidence is admissible as well as being reliable and credible and that there are no public interest reasons why the case should not be prosecuted (known as the 'full code test').

## 4.3.1 Vulnerable Clients

We have discussed in Chapter 2 why it is important to always act on the client's instructions. However, there may be instances when a client cannot give clear instructions, for example, because they lack mental capacity under the Mental Capacity Act 2005 or because of their age. Such clients are regarded as 'vulnerable'. Those who lack mental capacity are defined under the Mental Capacity Act 2005 as being "unable to make a decision for himself in relation to the matter because of an impairment of, or a disturbance in the functioning of, the mind or brain" (see s. 2 of the 2005 Act). The 'impairment' can be temporary or permanent.

There may be circumstances where a vulnerable client cannot participate at all in criminal proceedings, in which case, to continue with a trial would be a breach of Article 6 of the European Convention on Human Rights. The case of *SC v the United Kingdom* (2005) 40 EHHR 10 states that it is not necessary for a defendant to be capable of understanding every detail of the evidence or every point of law, but it is a requirement that they have a broad understanding so that they can:

1. Explain his/her version of events to the legal representative acting for them.
2. Be able to make his/her legal representative aware of facts that might be important to the defence.
3. Follow the oral evidence given by prosecution witnesses.
4. Point out any facts that they dispute.

An advocate will always need to be attuned to the fact that a vulnerable client appearing in court may need an order imposing reporting restrictions to prevent the media from reporting on the case. Whilst Youth Courts are not open to the public, media representatives are allowed to attend. Crown courts and civil courts are, however, usually heard in public on the basis that (as for most cases) the administration of justice rests upon the principle of 'open justice'.

There must be evidence to support an application for reporting restrictions. Whilst reporting restrictions are automatic in a Youth Court for juveniles (see Children and Young Persons Act 1933, s. 49), they are discretionary in the Crown Court (see Youth Justice and Criminal Evidence Act 1999, Chapter IV) and the civil courts (see Children and Young Persons Act 1933, s. 39). An application for a discretionary reporting restriction can be made by following the procedure in CrimPR Part 6 (criminal proceedings) or CPR Part 39.2 (civil proceedings).

*Criminal Proceedings* – The criminal liability of a child begins as soon as they attain the age of ten (see Children and Young Persons Act 1933, s. 50). All defendants under the age of 18 will usually be dealt with in the Youth Court (a section of the Magistrates' Court). However, if a child is, for example, charged jointly with an adult or the offence involves a killing, they may be tried in the Crown Court, and this is becoming increasingly common (see Crime and Disorder Act 1998, s. 51(7)–(9)).

An advocate will therefore have a safeguarding role when dealing with a client who is a minor and there will be a duty to ensure the client's right to effective participation in court proceedings in accordance with Article 6 of the European Convention on Human Rights 1950 (right to a fair trial), Article 3.1 of the United Nations Convention on the Rights of the Child 1990 (consideration of the best interests of the child) and Article 12 of the 1990 Convention (right of the child to express their views freely and to be heard in judicial proceedings). Representation will also mean ensuring that a court complies with its duties under the Children and Young Persons Act 1933, s. 44(1) to have regard to the welfare of the child, particularly as the principal aim of the youth justice system is to prevent offending by children (see Crime and Disorder Act, s. 37(1)). An advocate will need to develop their relationship not just with the minor but also with their parents or guardian who may also take on the role of an 'appropriate adult'.

A vulnerable suspect who has been arrested will be entitled to have an 'appropriate adult' present during questioning in addition to a legal adviser. This may be the parent or guardian but can also be a person from the local authority (if the child is in care) or a social worker or a member of the Youth Offending Team ('YOT'). The role of an appropriate adult is to safeguard the vulnerable person's rights by making sure they understand their rights when at the police station. An appropriate adult will also help the vulnerable suspect to communicate with the police and their legal adviser and can also be present during intimate searches of the suspect's body.

There is even a specific sentencing guideline for young offenders (see the Sentencing Council's 'Sentencing Children and Young People – Overarching Principles' definitive Guidelines'). In addition, the Criminal Practice Direction 2015 (as amended) Division I 3G prescribes a process for dealing with all vulnerable defendants (including those with a mental disability). An advocate should therefore familiarise themselves with the appropriate procedural rules.

In criminal proceedings, a defendant who lacks mental capacity may not be fit to enter a plea of guilt or innocence. Fitness to plead may also be affected by a defendant's learning disability or a communication disorder of some kind. In such circumstances, the court will have to hold a 'Fitness to Plead' hearing to determine capacity. The court currently uses the 'Pritchard Test' set out in *R v Pritchard* [1836] EWHC KB1 to determine a defendant's capacity to enter a plea. This test has been criticised as outdated by the Law Commission (2016). It requires the court to consider the veracity (truthfulness) of the defendant's claim to lack capacity, followed by a consideration as to whether the defendant can realistically enter a plea and if so to consider whether the defendant has sufficient intellect to enable him/her to understand the nature of the proceedings. The determination is made on 'a balance of probabilities' if raised by the defence but changes to 'beyond reasonable doubt' if the prosecution takes on the burden of disproving and challenging the allegation of unfitness to plead.

For indictable cases, the procedure is set out under ss. 4 and 4A of the Criminal Procedure (Insanity) Act 1964. As the 1964 Act only applies to indictable offences it does not apply in the Magistrates' Court or the Youth Court. However, those courts have discretion to abandon usual procedures if a defendant is suffering from a mental disorder (see s. 37(3) Mental Health Act 1983) or learning or other disabilities (see s. 11(1) Power of the Criminal Courts (Sentencing) Act 2000).

It is for the court to make a finding of fitness to plead and this is governed by s. 4 of the Criminal Procedure (Insanity and Unfitness to Plead) Act 1991 (as amended by s. 22 of the Domestic Violence, Crime and Victims Act 2004). A finding can only be made on the written or oral evidence of at least two medical practitioners (one of whom needs to be an approved medical practitioner for these purposes).

Part of your responsibility as an advocate (if acting for the defence) is to ensure that you have obtained a psychological profile on the vulnerable defendant client to ensure that the court has the necessary evidence and information to reach the correct determination. You should also ensure that the expert psychologist addresses the Pritchard criteria in their written report. An advocate acting for the prosecution will need to consider what evidence is needed to prove the defendant is able to enter a plea.

If a defendant is not able to enter a plea or pleads a defence of insanity due to the 'M'Naghten Rules' during the trial, then under s. 1 of the Criminal Procedure (Insanity and Unfitness to Plead) Act 1991 the jury may return a 'Special Verdict' of 'Not Guilty by Reason of Insanity'. The burden of proving insanity under the M'Naghten Rules is placed on the defendant who must prove on a balance of probabilities (evidence pointing to a likelihood of more than 50%) that he/she was:

1. Suffering from a defect of reason at the time of the offence (i.e. their mental faculties of reason, memory and understanding were affected), and
2. That defect of reason was caused by a disease of the mind, and

3.  He/she did not know the nature and quality of the act that they were committing, and
4.  He/she did not know that what they were doing was wrong.

The court has powers to make various orders in this situation and these are set out in the Domestic Violence, Crime and Victims Act 2004, s. 24 such as a hospital order (with or without supervision), a supervision order on its own or an order for absolute discharge. An absolute discharge is more likely to be reserved for situations where the insanity is temporary and arises from 'automatism' (involuntary and total loss of control of bodily movements during the criminal act) and does not relate to a serious offence such as murder.

Vulnerable defendants may require special arrangements to be made as to how they testify in court ('known as special measures') and this is discussed later in this chapter. It might also be appropriate to apply for separate trials if a vulnerable defendant has been charged with a non-vulnerable defendant. The court will usually hold a special hearing known as a 'grounds rule' hearing to determine how a trial involving a vulnerable defendant should proceed (see Criminal Practice Direction 2015 (as amended) Division I 3E).

*Civil Proceedings* – a child under 18 can sue or be sued through a nominated person known as the 'litigation friend'. The procedure is set out in CPR Part 21 although the court does have the power to permit a child to conduct proceedings without a litigation friend (see CPR Part 21.2 (3)). A litigation friend can be appointed by the court, or a person can make an application to become a litigation friend by following the procedure in CPR Part 21.5 and 21.6 and filing a 'Certificate of Suitability'.

In the case of vulnerable claimants who suffer a metal disability within the meaning of the MCA 2005, a litigation friend would be appointed in civil proceedings to act on behalf of such a person who will be referred to as 'a protected party' (see CPR Part 21.2) and may also have a deputy from the Court of Protection who has been appointed to act on their behalf.

The relationship that an advocate will develop in the case of those who lack capacity (whether children or those with a recognised mental disorder in law), will be predominantly with the litigation friend or the Court of Protection.

## 4.3.2 Disagreements with the Client
In the event that a client is unhappy with the level of service provided or the way in which their case has been handled, they may wish to complain. The SRA Standards and Regulations requires all firms to have a complaints procedure in place (8.2) and inform the client in writing about their complaints procedure, including their right to formally complain to the Legal Ombudsman (8.3). This is to be at the time of engagement and so will be included in the initial 'retainer letter'. All complaints are to be dealt with free of charge (8.4).

Any disagreements with the client should firstly be resolved by talking to the client. This is in order to enable you to understand their concerns whilst also managing their expectations in terms of what you can realistically achieve for them based on any limitations in the law, the facts of their case or any professional rules that you are bound by. If you are not able to resolve matters personally with the client then you should refer them either to a supervising solicitor or a senior partner or member of staff within your firm or organisation, or such other person as stated in the firm's complaints procedure.

The SRA Standards and Regulations provide that any internal complaints process should be resolved within eight weeks (8.4) and if it is not, then the client should be informed of their right to make a formal complaint to the Legal Ombudsman. If the client's complaint is about misconduct, then they have the option to file a complaint with the Solicitors Regulation Authority for investigation.

If at any stage you are concerned that the client is asking you to take action which might be unlawful or unethical and therefore risks breaching your professional obligations so that you are 'professionally embarrassed', then there are steps that you can take:

a)  Refuse to take the steps/action that your client has instructed you to take and explain why.
b)  If the client insists that they want you to follow their instructions then tell the client that you can no longer act for them and that they should instruct new lawyers. You are bound by a duty of confidentiality and so there is no obligation to inform any new solicitors of the reasons why you have stopped acting for the client.
c)  It may be that the client has simply stopped responding to your communications and you can no longer get instructions. In those circumstances you should apply to come off the record if court proceedings are already underway.
d)  The client should file a 'Notice of Change of Solicitor' at court if court proceedings have started and they wish to change solicitors.
e)  If the client fails to file the 'Notice of Change of Solicitor' you should apply under CPR Part 42.3 (civil) or CrimPR 46.3 (criminal) for an order that you have ceased to act for the client.

Steps to remove yourself from the court record should only be taken after careful thought and where discussions with the client have not achieved a resolution. This is because removing yourself from the court record when litigation is already underway is likely to cause delays and possibly prejudice to the client.

# Understanding the Court System and Responsibilities to the Court

## 4.4 Maintaining Effective and Professional Relationships with the Court

It is not enough for an advocate to be knowledgeable about the subject matter of a case and to know how to present arguments in court, an advocate will also be expected to understand the inner workings of the judicial system and how to operate within it. Acquiring the necessary skills needed to build relationships with people in a court setting is an essential part of an advocate's work and also involves the skill of assimilation into new environments. In this section we will also look at how the advocate can learn much about the application of the law, the use of discretion and interpretation of rules constructed to ensure fairness and prevent injustices by learning from others within the court system and understanding how the judicial system is structured.

### 4.4.1 Rights of Audience

Legal professionals are permitted to appear at court to represent clients and present cases, as long as they meet certain qualification requirements. The Legal Services Act 2007, Part 3, s. 12 and Schedule 2 reserve certain legal activities to trained and qualified practitioners and these include the exercise of a right of audience (appearing and speaking in court) and the conduct of litigation (issuing proceedings, conducting, defending or prosecuting proceedings or taking action that is linked to these activities).

Legal professionals must be authorised to carry out these 'reserved activities' (see s. 13(2) of the Legal Services Act 2007). Individuals admitted to the 'Roll of solicitors' or who are registered are authorised by the SRA automatically gain rights of audience in the lower courts (see SRA Authorisation of Individuals Regulations 2021). Registered European Lawyers must also exercise certain rights under supervision (see the European Communities (Lawyer's Practice) Regulations 2000, s. 11 and the Services of Lawyers and Lawyer's Practice (Revocation etc.) (EU Exit) Regulations 2020.

### 4.4.1.1 *Rights of Audience in the Lower Courts*

Trainee solicitors or those undertaking Qualifying Work Experience must show that their work includes assisting in the conduct of proceedings and that they are supervised. They will be regarded as employees with limited rights of audience as permitted under Schedule 3, para 1(7)(a)–(c) of the Legal Services Act 2007 and can conduct

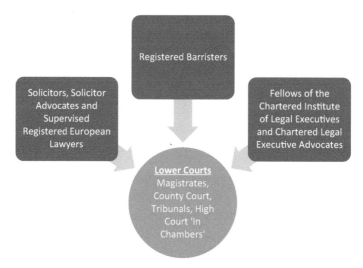

**Figure 4.3**  Rights of Audience in the Lower Courts.

**Figure 4.4**  Higher Rights of Audience.

interim hearings that are held in chambers. This is a private hearing in the judge's room and does not take place in open court. 'In Chamber' applications can take place in the County Court as well as the Family Court and the High Court.

### 4.4.1.2  Higher Rights of Audience

Solicitors and RELs can only exercise the right to appear in the higher courts once they have undertaken further assessment to meet the Solicitors' Regulation Authority's ('SRA') Rights of Audience Competence Standards (this is in order to comply with the SRA Authorisation of Individuals Regulations). They will then become 'Solicitor Advocates' with the right to appear before judges in the higher courts.

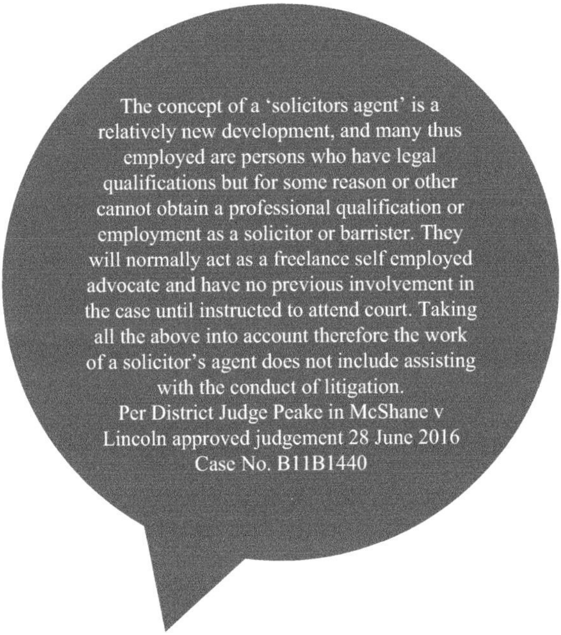

> The concept of a 'solicitors agent' is a relatively new development, and many thus employed are persons who have legal qualifications but for some reason or other cannot obtain a professional qualification or employment as a solicitor or barrister. They will normally act as a freelance self employed advocate and have no previous involvement in the case until instructed to attend court. Taking all the above into account therefore the work of a solicitor's agent does not include assisting with the conduct of litigation.
> Per District Judge Peake in McShane v Lincoln approved judgement 28 June 2016
> Case No. B11B1440

**Figure 4.5** Status of 'Solicitor Agents'.

It is a criminal offence for someone who does not have rights of audience or the right to conduct litigation to exercise that right (see Legal Services Act 2007, s. 14). The penalty is a maximum sentence of 12 months in the Magistrates' Court or two years in the Crown Court. However, it will be a defence if the person did not know or could not have known that they were committing such an offence.

Always ensure that you have checked whether you have the right to appear in a particular court and before a judge of a particular level of seniority. An unqualified solicitors' 'agent' will not be regarded as having rights of audience because unlike a solicitor's clerk, legal executive or paralegal, they will not usually have assisted with the preparation of the case (see Figure 4.5).

Not only will you be in breach of professional regulations and the law, but if you fail to observe when you have rights of audience, you will also invite the ire of the court as such a mistake will be considered to be disrespectful to the operation and traditions of the court.

## 4.4.2 Courtroom Etiquette
Advocates will be expected to respect the seniority and rank of judges by following certain traditions such as standing when the judge enters the courtroom (the court usher will usually say 'all rise' to signal when the judge is entering the courtroom). Advocates should not sit until the judge has taken his/her seat and should only stand

to address the judge when it is their turn to speak. If it is necessary for an advocate to leave the courtroom before the session has finished, an advocate should bow to the judge before leaving the courtroom.

For applications that are heard in private chambers the judge will already be seated in the room across a table when the parties enter. There is no usher in the room and no need to adhere to the tradition of rising unless the judge rises during the proceedings. Rowden and Others (2018) argue that the increasing use of technology in courtrooms, such as video conferencing affects the image that advocates and the public have of the judiciary and acts to break down barriers. Judges now work more in partnership with others affecting the traditional style of judging and moving it towards a more collaborative rather than separatist style. The collaborative approach can be seen, for example, in agreed practices such as the judge seeking counsel's input into the phrasing of wording in judgments and orders or the wording of jury directions and warnings. Hollingsworth (2013), argues the collaborative approach should go further in the Youth Courts to bridge a 'theory gap' that exists and this can be achieved by judges drawing on theory and empirical research from academics to address some of the embedded deficiencies in children's rights within the criminal justice system.

### 4.4.3  Advocate's Responsibilities to the Court
An advocate has a number of responsibilities to the court. For example, the SRA Standards and Regulations Code 2 sets out the standard of professionalism expected from advocates when they are involved in legal proceedings. These include refraining from misusing or tampering with evidence (2.1), or attempting to bribe witnesses (2.3), or putting forward false statements or making false representations to the court or others (2.4) or wasting the court's time (2.6). Therefore, the relationship that an advocate is expected to have with the court is both a professional and an ethical one.

In addition, in criminal proceedings CrimPR 3.3(2) explicitly places a duty on parties to actively assist the court by maintaining communication with the court officer to relay important information such as the likely plea of the defendant, the likely issues in agreement and in dispute in the proceedings, the nature of materials disclosed to the other party and whether any particular court directions are likely to be needed. The overriding objective in Part 1 of both the CrimPR and the CPR (discussed below) places further obligations on advocates to assist the court in managing cases.

### 4.4.4  Upholding Undertakings Given to the Court
An undertaking is a promise to do something or refrain from doing something. Unlike a simple promise, undertakings can have repercussions if the promise is broken. In order to be considered an undertaking, the promise must be given by a lawyer in their professional capacity rather than in a personal or business capacity. Solicitors will give undertakings as part of practice, for example in a conveyancing transaction

they may undertake on receiving mortgage monies from a lender to use the monies for the purchase price and not to release the monies directly to the client.

Failure to honour an undertaking can lead to disciplinary proceedings by the SRA. The court will usually request that undertakings are given in writing by an individual lawyer. Honouring an undertaking is considered to be part of the trust and integrity that is important to the legal profession as a whole. In *Briggs v The Law Society* [2005] EWHC 1830 Smith LJ explained that "[t]he recipient of an undertaking must be able to assume that once given it will be scrupulously performed" [35].

An advocate may give an undertaking to the court during proceedings at some point in their career. An undertaking to the court is considered to be serious and if broken can lead to the court exercising its 'supervisory powers' over a solicitor. This might include making wasted costs orders that impose costs on the solicitors' firm as a means of punishment for poor professional conduct in court. Alternatively, the court might make contempt of court orders with the threat of a short period of imprisonment in more serious cases. Failure to honour a court undertaking is therefore viewed as serious professional misconduct.

An advocate should therefore be very careful about wording a promise as an undertaking and consider whether an undertaking is necessary and can realistically be adhered to.

In *Assaubayev v Michael Wilson and Partners Ltd* [2014] EWCA Civ 1491 the Court of Appeal held that the court's supervisory jurisdiction to punish for failure to honour an undertaking only extends to powers over solicitors as officers of the court and does not extend to limited liability partnerships or companies through which a solicitor practices. This was reconfirmed in *Harcus Sinclair LLP and Another v Your Lawyers Ltd* [2021] UKSC 32 in which the Supreme Court noted that the Legal Services Act 2007 had widened the legal market to permit different types of providers to enter the market and the Limited Liability Partnership Act 2000 further enabled partnerships to be incorporated as LLPs. However, the supervisory powers over these new bodies were lacking in legislation in terms of remedies for failures to honour undertakings. This had created a 'lacuna' (gap) in terms of the court's authority over these new entities and will require future legislation.

## 4.4.5 The Overriding Objectives

The Civil and Criminal Procedure Rules impose a duty on those participating in cases to adhere to principles of fairness and transparency and to assist the court at all stages of the litigation process. As such, each of the procedural rules that govern criminal and civil cases begins with an overriding objective. These are to be found in Part 1 of each set of procedural rules. These objectives also govern how an advocate will deal with other people involved in court cases.

| Criminal Procedure Rules ('CrimPR') Part 1 – Overriding Objective | Civil Procedure Rules ('CPR') Part 1 – Overriding Objective |
|---|---|
| • Criminal cases should be dealt with **justly** which includes:<br><br>a) Acquitting the innocent and convicting the guilty<br>b) Treating all participants with politeness and respect<br>c) Dealing with the prosecution and the defence fairly<br>d) Recognising the rights of a defendant, e.g. those under Article 6 European Convention on Human Rights<br>e) Respecting the interests of witnesses, victims and jurors and keeping them informed of the progress of the case<br>f) Dealing with cases efficiently and expeditiously<br>g) Ensuring that appropriate information is available to the court when considering bail and sentence<br>h) Dealing with cases in ways that take account of (1) the gravity of the offence alleged, (2) the complexity of what is in issue, (3) the severity of the consequences for the defendant and others affected and (4) the needs of other cases | • Enable the court to deal with cases **justly and at proportionate cost** which includes:<br><br>a) Ensuring that the parties are on an equal footing<br>b) Saving expense<br>c) Dealing with the case in ways which are proportionate to (1) the amount of money involved, (2) the importance of the case, (3) the complexity of the issues and (4) the financial position of each party<br>d) Ensuring that the case is dealt with expeditiously and fairly<br>e) Allotting an appropriate share of the court's resources to the case whilst taking into account the need to allot resources to other cases<br>f) Enforcing compliance with rules, practice directions and orders |

When conducting litigation, an advocate should always be mindful of whether they are adhering to the overriding objective during case preparation and case presentation.

## 4.4.6 Adhering to Time Limits

An advocate needs to have a good grasp of any procedural time limits imposed by the criminal and civil procedure rules because any documents which have not been served or issued within set time limits may render a prosecution or action invalid or the court may impose sanctions for a failure to observe the rules. In *R (Hysai) v Secretary of State for the Home Department* [2014] EWCA Civ 1633 Moore-Bick LJ gave a stern reminder that "[i]gnorance of the rules will rarely, if ever, provide a good reason for failing to comply with them, especially where professionals are involved" [52].

Time limits punctuate the procedural rules. For example, in criminal proceedings, the time limit for issuing warrants, summonses and applications is set out in s. 1 and s. 127 of the Magistrates' Court Act 1980. Unless legislation exists to the contrary, application to start a prosecution would normally be issued within six months of when the offence was committed, or a complaint arose (e.g. from the date of charging the defendant with the offence).

Civil proceedings have similar stringent rules about starting proceedings. For example, when starting proceedings, a claimant will set out the nature of their case in a 'claim form'. The claim form can give brief details of the claim with fuller details given later in a document known as the 'particulars of claim'. A claim form that is to be served on an opponent within the court's jurisdiction (England and Wales) must be served within four months of being issued by the court. The time period is extended to six months for claims served out of the jurisdiction (see CPR 7.5(2)). If a particulars of claim has not been set out within the claim form itself but is to be served separately then the claimant has an additional 14 days from service of the claim form to serve any particulars of claim (see CPR Part 7.4(1)(b)).

Each of the procedural rules has its own guidelines as to when a served document will be deemed to have been received. This is contained in CrimPR 4.11 in the case of criminal proceedings and in the case of civil proceedings CPR 6.14 and 6.26. Other examples of important civil time limits include preparation and service of trial bundles in civil proceedings. These must be filed in court not more than seven days and not less than three days before the trial (see CPR 39.5).

In criminal proceedings an advocate can expect to receive service of the prosecution evidence within a particular time period when a Magistrates' Court sends the defendant to the Crown Court for trial. Under CrimPR Part 3.19 this will be no more than 50 days after sending for trial (if the defendant is in custody) or no more than 70 days after sending for trial (if the defendant is on bail).

The rules contain sanctions for failure to comply with any of the procedural rules including time limits. The sanctions may include a wasted costs order or the striking out of a claim. However, the procedural rules do include provisions for time limits to be varied by the court or by agreement between the parties. In criminal proceedings this is contained within CrimPR Part 3.7 and in civil proceedings in CPR Part 3.8 (4). The sanctions contained in the rules for failure to comply with a particular rule will apply unless a party applies for relief from those sanctions.

In *Denton v TH White Ltd* [2014] EWCA Civ 906 the court gave guidance on the factors a judge should consider when deciding whether to grant relief from sanctions in civil proceedings. These are to be found at para 24 of the judgment. The court is expected to:

1.  Identify and assess the seriousness and significance of the failure to comply with the rules, practice direction or court order that is in question.
2.  Consider why the failure to comply occurred. And

3.   Evaluate all the circumstances of the case that would enable the judge to deal justly with the case (this involves taking account of CPR Part 3.9(a) and (b) which relate to the need for litigation to be conducted efficiently and at proportionate cost) and to enforce compliance with rules, practice directions and orders.

Certain causes of action must be litigated within particular time periods as set out in the Limitation Act 1980. For example, in the case of personal injury actions the limitation period is three years which runs either from the date of the accident or the date of knowledge. However, sometimes an accident may happen very close to the beginning of the next day in which case there is an issue about when to start counting the time period. In *Matthew and Others v Sedman and Others* [2021] UKSC 19 the Supreme Court confirmed an earlier Court of Appeal decision that a fraction of a day is not recognised for the purposes of counting the limitation period and the counting must start on the following day. In 'midnight deadline' cases the cause of action will arise at midnight and not the day after as there cannot be said to be an issue about the calculation of a fraction of a day.

In criminal proceedings, an advocate should observe time limits relating to when defendants may be held on 'remand' (placed in custody whilst awaiting trial). These time limits are set out in the Prosecution of Offences (Custody Time Limits) 1987 as amended by the Prosecution of Offences (Custody Time Limits) (Amendment) Regulations 2000.

## Confidence Exercise

Try This One on Your Own

Fill in the following time limits and limitation periods that apply under the various procedural rules and Limitation Act 1980 in the table below:

| Source/Authority | Description | Time/Limitation Period |
|---|---|---|
| Limitation Act 1980, s. 2 | Bringing a tort action | ? |
| Criminal Procedure Rules Part 10.4 | Serving a draft indictment on the Crown Court after sending a case from the Magistrates' Court | ? |
| Civil Procedure Rules Part 31.5 (3) | Disclosure report to the Court | ? |
| Criminal Practice Directions IX 39F.2 | Serving appellant's skeleton arguments for an appeal | ? |
| Limitation Act 1980, s. 9 | Recovering sums under statute | ? |

Under the Limitation Act 1980, a discretion is given to the court to dis-apply certain time limits and this discretion can be found in s. 32 of the 1980 Act (for defamation and malicious falsehood claims) and s. 33 (for personal injury or death claims). An advocate who has missed an important time limit under the Act may therefore be able to apply for the court to dis-apply the time limit so that the action can proceed.

As well as any time limits imposed by procedural rules or legislation, it is also important for an advocate to keep to any timetable imposed by the court. For example, in civil proceedings the court may direct that witness statements, experts' reports and other evidence is filed in court and served on the opposing party within a given period of time. Failure to adhere to this could lead to the court making an 'unless order'. This is an order that provides that if the action is not taken by the extended deadline, then certain consequences will arise such as the court striking out a statement of case. CPR Part 2.9 provides that compliance by taking particular steps must be expressed by a calendar date and include the time of day rather than being loosely expressed as, for example, "within seven days". In the case of an unless order, if it is not expressed as a calendar time and date it should be expressed with reference to the date of the unless order. For example, "within seven days of service of this order" (see CPR PD Part 40B para 8.1 and 8.2). The recent case of *Poule Securities Limited v Howe and Others* [2021] EWCA Civ 1373 confirms that 'unless orders' must be clearly worded.

Both the civil and criminal courts do of course have case management powers to extend time limits as we have discussed previously.

## 4.4.7  Privilege and Public Interest Immunity

Whilst court proceedings involve an investigation of the truth and disclosure of information between the parties is encouraged, there are instances when information can be legitimately withheld. An advocate may claim that documents or information are subject to privilege or public interest immunity ('PPI').

Privilege means that the document is protected due to confidentiality and may arise in three ways: (1) the information is subject to the privilege against self-incrimination where to provide information or evidence as a witness would then expose that witness to criminal charges, other penalties or forfeiture under UK law, (2) the information is subject to 'legal professional privilege' – this may relate to communications between the client and their legal adviser, regardless of whether litigation is contemplated (known as 'legal advice privilege') or between the client and third parties or the legal adviser and third parties where litigation is in progress or is pending (known as 'litigation privilege') or (3) the information is protected as a 'without prejudice' communication which arose in an effort to negotiate or reach a settlement. A claim to privilege can be made by any party before or at the trial itself.

For the purposes of legal professional privilege, the communication can be both oral or in writing and can include emails and memorandums sent internally within a company if an employee is asked to send such documents to receive legal advice or in contemplation of proceedings (see *Three Rivers District Council & Others v The Governor and Company of the Bank of England (No. 5)* [2003] EWCA Civ 474). In the case of legal advice privilege the dominant purpose of the correspondence must be legal advice (see *Civil Aviation Authority v The Queen on the Application of Jet2.Com Limited and the Law Society of England and Wales* [2020] EWCA Civ 35).

Privilege is a personal right of the originator of the information and this right can be waived and disclosure can be voluntarily made.

An advocate will normally rely on the duty of confidentiality that exists between them and the client. Such communications and information will also be protected by privilege. Whilst the client can waive that privilege from disclosure, the legal adviser cannot. The case of *R v Seaton* [2010] EWCA Crim 1980 clarifies that where the defendant waives his privilege to give evidence about what was said between him and his solicitor at the police station, this does not mean that the defendant is waiving the privilege to all the communications that have occurred between him and his solicitor in the course of their dealings. The facts of this case involved a defendant who alleged in his evidence-in-chief that he had made a witness statement to his solicitor which initially contained an error of identification. He alerted his solicitor to this fact. He maintained that the subsequent correct identification that he gave in his evidence at court was not a recent fabrication because he had made this same corrected identification to his solicitor before the trial. The judge held this evidence could amount to a waiver of the legal privilege between himself and his solicitor on this point alone and that the trial judge had been entitled to invite the jury to draw their own conclusions from the fact the solicitor had not been called to give evidence.

There is another instance in which disclosure may be refused and this is public interest immunity. This is where evidence is withheld or excluded on the grounds of public policy, for example, because the evidence might adversely affect the interests of the state (e.g. national security) or the administration of justice. Such documents or communications have an element of secrecy.

According to *Conway v Rimmer* [1968] AC 910 it is for the court to decide whether public interest immunity can be claimed and this will usually involve adopting the 'Bangs' procedure in court of (a) identifying exactly what material or parts of materials a public interest immunity claim is sought, (b) the basis for that claim and (c) whether the material is relevant to the issues in the case (see *Commissioner of the Police of the Metropolis v Bangs* [2014] EWHC 546).

Even the identity of a witness can be withheld on public interest immunity grounds, for example, if a witness in a criminal trial is on a witness protection programme and their name and address cannot be revealed in open court. An advocate will therefore need to understand and identify questions of confidentiality and secrecy when dealing with clients and experts to ensure that communications and information are not inadvertently disclosed where they would ordinarily be covered by privilege or public interest immunity. We will look at privilege and public interest immunity in more detail in Part B.

## 4.4.8  Observing Evidential Rules in Court

In Part B we will discuss some of the key evidential rules that an advocate will come across at trial. It is important that an advocate is mindful of these rules and the judge's discretionary powers when deciding what evidence to bring before the court.

The trial judge's decision to admit or exclude a piece of disputed evidence can have a crucial influence on the outcome of a case. For example, if the trial judge decides to let the jury hear a defendant's confession to the police or lets the jury hear about a defendant's previous convictions then the defence position is seriously weakened – yet this is what happens regularly in Crown Court trials. An advocate must know when it is appropriate to ask the judge to exercise their discretion to exclude or admit evidence and in what circumstances this is permitted. This is a further example of the collaborative relationship between the judge and the advocate. A trial judge has obligations placed upon them to provide written reasons for some decisions on admissibility. We will discuss this further in Chapters 5, 6 and 7.

## 4.4.9  Respecting the Hierarchy of the Courts and their Precedents

We discussed in Chapter 2 the importance of legal research in the preparation of a case, particularly in relation to the use of case law. To ensure justice, the UK legal system functions on a fundamental principle that similar cases should be treated in a similar way. In this section we will begin by considering the hierarchical structure of the court system and then consider how an advocate would be expected to work within that system.

The court structure in England and Wales is divided in three main ways:

1. By Authority (the ability to bind other courts through a hierarchical structure).
2. By Jurisdiction (depending on the type and complexity of the case).
3. By Determination (ability to hear and decide cases and/or appeals).

The use of cases as precedent relies upon an efficient system of law reporting. As discussed in Chapter 2, there are several different law reports. However, the Practice Direction: Citation of Authorities 2012 states that where a case is reported in the official law reports of the Incorporated Council of Law Reporting (AC, QB, ch, fam reports) then those reports *must* be cited as they are regarded as the most authoritative reports. The doctrine known as 'stare decisis' (meaning let the decisions stand) provides that a decision made by a court in one case is binding on other courts in later cases that involve similar facts.

The doctrine of stare decisis is also subject to the level of seniority of the court making the original decision. Only decisions made in certain courts of a particular seniority will bind the decisions made in lower courts. The higher the court in terms of its place of seniority in the court structure, the more weight its decisions will have in terms of being authoritative and capable of binding the lower courts that must follow those decisions. However, the question as to whether a senior court should be bound by its own earlier decisions has been more problematic. As we will see in the section below, some of the senior courts have developed their own exceptions as to when they are bound by their own decisions.

The senior court structure in England and Wales can be illustrated by the diagram in Figure 4.6.

The lower court structure in England and Wales can be illustrated by the diagram in Figure 4.7.

## 4.4.10  The Courts' Jurisdiction

It is important to ensure that proceedings are brought in the correct court and that the judge has the necessary powers and jurisdiction to deal with the case. This ensures an efficient working relationship between the advocate, the judiciary and court staff.

In civil proceedings, CPR PD 7A para 2 sets out details of when a case should be brought in the County Court or the High Court. In criminal cases all cases start their

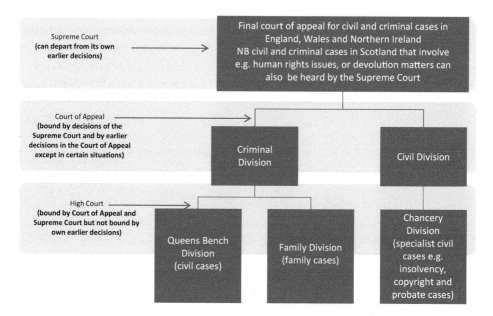

**Figure 4.6** The Senior Court Structure.

## Criminal Jurisdiction

| Crown Court |
| :---: |
| (bound by decisions of the senior courts. Not bound by own previous decisions) |

| Magistrates' Court |
| :---: |
| (bound by decisions of the senior courts. Not bound by own previous decisions) |

## Civil Jurisdiction

| County Court |
| :---: |
| (bound by decisions of the senior courts. Not bound by own previous decisions) |

| Magistrates' Court |
| :---: |
| (bound by decisions of the senior courts. Not bound by own previous decisions) |

## Family Jurisdiction

| Family Court |
| :---: |
| (NB with judges at all levels) |
| (bound by decisions of the senior courts. Not bound by own previous decisions) |

**Figure 4.7** The Lower Court Structure.

journey in the Magistrates' Court regardless of the complexity and seriousness of the charges. After the first hearing in the Magistrates' Court (where the defendant will usually enter a plea of guilty or not guilty) a process then takes place to determine the correct criminal court based on the severity of the charges. The less serious charges are known as 'summary only' and will be tried in the Magistrates' Court, including sentencing (see s. 2 of the Magistrates' Courts Act 1980). Examples of 'summary only' offences are most road traffic offences.

Offences that are regarded as of medium seriousness are known as 'triable either way offences' because they can be tried in either the Magistrates' or Crown Courts and the defendant is given a right to choose their preferred jurisdiction (known as 'a right of election') in a 'Mode of Trial' procedure that takes place in the Magistrates' Court (see s. 17A and s. 18 of the Magistrates' Courts Act 1980). The offences that are 'triable either way' are set out in s. 17 and schedule 1 of the Magistrates' Courts Act 1980 and include the common law offence of outraging public decency, as well as certain offences under the Offences Against the Person Act 1861 such as threats to kill, assault occasioning bodily harm ('ABH') and concealing the birth of a child.

Finally, 'indictable only' offences are the most serious offences and include murder and rape. These cases will be sent to the Crown Court for trial and sentencing in accordance with the procedure in s. 51 of the Crime and Disorder Act 1998 (as amended by the Criminal Justice Act 2003). The transfer procedure can take place in the absence of the defendant if the court grants permission as confirmed in the case of *R v Umerji* [2021] EWCA Crim 598. The Magistrates' Courts also have powers to hear an indictable case involving a child under 18 as if it were a summary trial (see Magistrates' Courts Act 1980, s. 24).

In the criminal courts, non-magistrate court judges can constitute their own courts into Magistrates' Courts and assume the role and function of a District Judge in the Magistrates' Court. This is the interpretation given in the case of *Gould and Others v R* [2021] EWCA Crim 447 to the powers conferred on judges by s. 66 of the Courts Act 2003. However, if a judge decides to constitute their own court into a Magistrates' Court to correct technical errors that were made in the documents before a Magistrates' Court, they must follow the entire procedure that would have taken place in the Magistrates' Court. They must then restore the case back to their own court's jurisdiction. The court in question must also according to the *Gould* principles record what has taken place and inform the relevant Magistrates' Court (see CrimPR Part 5.4(3).

Whilst normally in the civil courts an advocate will appear before either a District Judge or a Circuit Judge in the County Courts, other judges have the right to sit as County Court judges including the Master of the Rolls, the Lord Chief Justice and the President of the Family Division (see s. 5 of the County Courts Act 1984). As such, an advocate should always check the rules governing jurisdiction before starting or defending proceedings. If in doubt, contact the court for clarification.

## 4.4.11  The Role of the Jury

Lord Devlin (1956) described the jury as having the important function of assisting the judge to reach the correct decision and as fundamental to the principles of freedom in a democracy. This has been echoed by Bingham (2010) who considers jury trials to be fundamental to the rule of law. The right to a fair trial is also considered an important aspect of a defendant's human rights and involves a determination by an independent and impartial tribunal under Article 6.1 of the European Convention on Human Rights 1950 as enshrined in the Human Rights Act 1998.

As stated in *R v Pope* [2012] EWCA Crim 2241 jury primacy means that the ultimate responsibility for findings of innocent or guilt rest with the jury rather than the trial judge. In this case the Court of Appeal observed "[I]t is not open to the Court to set aside the verdict on the basis of some collective, subjective judicial hunch that the conviction is or may be unsafe" [14].

Each member of the jury must swear an oath or affirm in the same way that witnesses are expected to do. However, the wording of the oath/affirmation is slightly varied (see CrimPR Part 25.6(9)):

> "I swear by (*include religious beliefs e.g. 'Almighty God'*) that I will faithfully try the defendant and give a true verdict according to the evidence".

> OR

> "I do solemnly, sincerely and truly declare and affirm that I will faithfully try the defendant and give a true verdict according to the evidence".

The jury makes their determination in secret in the sense that the parties and judge are not permitted to ask what happened in the jury room. However, research by Thomas (2010) found that despite the secretive nature of jury determinations they were fair overall, although geographical factors meant that the pool for selection of juries could affect whether there was a sufficient mix of diversity amongst jurors. In addition, Thomas found from her study that most trials did not require a jury deliberation because defendants pleaded guilty during the trial or trials were halted for technical reasons. 59% of all charges result in a guilty plea according to the research.

Developing a relationship of trust with the jury will be important to any appearance in a Crown Court for criminal cases (and for some civil disputes). It is important to note that a jury trial is not available routinely. For example, s. 17 of the Domestic Violence Crime and Victims Act 2004 limits the use of jury trials in indictable criminal cases involving multiple counts and it would be impracticable to hold a trial by jury. Section 22 of the same Act removes the role of the jury to determine the question of a defendant's fitness to plead in a criminal case. Sections 45 and 46 of the Criminal Justice Act 2003 provide that jury trials are not to be used in the criminal courts where there is a perceived danger or evidence of the possibility of jury tampering in an indictable case. Section 11 of the Defamation Act 2013 exempts defamation cases from trial by jury unless the court orders otherwise. Under s. 69 of the Senior Courts Act 1981, certain civil cases, for example, fraud, malicious prosecution and false imprisonment cases heard in the High Court can be tried with a jury.

This tribunal of fact comprises 12 men and women who have the responsibility to determine questions of fact and the 'ultimate issue' of guilt, innocence or liability. A jury is also responsible for evaluating the evidence that is heard in court to decide on its reliability, accuracy and truthfulness and how much 'weight' (reliance, value, credence) to place on such evidence. Its role, function and responsibilities are set out in the Juries Act 1974. The jury decides whether the evidence taken as a whole is enough to convict the defendant beyond a reasonable doubt in criminal cases and on a balance of probabilities in civil cases. In assessing the weight of evidence, the jury will use their logic and experience. Typical ways of assessing evidence include evaluating whether the piece of evidence contains internal inconsistencies or is inconsistent with undisputed facts or contains glaring omissions or inaccuracies. With the testimony of live witnesses, it is also possible to assess their demeanour whilst giving evidence or being cross-examined. This observation of a witness is a means of testing the reliability of their testimony.

The jury is encouraged to reach a unanimous verdict but the 1974 Act does permit a judge to accept a majority verdict where the jury has been unable to reach a unanimous one. A majority verdict will consist of ten out of 12 jurors being in agreement. If there are only ten jurors (because the numbers have been reduced for example by death or discharge of a juror) then a majority verdict will be nine out of ten of those remaining jurors who are in agreement – see s. 17 of the Juries Act 1974 and the Criminal Practice Direction VI 26C–26M).

An advocate will need to apply the communication skills of persuasion (discussed in Chapter 3) to influence the jury into seeing the strengths of their case. Whilst taking on the role of the storyteller, an advocate must avoid making themselves the centre of the story. The jury should remain focused on the facts and the evidence to support those facts, not on the advocate. The role of the advocate is to serve the information to the jury artfully, even creatively but always in a reasoned way. This is not to say that the personality of the advocate is unimportant. An advocate's exuberant personality may mean that they are the one who is remembered by the jury at the end of submissions. However, this should be for positive and not negative reasons. It is the advocate's words that must find their way into the jurors' memory.

# Handling Witnesses

## 4.5 Maintaining Effective and Professional Relationships with Witnesses

Witnesses can win or lose a case for an advocate depending on their performance on the day of the trial. Whilst witnesses should never be 'coached' into what to say, they should not present any surprises at trial either. All witnesses who are to be called should be 'proofed' beforehand by taking a detailed summary of the evidence that they intend to give at court. The SRA Standards and Regulations provide that witnesses should not be offered inducements or other benefits to testify (2.3). It is permissible to discuss with a witness what to expect at court in terms of court formalities and the various orders of questioning. In order for a witness to give evidence they must be competent and compellable to attend court.

### 4.5.1 Competent and Compellable Witnesses

Competency refers to the ability of a witness to testify. If a witness is not competent, they will be barred from testifying. Testimony takes place either on oath or, in some cases, unsworn (e.g. in the case of children under 14 and mentally defective adults).

In criminal proceedings there is a general test for competency which can be found in s. 53 of the Youth Justice and Criminal Evidence Act 1999. The starting point is that all witnesses (regardless of age) are competent to give evidence in court (see s. 53(1)). However, this presumption is rebuttable if the witness is not able to understand questions put to him/her as a witness or give intelligible answers (see s. 53(3) of the Act).

A competent witness will also be compellable which means that the witness can be forced to attend court to testify. A witness summons can be issued to force a witness to come to court. Failure to abide by a witness summons will be regarded as contempt of court and a witness could therefore ultimately be sent to prison for this breach.

An advocate will need to undertake their own initial assessment as to whether a witness can be regarded as competent and decide whether expert evidence should be called on this issue. A challenge can be made to a witness's competency either before or during the trial. An advocate will also need to assess whether the lack of competency of a witness can be corrected by offering 'special measures' (see below) and discuss this with the judge at a case management conference or specially arranged 'ground rules' hearing.

All witnesses (unless they are a party, or in some cases an expert) are expected to wait outside the courtroom until called to give evidence so that their evidence is not influenced by the evidence they have heard in court (see for example CrimPR Part 24.4(2)).

Witnesses must also take an oath or affirm unless legislation provides otherwise. An oath requires a witness to swear on their holy book and repeat the words:

> I swear by (*insert according to religious belief e.g. 'Almighty God'*) that the evidence I shall give shall be the truth the whole truth and nothing but the truth.

In the case of an affirmation (for those without a particular religious belief) the wording is usually:

> I do solemnly, sincerely and truly declare and affirm that the evidence I shall give shall be the truth the whole truth and nothing but the truth.

In the youth court, a child between 14 and 18 can give an oath but it will be known as a promissory oath and will usually follow the wording below:

> I promise before (*insert according to religious belief e.g. 'Almighty God'*) that the evidence I shall give shall be the truth the whole truth and nothing but the truth.

Similarly, a child can choose to give an affirmation as follows:

> I do solemnly, sincerely and truly declare and affirm that the evidence I shall give shall be the truth the whole truth and nothing but the truth.

Children under 14 can give unsworn evidence. An advocate should ensure a witness understands these formal procedures by explaining what will happen in court, including the court layout and traditions.

## 4.5.2 Vulnerable Witnesses

In the same way that an advocate should be sensitive to the needs of a vulnerable client (see discussion in 4.3.1), an advocate should also be attuned to whether a witness might have a vulnerability both seen and unseen. This is important as it may make it difficult for them to fully participate in a trial. This can usually be determined in a meeting with the person concerned and a full discussion should take place about how they could be assisted in court.

There are certain categories of witnesses who are given special protection and treated differently during the course of a trial because their vulnerability may impact their ability to fully participate or may affect the quality of their evidence. These categories of witnesses include minors (those under 18) and those suffering from a physical or mental disability as well as witnesses who are 'in fear'. Such witnesses may be entitled to give their evidence with special assistance known as 'special measures' (see discussion in 4.5.3).

In criminal proceedings, a 'ground rules hearing' is also routinely held in the case of vulnerable witnesses and this is covered by CrimPR Part 3.9. This is a pre-trial case management hearing where the court will decide on the appropriate level of questioning and treatment of a vulnerable witness at the trial.

In civil proceedings, CPR PD 1A provides that the court and advocates should identify any vulnerable witnesses at an early stage and decide whether appropriate orders or directions are needed. The category of witnesses who may be regarded as 'vulnerable' is much wider, as under para 4 of the Practice Direction it includes not just age and physical and mental condition but also the impact that the subject matter of the trial might have on the witness, any social, domestic, and cultural circumstances and the witness's relationship to a party or another witness in the proceedings.

The civil courts can also hold a 'ground rules' hearing (see para 8 CPR PD 1A) to determine the nature of a witness's vulnerability before they give evidence and to decide what directions to make. CPR Part 32.1(1)(c) gives the court the power to control the way in which the court receives evidence, and this includes making special measures for witnesses.

As discussed in Chapter 3, when questioning vulnerable witnesses an advocate will need to be flexible and move away from traditional styles of questioning. It is important for an advocate to avoid what is known as 'tag' questions which are questions that are too long or complex in nature. Questions should be non-confrontational, and an advocate should avoid distressing a witness or using leading questions.

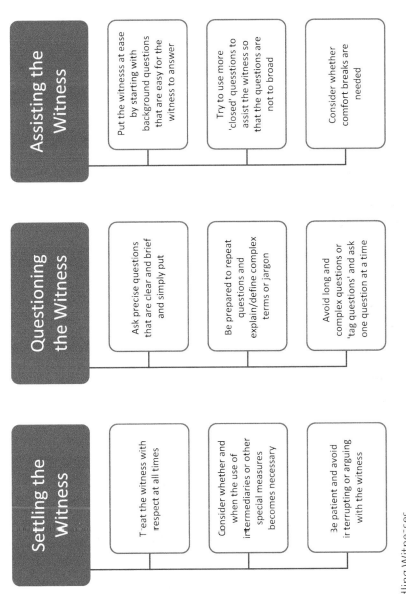

**Assisting the Witness**

Put the witness at ease by starting with background questions that are easy for the witness to answer

Try to use more 'closed' questions to assist the witness so that the questions are not to broad

Consider whether comfort breaks are needed

**Questioning the Witness**

Ask precise questions that are clear and brief and simply put

Be prepared to repeat questions and explain/define complex terms or jargon

Avoid long and complex questions or 'tag questions' and ask one question at a time

**Settling the Witness**

Treat the witness with respect at all times

Consider whether and when the use of intermediaries or other special measures becomes necessary

Be patient and avoid interrupting or arguing with the witness

**Figure 4.8** Handling Witnesses.

### 4.5.3 Special Measures

A criminal court can make a 'special measures direction' under s. 19 of the Youth Justice and Criminal Evidence Act 1999. This is possible if a witness is eligible for such measures due to age or mental incapacity (s. 16) or because they would otherwise be unable to testify due to fear or distress (s. 17).

### 4.5.3.1 Vulnerable Witnesses

Various special arrangements can be put in place for a witness and these are set out in ss. 23–30 of the 1999 Act. For example, under s. 27 of the Act a court can grant 'special measures' to enable a child witness to give their oral evidence-in-chief by way of a video recording if it is in the interests of justice to do so. Under s. 30 of the same Act a court can order that a person suffering from a particular disability or disorder is provided with an appropriate device in court to enable questions and answers to be communicated to that witness. An advocate should be prepared in these circumstances to ensure that their vulnerable witness receives an appropriate special measures order (where applicable) and this will involve persuasive arguments about why the quality of the evidence might be diminished by the witness's vulnerability.

For Crown Courts in certain geographical areas such as Durham, Harrow, Isleworth and Wood Green, the court also has the power to make a special measures direction for video-recorded cross-examination (see s. 28 of the Youth Justice and Criminal Evidence Act 1999 brought into effect on 30 September 2021 by the Youth Justice and Criminal Evidence Act 1999 (Commencement No. 22) Order 2021).

Special measures are not usually available for defendant witnesses in criminal proceedings although the court can exercise its inherent jurisdiction (power of the judge to make a decision where there is no applicable law) to order any special measures that might accommodate any special needs of a defendant. An example might be permitting the use of an interpreter or reading documents out loud if a defendant is unable to read.

Special measures can however be made for child defendants who are under the age of 18 or an adult defendant who suffers from a mental disability. They may be permitted to give their evidence by live video link (see s. 33A of the Youth Justice and Criminal Evidence Act 1999 as inserted by the Police and Justice Act 2006, s. 47). The process under CrimPR Part 18.14–17 should be followed to apply for permission from the court to put in place special measures at the trial for a vulnerable defendant.

Special measures have also been used in civil proceedings, for example, in *Polanski v Conde Nast Publications* [2005] UKHL10 the House of Lords confirmed that where a witness was unable to travel to the UK due to a fear of being extradited, a video conferencing order could be made to hear the witness's testimony.

Even if a witness does not fall into the category of witnesses eligible for a special measures direction under ss. 16 and 17 of the 1999 Act, an advocate can still argue that the court should use its inherent jurisdiction under s. 19(6) of the 1999 Act to make a special measures direction.

### 4.5.3.2 A Witness in Fear

A witness may also be regarded as vulnerable because they are 'in fear' and will only testify if their identity is concealed. This may be because of fear of the defendant or his/her associates. In those circumstances, a court also has powers to grant an 'anonymity order' under the Coroners and Justice Act 2009 (see CrimPR Part 18.18–22). An advocate should be prepared in these circumstances to ensure that their witness receives an appropriate anonymity order (where applicable) and this will again involve persuasive arguments but this time about why the quality of the evidence might be diminished by the witness's fear or distress. The criteria set out in s. 88 of the 2009 Act must be met in addition. These involve showing, for example, that the order is necessary to protect the safety of a witness or another person or to prevent serious damage to property or harm to the public interest ('condition A'), that making an order would be consistent with the defendant receiving a fair trial ('condition B') and that it is in the interests of justice for the witness to testify and they would not testify unless an order is made or there would be a risk of harm to the public interest if the witness were allowed to testify without an anonymity order being made ('condition C').

## Handling Experts

## 4.6 Maintaining Effective and Professional Relationships with Experts

Experts are important witnesses in any trial or hearing that involves complex matters which are beyond the ordinary knowledge or understanding of the judge or jury. However, an expert must be independent, unbiased and give evidence that is based on their expertise. They do not necessarily need to have qualifications. For example, a police officer who has extensive experience of watching and analysing CCTV footage may be permitted to give expert evidence about particular CCTV footage.

Although an expert is not an advocate, their role, like an advocate, is to assist the court. An expert should not stray beyond their field of specialism when giving evidence or this could amount to opinion evidence that does not fall within the exceptions to the hearsay rules (see Chapter 5). An expert's report must be disclosed to the other party if it is to be relied upon at trial (see CPR Part 35.13 and CrimPR Part 19.3).

Ward (2020) argues that the lack of a clear test as to the reliability of expert evidence is problematic and argues that the courts should move to formalise a more stringent test in line with the safety test in hearsay evidence (we will discuss hearsay evidence in Part B). The common law has essentially developed a loose test that the expert's evidence must have a sufficiently reliable scientific basis before it can be admitted into evidence (see for example the Australian case of *R v Bonython* (1984) 38 SASR 45 that has been cited by the English courts).

## 4.6.1  The Expert's Duty

Regardless of which party instructs and pays the fees of an expert, the expert's duty is to the court. This means that their report is prepared for, and addressed to, the court and they can apply to the court for any orders or directions if they feel they are being unduly pressured by the party instructing them. The bi-partisan nature of an expert is clearly set out in civil proceedings under CPR Part 35 and in criminal proceedings under CrimPR Part 19.

In civil proceedings an expert has an overriding duty to help the court on all matters within its expertise (see CPR Part 35.3). Similarly in criminal proceedings CrimPR Part 19.2 imposes an overriding duty on an expert to, in addition, give objective and unbiased opinion and assist the court in fulfilling its case management functions. Like advocates, experts are also expected to help the court achieve the overriding objective.

## 4.6.2  The Expert's Written Report

The court decides whether expert evidence can be used. For example, in civil proceedings this power is found in CPR Part 35.4 and Civil Evidence Act 1972, s. 2. The use of an expert will usually be restricted to one expert per party from a particular field (e.g. one medical expert, one forensic accountant expert, etc). In civil proceedings it is not necessary to call an expert to testify if the parties agree to rely on written evidence. In criminal proceedings an expert is usually required to be called to testify (see CrimPR part 19.3(4)(b)) unless the parties agree or the court directs the expert need not attend.

The format of an expert's report is also prescribed by the procedural rules. CPR Part 35.10 and PD 35 paras 3.1–3.3 set out what an expert's report should contain in civil proceedings. In criminal proceedings this is to be found in CrimPR Part 19.4. An advocate should ensure that when perusing expert reports the report is in the correct format and contains the information required by the relevant court under the relevant procedural rule. Generally, reports should include details of an expert's qualifications, details of the literature the expert has used, summarise a range of differing opinions of the topic under examination and summarise the expert's own opinion with reasons for those opinions.

In criminal proceedings an expert is expected to serve with their report anything which the party serving the report is aware might (1) be thought capable of undermining the reliability of the expert's opinion or (2) detracting from the credibility or impartiality of the expert and (3) an explanation of how facts stated in the report are admissible as evidence (see CrimPR Part 19.3(3)(c)). In addition, if a witness of fact gives evidence where any part of it may be regarded as expert evidence then that evidence may have to comply with the requirements for an expert under CrimPR Part 19 although the court can make adaptions to those rules (see CrimPR Part 19.1(3)).

An expert must also give certain declarations about the validity of their report. For civil proceedings an expert's report must contain a statement of truth (see CPR PD 35 para 3.3). In criminal proceedings the expert's report must contain a 'declaration of truth' (see CrimPR Part 19.4(k) and CrimPR Part 16.2(b)).

### Expert's Declaration of Truth in Criminal Proceedings

I declare that this report is true to the best of my knowledge and belief and that I am aware that if it is introduced in evidence, then it would be an offence wilfully to have stated in it anything that I know to be false or do not believe to be true.

### Expert's Statement of Truth in Civil Proceedings

I confirm that I have made clear which facts and matters referred to in this report are within my own knowledge and which are not. Those that are within my own knowledge I confirm to be true. The opinions I have expressed represent my true and complete professional opinions on the matters to which they refer. I understand that proceedings for contempt of court may be brought against anyone who makes, or causes to be made, a false statement in a document verified by a statement of truth without an honest belief in its truth.

Under CPR 35.6 a party may put written questions to an opponent's expert about their report and where possible experts are expected to narrow the issues that are in dispute to save court time. The court also has the power to decide that only one single expert is used in the case (see CPR 35.7 and CrimPR Part 19.7) rather than an expert for each party. An advocate should ensure that the expert understands their duties and responsibilities under the relevant civil procedure rules.

## Working with your Opponent and Other Legal Professionals

## 4.7 Maintaining Effective and Professional Relationships with Other Legal Professionals, Litigants-in-Person and McKenzie Friends

If an opponent is represented by a legal professional, then an advocate will develop their relationship with that legal professional. This is an easier relationship in the sense that the behaviour of other legal professionals will be prescribed by codes and rules of conduct, and they will have a good understanding of procedural rules and the requirements of the court.

However, not all opponents will be represented by a legal professional. Some opponents may represent themselves (litigants-in-person) or may have the assistance of a layperson known as a 'McKenzie Friend'.

*The Equal Treatment Bench Book* suggests that where a legally qualified advocate represents a party, but the other party is a litigant-in-person, the judge should invite the advocate to make closing submissions first so that the litigant-in-person can see how advocacy should be conducted. As such, legally qualified advocates should be prepared for the court to depart from normal conventions when appearing opposite a party who is acting as a litigant-in-person.

In the civil courts the judiciary have published a helpful guide for litigants-in-person known as *A Handbook for Litigants-in-Person* that provides a summary of the key procedural rules and the structure of litigation.

In addition, the *Equal Treatment Bench Book* includes information for judges on how to assist litigants-in-person to conduct proceedings but in an even-handed way. This guidance applies to both the criminal and civil courts.

A 'McKenzie Friend' is usually an unqualified person who assists the litigant in person (see *McKenzie v McKenzie* [1971] P 33). The court has issued guidelines regarding the conduct of litigants-in-person and McKenzie Friends in court. For example, the 2010 *Practice Guidance: McKenzie Friends (Civil and Family Courts)* provides that whilst a litigant-in-person has a right to reasonable assistance from a layperson there is not a corresponding right of a McKenzie Friend to provide assistance. Their presence in court is at the court's discretion. A court can refuse to allow a McKenzie Friend to assist in court if the court is satisfied that the litigant-in-person does not need to receive such assistance to ensure justice and fairness. This might be because the litigant-in-person has made the choice to be unrepresented, or the case is a simple and straightforward one or the other party is unrepresented too.

The Practice Guidance also states at para 4 that a McKenzie Friend cannot sign court documents on behalf of a litigant-in-person or address the court or examine witnesses.

The Practice Guidance recognises the right of a McKenzie Friend to charge a fee to the litigant-in-person (see paras 27–30) but the fees cannot be recovered from the opposing party without permission of the court.

The Practice Guidance also provides that the McKenzie Friend should contact the court indicating a wish to act as a McKenzie Friend and provide a copy of their CV setting out their relevant experience and confirming that they understand the role of a McKenzie Friend. They will be bound by a duty of confidentiality and must not have a conflicting interest in the case. A McKenzie Friend's application is less likely to be approved by the court if the case is being heard in 'closed court' (private proceedings in chambers or where the proceedings involve sensitive information). The court does, however, have the power to grant a McKenzie Friend the right to offer further 'reasonable assistance' (including exercising a right of audience) to the litigant-in-person if the case and circumstances justify this (see paras 5–8 and 18–26 of the Practice Guidance 2010).

If a McKenzie Friend is permitted to assist a litigant-in-person, they do not acquire rights of audience and cannot conduct the litigation. They can merely provide moral support, advice and guidance to the litigant (including taking notes) but the litigant-in-person must conduct the litigation themselves and speak to the judge. The McKenzie Friend must remain silent in court.

In *Leigh Ravenscroft v Canal and River Trust* [2016] EWHC 2282 a McKenzie Friend (Mr Moore) sought rights of audience to act for a litigant-in-person in a dispute relating to the seizure of a canal boat by the Canal and River Trust and the imposition of a penalty by way of licence fees. The court had to consider all the circumstances in the case including representations that the litigant-in-person was unable to conduct proceedings on their own behalf. It was argued that this was because the litigant-in-person was illiterate. A further argument was that the litigant-in-person was so emotionally involved with the facts of the case he would be unable to present his own case calmly. Whilst noting that rights of audience to McKenzie Friends would only be granted in exceptional circumstances, the court held that when deciding on whether to grant a McKenzie Friend rights of audience, it was necessary to consider both the litigant-in-person's personal circumstances and the context in which the application for the rights of audience arises. Mr Moore was granted permission to act as an advocate on the understanding that it was permission that was not finite and could be withdrawn at any stage.

If an advocate has an unrepresented party as an opponent, it may be prudent to ensure as a matter of courtesy that the litigant-in-person is aware of the *Litigants-in-Person Handbook* and that they can also seek advice from the Personal Support and Citizen's Advice Bureau located in the High Court (civil cases only) or use a McKenzie Friend to offer assistance. Advocates should not seek to take advantage of the lack of legal knowledge of a litigant-in-person or a McKenzie Friend.

An advocate should never mislead or attempt to mislead an opponent or other legal professionals and should always act fairly in order to maintain trust (see SRA Standards and Regulations 1.2 and 1.4). An advocate should always provide requested information (that is not privileged or otherwise protected) to other solicitors within a reasonable period of time on request and make appropriate enquiries in order to progress the client's case.

An advocate should as a matter of professional courtesy ensure that they confirm any such facts or criticisms if these are to be made the basis of an appeal. However, an advocate must also remember that there are competing responsibilities and obligations in relation to confidentiality that may prevent full disclosure by other solicitors.

# In Summary

## Maintaining Effective and Professional Relationships with Clients

A competent advocate will be able to:

- Keep clients informed of the progress of the work including any complications, risks, additional costs and important time limits.
- Allow the client to make decisions by providing them with all the relevant information and evidence, including complaint processes.
- Ensure clients are aware of any risks or additional costs relating to their case and keep them appraised of progress on their case at all times.
- Build a relationship of trust with the client by addressing their concerns and responding sensitively to their needs.
- Be respectful to all clients and act in a way that promotes equality, diversity and inclusion.
- Identify when a client may be regarded as 'vulnerable' and ensure provisions are made available to the client to fully access legal services both before and at trial.
- Provide advice and guidance that is tailored in language and style according to the clients' emotional, physical, neurodiverse, cultural or other needs.
- Handle sensitive situations as they arise by diffusing tensions, offering comfort and empathy where needed and avoiding patronising the client.
- Maintain the security and confidentiality of communications.
- Be able to assess when and if they should apply to be removed from the court record.

## Maintaining Effective and Professional Relationships with Others

**(SQE Advocacy Assessed skill – see www.sra.org.uk)**

### 1. The Court

A competent advocate will be able to:

- Treat court personnel and visitors with courtesy and respect including observing equality, diversity and inclusivity.

- Observe the 'overriding objective' at all times when managing and progressing cases and during a trial.
- Understand the commercial, organisational and financial context in which courts work to avoid errors and/or lack of care, recklessness or dishonesty that impacts others.
- Use court processes in an efficient way observing and complying with court rules, procedure, processes and traditions.
- Meet timescales and other court requirements and avoid procedural irregularities.
- Comply with disclosure and understand when material may be exempt from disclosure due to privilege or public interest immunity.
- Understand the seriousness of giving and breaching undertakings to the court.
- Avoid placing themselves in a position where they would be in contempt of court or subject to a wasted costs order.
- Avoid wasting the court's time.
- Progress cases in ways that are honest, transparent and fair and avoid the misuse of evidence, tampering with evidence or producing false evidence.
- Adhere to court rules and procedures.

## 2. Witnesses
A competent advocate will be able to:

- Treat witnesses with courtesy and respect including observing equality, diversity and inclusivity.
- Assess whether a witness is competent and compellable to give evidence in court.
- Avoid offering witnesses inducements or benefits in exchange for their testimony.
- Recognise when a witness may be 'vulnerable' and in need of special measures to testify (if eligible).
- Be prepared to adapt and tailor their style of questioning appropriate to 'vulnerable' or 'protected' witnesses.

## 3. Experts
A competent advocate will be able to:

- Treat experts with courtesy and respect including observing equality, diversity and inclusivity.
- Provide clear instructions to experts about the nature of their instructions and the scope of the client's objectives and provide all relevant evidence to assist the expert to reach an opinion.
- Ensure an expert's report is in the correct format as required by the relevant procedural rule, including statements or declarations of truth.
- Cooperate and assist in the process of helping experts to narrow the issues between them.

- Recognise when to seek help from other experts including delegating matters beyond the expertise of the chosen expert.
- Ensure the chosen expert(s) is aware of their duties and obligations to the court.

## 4. Your Opponent

- Always treat your opponent and other legal professionals with respect and courtesy.
- Be prepared to assist (to a degree) an unrepresented party who does not have a McKenzie Friend.
- Be cooperative when asked to provide information to other legal professionals and do so in a prompt and timely way (this excludes information that is confidential or where your client objects to the provision of the information and you are not under a compulsion to reveal the information).

### Key Practice Case

The case of *R v Achogbuo* [2014] EWCA Crim 567 is a reminder of the need for lawyers to communicate with each other and avoid making misconceived applications to the court due to a failure to conduct independent enquiries and to avoid relying solely on a client's word or recollection.

In this case the defendant had been convicted in the Crown Court of two counts of sexual assault on a child under 13 contrary to s. 7 of the Sexual Offences Act 2003. The defendant then instructed two new solicitors to lodge an appeal. The first solicitors applied for the case file which they received by email and then took no further action. The defendant then instructed the second set of solicitors who requested the client's case file from his trial solicitors but there was a delay of some three months which became the subject of a complaint to the Legal Services Ombudsman and required intervention by the Solicitors Regulation Authority.

The papers were then received by the defendant's new solicitors, and they lodged an appeal notice based on the ground that an application to admit hearsay evidence by the prosecution should have been refused by the trial judge. However, when the appeal notice was received by the court, they requested a transcript of the original trial which revealed that no hearsay application had in fact been made or granted at the trial. The solicitors agreed to withdraw the application. They then made a second appeal application some four months later based on allegations of incompetence by the previous trial lawyers. The allegation was that the trial lawyers had failed to advise the defendant about his right to waive legal professional privilege and discuss the advice given to him to give a 'no comment' interview to the police. The application also requested an extension of time to file the appeal. The application however failed to mention the previous application that had been made to the court. The court then obtained permission from the defendant's solicitors to write to the previous trial solicitors and counsel to establish what advice had been given about the no comment interview. It was established that the defendant had been fully advised and had been made aware that the jury could draw adverse inferences at trial based on his silence at the police interview. The court reached the conclusion from these enquiries that the appeal had no prospect of success; in addition, it was a frivolous and vexatious application as the court had not been informed of the previous unsuccessful appeal application.

The court stated:

> The court expects not only the highest standards of disclosure but also strict compliance with the duties of solicitors and advocates. It is the fundamental duty of advocates and solicitors to make applications to this court after the exercise of due diligence. In cases where the incompetence of trial advocates or solicitors is raised, the exercise of due diligence requires, having made enquiries of trial lawyers said to have acted improperly, taking other steps to obtain objective and independent advice before submitting grounds of appeal to this court based on allegations of incompetence.
>
> [20]

The court went further in the case of *R v McCook* [2014] EWCA Crim 734 and stated that

> [i]n any case where fresh solicitors or fresh counsel are instructed, it will henceforth be necessary for those solicitors or counsel to go to the solicitors and/or counsel who have previously acted to ensure that the facts are correct, unless there are in exceptional circumstances good and compelling reasons not to do so.
>
> [11]

## Practice Tips

- Apply common sense to everyday situations and ensure that client care and professional conduct rules remain at the forefront of your mind when dealing with the client and others.
- Remember that an advocate who is able to respect others will gain the trust and confidence of others.
- Always make informed decisions based on client and witness needs and the type and nature of evidence in the case and the permissible routes that you can take within the confines of the procedural rules and legislation.
- Each case will differ in nature and degree and you should be prepared to be flexible and adaptable in the way you handle cases particularly if vulnerable or protected persons or litigants in person are involved.
- Your relationship with the court is a special one built on traditions, customs, rules and legislation. The court exercises a supervisory role over your management and conduct of cases and expects high standards and you should bear this in mind at all times.

## Practice Risks

- Ignoring the overriding objective and, where applicable, pre-action protocols when preparing, progressing and presenting a case in court will draw criticism from your opponents and the court and could lead to wasted costs or the striking out of a claim or statement of case.
- Issuing proceedings in the wrong court or jurisdiction will cause undue delay and unnecessary costs for the client.
- Focusing solely on the case and not meeting the important administrative aspects in terms of keeping timescales, keeping the client informed of progress, costs, risks and the complaints procedure could lead to allegations of misconduct.
- Assuming litigants-in-person or third parties such as experts will always understand the requirements of procedural rules may mean that your case is affected or delayed by procedural irregularities.
- Failing to manage your client's expectations could mean that you have to terminate your retainer with the client due to disagreements that could compromise your professional integrity.

## EXERCISE A

### Test Your Knowledge – Problem Scenario

You are a trainee solicitor. You are asked to attend a possession hearing in open court to represent a landlord. The barrister who was due to attend has been involved in an accident on the way to court. You have never dealt with a possession case before and the training you have received so far has largely been in criminal law matters. However, given that this is an emergency, you agree to go to court to "give it a go". When you arrive at court you tell the court clerk that you are a lawyer acting for the claimant landlord. You then proceed to make representations in court on behalf of your client and you successfully obtain a possession order.

What issues of competence and relationship breaches arise from your actions?

**Go to Part C for a suggested answer.**

## EXERCISE B

### Test Your Knowledge – Multiple Choice Tests

#### *Test One*

You are acting for a client in a clinical negligence action against a local hospital. Your client's claim alleges that he sustained injuries following heart surgery which was negligently performed. You have received a report from your expert which contains a number of errors. Identify below which of the following from the expert's report would *not* be regarded as an error under the appropriate civil procedure rule CPR Part 35 and CPR PD 35 (you will need to read this rule and practice direction):

1. The report has been addressed to your firm.
2. The report states the substance of instructions but does not contain the expert's qualifications.
3. The report contains a statement that the expert understands their duty to the court and has complied with that duty.
4. The report contains a statement of truth with the following wording: "I confirm that I have made clear which facts and matters referred to in this report are within my own knowledge and which are not. I am aware that if my report is introduced in evidence, then it would be an offence wilfully to have stated in it anything that I know to be false or do not believe to be true."
5. The report contains details of the literature or other material that the expert has not read when writing the report.

### Test Two

You are acting for a 13-year-old child in criminal proceedings for theft. Which of the following would be regarded as the most appropriate and correct action to take?

1. Inform the prosecution that they have incorrectly commenced proceedings against the child as the age of criminal liability is 14.
2. Confirm to the court that your client will be giving unsworn evidence.
3. Advise your client that they will have a right of election for their case to be heard in the adult Crown Court.
4. Seek special measures on the basis that your client is a protected client who lacks capacity under the Mental Capacity Act 2005.
5. Seek an 'anonymity order' that your client can give evidence without disclosing their identity.

**Go to Part C for the suggested answers.**

# Self-Reflection Checklist

| What **three** important things have you learnt from this chapter? | 1 | 2 | 3 |
|---|---|---|---|
| Set out **three** additional steps that you need to take to learn the skills in this chapter in more detail | 1 | 2 | 3 |

# References

## Books

T Bingham, *The Rule of Law* (Penguin Books, 2010).
P Devlin, *Trial by Jury: The Hamlyn Lectures 8th Series* (Stevens and Sons Ltd, 1956).

## Journal Articles

K Hollingsworth, 'Theorising Children's Rights in Youth Justice: The Significance of Autonomy and Foundational Rights' (2013) 76 (6) Modern Law Review 1046.
E Rowden and A Wallace, 'Remote Judging: The Impact of Video Links on the Role of the Judge' (2018) 14 (4) International Journal of Law in Context 504.
T Ward, 'Explaining and Trusting Expert Evidence: What is a 'Sufficiently Reliable Scientific Basis?' (2020) 24 (3) Journal of Evidence and Proof 233.

## Cases
*Assaubayev v Michael Wilson and Partners Ltd* [2014] EWCA Civ 1491.
Briggs v The Law Society [2005] EWHC 1830.
*Civil Aviation Authority v The Queen on the Application of Jet2.Com Limited and the Law Society of England and Wales* [2020] EWCA Civ 35.
*Conway v Rimmer* [1968] AC 910.
*Commissioner of the Police of the Metropolis v Bangs* [2014] EWHC 546.
*Denton v TH White Ltd* [2014] EWCA Civ 906.
*Gould and Others v R* [2021] EWCA Crim 447.
*Harcus Sinclair LLP and Another v Your Lawyers Ltd* [2021] UKSC 32.
*Matthew and Others v Sedman and Others* [2021] UKSC 19.
*McKenzie v McKenzie* [1971] P 33.
McShane v Lincoln [2016] unreported approved judgment 28 June 2016. Case No B11B1440.
*Polanski v Conde Nast Publications* [2005] UKHL10.
*Poule Securities Limited v Howe and Others* [2021] EWCA Civ 1373.
*R v Achogbuo* [2014] EWCA Crim 567.
*R v Bonython* (1984) 38 SASR 45.
*R (Hysai) v Secretary of State for the Home Department* [2014] EWCA Civ 1633.
*R v McCook* [2014] EWCA Crim 734.
*R v Pritchard* (1836) EWHC KB1.
*R v Seaton* [2010] EWCA Crim 1980.
*R v Umerji* [2021] EWCA Crim 598.
*SC v the United Kingdom* (2005) 40 EHHR 10.
*Three Rivers District Council & Others v The Governor and Company of the Bank of England (No 5)* [2004] EWCA Civ 218.

## Legislation
Constitutional Reform Act 2005.
County Courts Act 1984.
Crime and Disorder Act 1998.
Criminal Attempts Act 1981.
Criminal Justice Act 2003, s. 45 & s. 46.
Criminal Procedure (Insanity Act) 1964, s. 4, s. 4A.
Criminal Procedure (Insanity and Unfitness to Plead) Act 1991, s. 1.
Defamation Act 2013, s. 11.
Domestic Violence Crime and Victims Act 2004, s. 17, ss. 22 & 24.
Equality Act 2010.
European Convention on Human Rights 1950, Article 6.3(d).
Human Rights Act 1998.
Legal Services Act 2007.

Limited Liability Partnership Act 2000.
Magistrates' Courts Act 1980.
Mental Capacity Act 2005.
Powers of Criminal Courts (Sentencing) Act 2000, s. 11(1).
Prosecution of Offences (Custody Time Limits) 1987.
Prosecution of Offences (Custody Time Limits) (Amendment) Regulations 2000.
Youth Justice and Criminal Evidence Act 1999, s. 27 & s. 30.
Legal Services Act 2007.
The Practice Statement (1966) 3 All ER, 77.

## Procedure Rules
Civil Procedure Rules Parts 1A, 2.9, 21, 42.
Civil Procedure Rules PD 40B, para 8.1, 8.2.
Criminal Procedure Rules Part 18.

## Practice Directions
Civil Procedure Rules Practice Direction 1A.
Criminal Procedure Rules Practice Direction: Evidence.

## Other
Equal Treatment Bench Book.
Equality and Human Rights Commission, 'Is Britain Fairer? The State of Equality and Human Rights 2018 (EHRC 2018).
A Handbook for Litigants in Person, Bailey, E (ed) and Boers, P, Hampton, A, Hodge D and Hughes, P accessed via www.judiciary.uk.
Law Commission, 'Unfitness to Plead': Volume 1 Report (2016) Law Com No. 364.
Magistrates' Court Adult Bench Book.
SRA Standards and Regulations Code of Conduct for Solicitors, RELs and RFLs Code 2 and Code 3.
Solicitors' Regulation Authority's Rights of Audience Competence Standards.
The Lammy Review 'An Independent Review into the Treatment of, and outcomes for, Black Asian and Minority Ethnic Individuals in the Criminal Justice System (David Lammy MP 2017).
Thomas, C 'Are Juries Fair?' (Ministry of Justice Research Series 1/10, 2010).

## Websites
www.judiciary.uk
www.legalombudsman.org.uk
www.sra.org.uk
www.supportthroughcourt.org

# PART B
## The Litigation Advocate

# 5

# An Introduction to Criminal Litigation

## Key Chapter Points

- Relevant evidence is usually admissible unless an exclusionary rule applies that prevents the jury from considering such evidence.
- Judicial discretion can be used in criminal cases to exclude or (in limited circumstances) include relevant evidence.
- In criminal proceedings the codes of practice of the Police and Criminal Evidence Act 1984 provide a further framework for determining the admissibility of evidence.
- Interim applications can be made before trial to seek orders for the progression or cessation of the case.

## 5.1 Introduction

In this chapter we will focus on (1) the admissibility of evidence in criminal proceedings and (2) how to make interim applications prior to a criminal trial. We will look at three types of interim hearings in our case study in this section: (1) a bail application, (2) a specific disclosure application and (3) an application for the admission of hearsay and character evidence.

An advocate is required by the criminal procedure rules to explicitly explain to the court how evidence (which goes beyond direct witness testimony) is admissible (see CrimPR Part 24.4(3) for the Magistrates' Court and CrimPR Part 25.11(3) for the Crown Court). The case of *Alec John Smith v R* [2020] EWCA 777 reminds us that "the Criminal Procedure Rules are not decorative. They are there for a reason" [50].

We will start by considering some of the key evidential rules on admissibility that an advocate will need to be aware of when conducting proceedings. In Appendix B at the end of Part B, you will find a helpful Table of Key Evidential Rules cross-referenced to relevant legislation and procedural rules.

DOI: 10.4324/9781003134770-8

# Exclusionary Rules

## 5.2  Excluding Evidence

In criminal proceedings there are a number of rules, both common law and statutory, that prevent certain pieces of evidence being admitted into the proceedings. This means they cannot be heard by the judge/jury at trial. Judicial discretion is used to exclude such evidence and the judicial discretion is found under s. 78 and s. 82(3) of the Police and Criminal Evidence Act ('PACE') 1984. However, certain pieces of evidence such as hearsay and character evidence have their own statutory provisions for the exercise of judicial discretion to exclude evidence and we will discuss these later in the chapter. Other pieces of evidence such as confessions have a statutory provision that mandates the exclusion of this type of evidence in certain situations and we will also consider this in this chapter.

In addition, breaches of the Codes of Practice to the Police and Criminal Evidence Act 1984 may lead to the exclusion of evidence obtained as a result of those breaches. A criminal advocate should familiarise themselves with all the different codes of practice of PACE (A–H) and these can be found on the government website www.gov.uk.

As we will see when discussing appeals, if a judicial discretion is used to exclude evidence (or in limited cases to include evidence) it is very hard to challenge this decision through an appeal, unless it can be shown that the exercise of the discretion was so perverse that no other judge would have made the same decision (this is known as 'Wednesbury unreasonableness').

In a criminal court the judge normally hears legal argument about issues of admissibility in the absence of the jury either before trial or during the trial in a procedure known as a '*voir dire*' (a trial within a trial when the jury is temporarily asked to leave the courtroom). The reason for the absence of the jury is so that if the judge makes a ruling that the disputed evidence is inadmissible the jury will not have heard the evidence and therefore cannot rely upon it when deciding the verdict.

Illegal searches, confessions and character evidence are types of evidence that would be subject to a *voir dire* to determine issues of admissibility.

## 5.2.1  Illegally or Improperly Obtained Evidence

This is evidence that has been obtained in a questionable or wrong way and has breached normal rules and procedures. Unlike the other categories of evidence that we will consider in this section, there is not a general exclusionary rule against evidence that has been obtained in an illegal or improper way; if the evidence is relevant, it is potentially admissible. However, there are rules to be found in legislation and common law that exclude certain types of improperly obtained evidence such as confessions or evidence obtained by torture. Generally, the court will exercise discretion in deciding admissibility.

Improperly obtained evidence may also involve breaches of the Police and Criminal Evidence Act ('PACE') 1984. For example, searches by the police (whether of a person or property) should be conducted in accordance with Code A and B of PACE 1984. Where evidence has been obtained illegally or unlawfully (such as a confession obtained by force or an illegal search or manufactured evidence by the police) the court has a discretion to exclude the evidence from trial and this is usually done through the discretion found under s. 78 PACE 1984. This section provides that "where in all the circumstances of the case the evidence would have an adverse effect on the fairness in the proceedings it ought not to be admitted". It is a statutory provision commonly used to exclude prosecution evidence.

Police trickery is false or misleading information and/or action that takes place after the crime has already been committed. The trickery may be used to obtain evidence against the defendant, for example, by illegally bugging the defendant's cell or falsely telling the defendant that his fingerprints were found at the scene of the crime. Whilst the police are allowed to use certain tricks in targeted operations these must be fair.

Evidence that has been obtained by police trickery may also lead to the evidence being excluded using s. 78. The judge also has an alternative exclusionary discretion that can be found under s. 82(3) PACE which is the courts' general power to exclude evidence in any form.

As stated by Viscount Dilhorne in *R v Sang* [1979] UKHL 3:

> evidence may be obtained unfairly but not illegally but it is not the manner in which it has been obtained but its use at the trial if accompanied by prejudicial effects outweighing its probative value and so rendering the trial unfair to the accused which will justify the exercise of judicial discretion to exclude it [10].

This principle is thought to have been preserved by the judicial discretion in s. 82(3) PACE 1984.

However, the availability of judicial discretion to exclude evidence does not mean it will always lead to evidence being excluded. For example, in *Khan v UK* (2000) 31 EHRR 45 secretly taped surveillance material was not considered to have been admitted in breach of Article 6 of the European Convention on Human Rights (right to a fair trial) because of the Sang principle and the *voir dire* all of which afforded a defendant an opportunity to challenge the material before a judge made a decision as to whether or not to exercise the judicial discretion to exclude.

Whilst evidence obtained by police trickery might escape exclusion if it is relevant and not so prejudicial as to outweigh its usefulness in proving an issue at trial, the same cannot be said of evidence obtained by 'entrapment'.

Entrapment can also be regarded as a type of trickery, but it takes place before the crime has been committed. It requires the police or their agents to incite a suspect to commit a crime they would not otherwise have committed (sometimes called 'state-created crime'). Entrapment is not a defence but is used as a mitigating factor that can lead to the complete cessation of the trial or the exclusion of evidence.

In *R v Smurthwaite: R v Gill* (1994) 98 Cr App R 437 in the Court of Appeal Lord Taylor gave some helpful guidelines in identifying when trickery might fall into the category of entrapment. The court listed questions that a court should ask itself when considering how the evidence was obtained such as, was the officer acting as an agent provocateur in the sense of enticing the accused to commit an offence he would not otherwise have committed? What was the nature of the entrapment? Does the evidence consist of admissions to a completed offence or the offence itself? How active or passive was the officer's role in obtaining the evidence? Did the officer abuse his/her role by asking questions which ought properly to have been asked as a police officer in accordance with Code C PACE? Whilst these guidelines have been criticised as too simplistic in later cases such as *R v Looseley* [2001] UKHL 53, they do provide a starting point for considering whether the extent of any police trickery might amount to entrapment.

Entrapment is regarded as so serious that according to *R v Looseley* [2001] UKHL 53 the appropriate remedy is to stop the criminal trial altogether. In criminal proceedings this is known as a 'stay of proceedings'.

However, an abuse of process requires the defence to make an application at the beginning of the trial and this may not always be possible if evidence of entrapment only comes out during the trial itself. In this situation it might be appropriate instead to exclude the evidence under s. 78 and this could exclude all prosecution evidence (for example, following a 'submission of no case to answer') so that the end result would be the same as a stay of proceedings. The trial however would have been brought to an end on wider considerations of the integrity of the justice system rather than because the proceedings were an abuse of process.

Equally, if the actions of the police or their agents simply created what Lord Nicholls in *Loosely* described as "an unexceptional opportunity to commit a crime" rather than being "so seriously improper as to bring the administration of justice into disrepute" (for example because the state had lured the defendant to commit the crime), then a consideration of the use of the s. 78 discretion rather than a stay of proceedings would be the more appropriate course of action.

In such situations the court would be assisted by applying Lord Steyn's balancing test in *R v Latif* [1996] UKHL 16 to decide whether the opportunity was an exceptional or unexceptional one and therefore whether to exercise judicial discretion or stay the proceedings. This test was expressed by Lord Steyn as "the judge must weigh in the balance the public interest in ensuring that those that are charged with grave crimes should be tried and the competing public interest in not conveying the impression that the court will adopt the approach that the end justifies the means". Using the s. 78 discretion in these circumstances would mean that evidence obtained by entrapment could be excluded if its admission would have such an adverse effect on the fairness in the proceedings it ought not to be admitted but the trial could still continue using the other available evidence. Lord Steyn recognised that there was some overlap between the court's jurisdiction to stay proceedings and the power to exclude evidence.

A court will have to consider all the factors in the case including the reason for the police operation and whether the intrusive nature of the investigation could be justified. The case of *R v Syed* [2018] EWCA Crim 2809 left open the question of whether the burden of proving that the defendant was lured into committing the crime should be on the defendant to prove.

## 5.2.2 Confessions

Confession evidence is defined by the Police and Criminal Evidence Act 1984 ('PACE'), s. 82(1) as including "any statements wholly or partly adverse to the person who made it, whether made to a person in authority or not and whether made in words or otherwise".

A confession will usually be produced at court in documentary form as a written transcript from a recorded interview whilst the defendant was in police custody.

Special exclusionary rules apply to the admission of confessions in a criminal trial. The definition of a confession under s. 82(1) of PACE 1984 makes clear that any statement "wholly or partially adverse to the person who made it", is capable of amounting to a confession and so an advocate needs to consider any statements made by the client at the police station with great care. An admission does not have to be as simple as "I did it" and may include an acknowledgement of being present at the scene of the crime or having a motive for committing the offence. A confession does not even have to be made to a person in authority such as a police officer. However, the statement must include some blameworthy aspects (known as 'inculpatory') rather than purely 'exculpatory' (removal of blame).

A defendant's confession is only admissible at trial if the prosecution can establish beyond reasonable doubt that it has not been obtained either by oppression (see s. 76(2)(a) of PACE 1984) or things said and done which would make the confession unreliable (see s. 76(2)(b) of PACE 1984). There must be a link between what was said and done and the confession subsequently being made by the defendant for s. 76(2)(b) to apply.

For the purposes of defining 'oppression' under s. 76(2)(a) the 1984 Act provides a partial definition as including "torture, inhuman or degrading treatment, and the use or threat of violence". However, conduct can be oppressive without involving violence as was seen in cases such as *R v Miller* (1993) 97 Cr App R 99 where the interrogation methods fell short of violence but were contrary to the spirit of PACE in that the questioning was oppressive, threatening and insulting and only just fell short of violent.

As such, police interrogation methods will be under the spotlight, in particular, whether Code C of PACE has been followed (requirements for the detention, treatment and questioning of suspects in police custody). Code H (requirements for the detention, treatment and questioning of suspects in police custody on terrorism offences) may also be relevant. Other relevant PACE codes of practice will be Code D (Identification procedure), Code E (audio recording of interviews with suspects at a police station) and Code F (visual recording with sound of interviews of suspects at a police station).

A suspect at a police station also has a right to consult a solicitor in private (see s. 58 of PACE 1984), this right can be delayed but not withdrawn completely. A suspect also has a right to inform someone of their whereabouts when they are taken to a police station (see s. 56 of PACE 1984). In addition, vulnerable suspects must have an independent person present when they are interviewed (see s. 77 of PACE 1984).

An advocate will need to read interview transcripts carefully to assess whether there has been a breach of any of the codes of practice of PACE. Breaches of PACE will not always amount to 'oppression' or 'things said and done' and it will very much depend on the seriousness of the breaches and whether, in the case of s. 76(2)(b) a causal connection can be found.

However, even if the prosecution can show that the confession was not obtained in a way that breached either s. 76(2)(a) or (b) it is still possible for a defence advocate to argue that the court should exercise its discretion under s. 78 of PACE on the basis that admitting the confession "would have such an adverse effect on the fairness in the proceedings" that it would be wrong to allow it to be admitted and heard by the jury. As established in cases such as *R v Walsh* (1989) 91 Cr App R 161 the breach of PACE must be "significant and substantial" for the court to exercise its discretion under s. 78 where a confession has not fallen foul of s. 76.

Lying to a suspect's legal representative has also been considered as a breach of PACE that will lead to the court using its discretion under s. 78 to exclude a confession which would otherwise have been admissible. For example, in *R v Mason* [1987] 3 All

ER 481 the police tricked the defendant into believing that his fingerprints had been found at the scene of the crime and repeated this lie to his solicitor. In *R v McGovern* (1991) 92 Cr App R 228 the police interviewed a pregnant and vulnerable suspect in the absence of a solicitor during which she made a confession. When the solicitor arrived, the police interviewed her a second time without revealing to the solicitor that an earlier interview had occurred. A second confession was obtained. The court exercised its discretion to exclude both confessions on the basis that the earlier breach of PACE tainted the second confession too.

If the weight of the evidence points to the confession being admissible under s. 76(2) (a) or (b) then the evidence must be excluded and a failure by the judge to exclude the evidence could provide the basis for an appeal if the defendant is subsequently convicted.

A court will usually hold a *voir dire* (a hearing in the absence of the jury) to determine whether or not the confession is admissible and not in breach of s. 76 or s. 78. However, if the only issue is whether the confession is true then that is a matter that can be left to the jury to decide (see s. 76(2) of PACE 1984).

It is important to note that even if a confession is excluded (by using a discretion) or ruled inadmissible (because of the rule of law under s. 76), any facts or other evidence discovered as a result of the confession may still be admissible even if the confession itself is not. Under s. 76(4)(a) any facts discovered as a result of a confession are admissible. Therefore, if for example, a defendant makes a confession that leads the police to the whereabouts of a murder weapon, the murder weapon will still be admissible as real evidence even though the prosecution cannot refer to the confession in explaining how they found the murder weapon. Under s. 76(4)(b) if the confession was useful in showing that a defendant spoke or wrote in a certain way that is important to a matter in issue in the trial, then those parts of the confession can be admitted. For example, in a case of rape where the complainant has not seen the perpetrator because she was blindfolded but can remember that the perpetrator pronounced a particular word in an unusual way, then any evidence from a recorded interview that would show the defendant pronounced words in the same way would be admissible even if it is part of a confession that is inadmissible or has been excluded.

Finally, it is important to note that where a case involves more than one defendant, an advocate may have to deal with a confession that has come from a co-defendant who is not the client. The confession however may help the defendant's case in terms of reducing their involvement or eliminating it altogether. Under s. 76A of PACE 1984 it is possible for a defendant to rely on a confession that has been made by a co-defendant. If the defendant wishes to admit a co-defendant's confession into evidence, they must still show that the confession was not obtained in breach of s. 76(2) (a) or (b) but the standard of proof will be on a balance of probabilities rather than the higher criminal standard that the prosecution would have to meet.

Whilst a confession is usually only admissible as evidence against the person who made it, in some very limited circumstances it can be used against other joint defendants and so an advocate will need to carefully consider whether they want to invoke s. 76A. In *R v Hayter* [2005] UKHL 6 the House of Lords held that once a jury was satisfied in a joint trial of two or more defendants that the confession of D1 has established D1's guilt, they could go on to look at whether D2 might also be guilty. Whilst D1's confession was not proof of D2's guilt it could be used in a limited way as evidence to consider D2's guilt once the jury was satisfied that D1 was guilty.

## 5.2.3  Criminal Justice Act Provisions on Hearsay

The next exclusionary rule to consider is that relating to hearsay evidence. The general principle on oral and documentary testimony is that the evidence should be original rather than second hand or copies. However, it is appreciated that this is not always possible and so exceptions have developed to the exclusionary rule.

Hearsay is defined in s. 114(1) of the Criminal Justice Act ('CJA') 2003 as "a statement not made in oral evidence in the proceedings" but which is to be admitted as "evidence of any matter stated". It is therefore statements made out of court, but which are to be used in court to prove the truth of the matters contained in the statement. Section115 of the 2003 Act defines a statement as "any representation of fact or opinion made by a person by whatever means; and it includes a representation made in a sketch, photofit or other pictorial form".

Therefore, if an advocate wishes to use a witness statement made by a witness who cannot attend court or to use maps or diagrams without calling the maker of those documents, then the advocate will need to make a formal application to admit the evidence as hearsay. This is only necessary if it is intended to rely on the truth of the information contained in the documents or witness statement. A formal application should be made in accordance with CrimPR Part 20 which involves a written notice to the other party and to the court identifying the evidence that is to be regarded as hearsay evidence.

If, however, the intention is simply to show that the statements were made but no reliance is being placed on its truth or importance it will simply be regarded as ordinary evidence subject to a judge or jury deciding how much weight to place upon it in determining the disputed issues.

### 5.2.3.1  Exceptions to the Hearsay Exclusionary Rule

Hearsay evidence is admissible if it falls into one of the exceptions set out in s. 116 of the CJA 2003 (unavailability of the witness), s. 117 (business documents and criminal investigation documents), s. 118 (certain common law exceptions), s. 119 (previous inconsistent statements) and s. 120 (previous consistent statements).

Even if hearsay evidence falls into one of the exceptions, it can still be excluded by the judge exercising judicial discretion under s. 126 of the CJA 2003. This section gives the judge an exclusionary discretion if "the court is satisfied that the case for excluding the statement, taking account of the danger that to admit it would result in undue waste of time, substantially outweighs the case for admitting it, taking account of the value of the evidence".

In addition, just like other evidence, the general discretionary powers under s. 78 and s. 82(3) that we have discussed earlier in this chapter, can be used to exclude hearsay evidence based on the fairness principle.

Hearsay is the only exclusionary rule that provides a judicial discretion to also include the evidence even where it would normally be inadmissible. This special discretion is found in s. 114(1)(d) and can be used if the court is satisfied that it is in the interests of justice to do so. This route to admissibility was described by the Law Commission (1997) as "a measure of last resort" at the time of their report into the proposed changes to hearsay which were subsequently included in the 2003 Act. However, it has been used to include otherwise inadmissible confession evidence (see *R v Y* [2008] EWCA Crim 10) and bad character evidence (see *R v Isichei* 2006] EWCA Crim 815).

According to cases such as *R v Musone* [2007] EWCA Crim 1237 the inclusionary discretion under s. 114(1)(d) can only be challenged on appeal if the decision to use it is 'Wednesbury unreasonable' in the sense that the judge's decision is considered to be perverse and no other judge would have made the same decision. The judge should look at, e.g. the probative value of the statement, what other evidence could be called, its importance to the case as a whole, the reliability of the maker, the extent of prejudice to the other party, etc (see s. 114(2)). Therefore, even if the hearsay evidence is not admissible because it does not fall into one of the exceptions provided for by the 2003 Act, an advocate should consider whether it is appropriate to call upon the judge to exercise his/her judicial discretion to include the evidence under s. 114(1)(d).

Refer to the useful table to understand when hearsay evidence can be admitted. An advocate can admit hearsay evidence if it falls into one of the exceptions identified in the CJA 2003 as set out in the table. Any admission is still subject to the judicial discretion to exclude.

| Method of Admissibility under CJA 2003 | Type of Hearsay | Criteria | Judicial Discretion |
|---|---|---|---|
| S. 114(1)(a) | Any hearsay evidence made admissible by statute, e.g. written witness statements (Criminal Justice Act 1967, s. 9), expert's reports (Criminal Justice Act 1988, s. 30) and bankers' books (Bankers' Books Evidence Act 1879, s. 3) | As set out in the relevant statute | S. 126 CJA 2003 (to exclude) or s. 114(1)(d) CJA 2003 (to include) or s. 78 and s. 82(3) PACE 1984 (to exclude – see s. 126(2)) |
| S. 114(1)(c) | All parties agree to the admission of the hearsay evidence | None | N/A |
| S. 114(1)(d) | All forms of hearsay | In the interests of justice | S. 114(2) factors for inclusion. There is no discretion to exclude once admitted by judge under s. 114(1)(d) |
| S. 116 | Witness ('W') unavailability due to:<br>1. W's death – s. 116(2)(a)<br>2. W's unfitness due to bodily or mental condition – s. 116(2)(b)<br>3. W is outside the UK and it is not reasonably practicable to secure their attendance – s. 116(2)(c)<br>4. W cannot be found and reasonably practicable steps have been taken to find them – s. 116(2)(d)<br>5. W is 'in fear' and does not give oral evidence for this reason – s. 116(2)(e) but **permission of the court is required to admit under this ground** | If the witness ('W') gave oral evidence on the matter at trial it would be admissible and W has been identified to the court's satisfaction. In the case of hearsay under s. 116(2)(e) the court must also be satisfied of the conditions under s. 116(4) | S. 126 CJA 2003 (to exclude) or s. 114(1)(d) CJA 2003 (to include) or ss. 78 and 82(3) PACE 1984 (to exclude – see s. 126(2)) |

| | | | |
|---|---|---|---|
| S. 117(1) and 117(4) | 1. Documents created in the course of a trade, business, profession or other occupation<br>2. Documents prepared for pending or contemplated criminal proceedings or investigation | 1. The person who supplied the information ('the relevant person') contained in the document had or may reasonably have had personal knowledge of the matters contained in it and if the information passed through others, then each person who supplied the information to the relevant person also received it in the course of a trade, business, profession or other occupation (see s. 117(2))<br>2. One of the s. 116(2) conditions above are satisfied or W cannot be reasonably expected to recollect the matters contained in the document | S. 126 (to exclude) or s. 114(1)(d) CJA 2003 (to include) or s. 117(6) and s. 117(7) CJA 2003 (to exclude due to unreliability)<br>ss. 78 and 82(3) PACE 1984 to exclude (see s. 126(2)) |
| S.118 | 1. Public documents, published works, records or evidence as to a person's age or date of birth – see s. 118(1)<br>2. Reputation as to character – see s. 118(2)<br>3. Reputation or family tradition – see s. 118(3)<br>4. Res gestae – see s. 118(4)<br>5. Confessions – see s. 118(5)<br>6. Admissions by agents – see s. 118(6)<br>7. Common enterprise – see s. 118(7)<br>8. Expert evidence – see s. 118(8) | None | S. 126 CJA 2003 (to exclude) or s. 114(1)(d) CJA 2003 (to include)<br>or<br>ss. 78 and 82(3) PACE 1984 (to exclude – see s. 126(2)) |
| S.119 | Previous inconsistent statements | The statement must be admitted as true by W or proved to be true under the Criminal Procedure Act 1865, ss. 3–5 | S. 126 CJA 2003 (to exclude) or s. 114(1)(d) CJA 2003 (to include)<br>ss. 78 and 82(3) PACE 1984 (to exclude – see s. 126(2)) |

*(Continued)*

| Method of Admissibility under CJA 2003 | Type of Hearsay | Criteria | Judicial Discretion |
|---|---|---|---|
| S.120 | Previous consistent statements<br><br>1. Used during oral evidence to rebut a suggestion of fabrication – s. 120(2)<br>2. Used during oral evidence to refresh memory while giving evidence – s. 120(3)<br>3. Used to identify or describe a person, object or place – s. 120(5)<br>4. Used to supplement W's oral evidence during cross-examination due to W's inability to recollect matters in the statement – s. 120(6)<br>5. Used to supplement oral evidence that has already taken place by producing evidence of a complaint made by W about a recent offence which is connected to the proceedings and would constitute the offence or part of the offence – s. 120(7) | For s. 120(3) – the criteria in s. 139 must be satisfied (see below).<br>For s. 120(5), (6) and (7) while giving evidence W must confirm that to the best of his/her belief the statement was made by them and states the truth<br>For s. 120(6) the statement must have originally been made when matters were fresh in W's memory.<br>For s. 120(7) the complaint must not have been made as a result of a threat or a promise | S. 126 CJA 2003 (to exclude) and s. 114(1)(d) CJA 2003 (to include)<br>ss.78 and 82(3) PACE 1984 (to exclude – see s. 126 (2)) |
| S. 121 | Multiple hearsay | The statements involved must be admissible either under s. 114(1)(c), s. 117, s. 119 or s. 120<br>OR<br>The court is satisfied that it should be admitted in the interests of justice | S. 126 CJA 2003 (to exclude) and s. 114(1)(d) CJA 2003 (to include)<br>ss.78 and 82(3) PACE 1984 (to exclude – see s. 126(2)) |
| S. 139 | Refreshing memory about any matter | The statement was made or verified by W at an earlier time and W states it records W's recollection of the matter at the time it was made and W's recollection of those matters is likely to be significantly better at the time it was recorded than when W is giving oral evidence | S. 126 CJA 2003 (to exclude) and s. 114(1)(d) CJA 2003 (to include)<br>ss.78 and 82(3) PACE 1984 (to exclude – see s. 126(2)) |

An advocate will need to be clear about what is to be proved in a trial in order to understand whether any out of court statements count as hearsay because they are intended to be used as evidence of 'any matter stated' within those statements.

Section 116(2)(e) is the only ground that requires leave of the court and the court will apply the 'interests of justice' test. An inquiry into the existence of 'fear' may take place first by the court considering any available evidence on fear and this can include the fearful witness being called to give oral evidence before the interests of justice test is applied. Fear is widely construed and includes fear of death or injury to another or financial loss and does not have to be directly attributable to the defendant (see *R v Horncastle* [2009] EWCA 964).

In *Al Khawaja and Tahery v United Kingdom* (2011) 54 EHRR 23 the court held that where fear is proven to be attributable to the defendant or those acting on his behalf, the defendant is taken to have waived his right to question witnesses and it is appropriate to allow the evidence of that witness to be read to the court, even if it is the sole or decisive evidence. In all other cases every effort should be made for the witness to give evidence and prosecutors should therefore apply for special measures or witness anonymity unless inappropriate or impracticable. According to *Al Khawaja* it would be a breach of Article 6(3)(d) for a witness who claims to be in fear to then be permitted to be both absent from court and to remain anonymous. This would offend the accused's right under this Convention "to examine or have examined witnesses against him and to obtain the attendance and examination of witnesses on his behalf under the same conditions as witnesses against him". Equally, anonymous hearsay should not be admitted under s. 114(1)(d) for the same reasons.

If hearsay evidence is admitted, the jury should be given a reminder during the judge's summing-up of where the burden of proof lies, the fact the hearsay evidence is disputed and the dangers of convicting solely upon such evidence. It is important that a jury is given a warning because of the potential unreliability of hearsay evidence. For example, if a witness does not give evidence the judge or jury will not have had an opportunity to see the demeanour of the witness to assess the truthfulness of their account. Much can be learnt about a witness by watching their body language. Also, a witness would ordinarily swear an oath before giving evidence, but hearsay evidence is not subject to an oath. A witness would also have their evidence tested in cross-examination if they appeared in court, but this opportunity is lost when hearsay evidence is admitted.

The judicial warning may vary slightly depending on the facts of the case and the type of hearsay evidence that has been admitted. For example, in respect of the admission of a previous consistent statement under s. 120, the judge might refer to the fact that having part of the evidence in writing might unintendedly give the evidence more prominence in the jury's mind. The Crown Court Compendium sets out examples of suggested wordings for a judge's warning to the jury following admission of each category of hearsay evidence.

It can sometimes to be difficult to assess when hearsay evidence might potentially be admissible as *res gestae* evidence under s. 118(4). *Res gestae* can be loosely translated as 'part of the matter'. It forms part of a witness's account even though it may relate to reported speech which is being used to prove the truth of the matter stated. There are three categories of *res gestae* that are potentially admissible under s. 118(4):

1.  Statements made by a person "so emotionally overpowered by an event that the possibility of concoction or distortion can be disregarded" – see *R v Andrews* [1987] AC 281.
2.  Statements that accompany an act and the act can only be properly evaluated as evidence if considered in conjunction with the statement.
3.  Statements that relate to a physical sensation or a mental state.

According to Lord Ackner's guidelines in the case of *R v Andrews*, a judge should consider whether there is an absence of concoction and that there is sufficient spontaneity and contemporaneity between the acts/events and the statement that would rule out the possibility of error or malice on the part of the declarant.

The admissibility of previous inconsistent statements is governed by s. 119 of the Criminal Justice Act 2003 (which applies to criminal proceedings only) and ss. 4 and 5 of the Criminal Procedure Act 1865 (which applies to civil as well as criminal proceedings).

Section 4 of the 1865 Act covers any oral statement made by a witness which is inconsistent with his/her present oral testimony (so does not have to be in writing) so long as the witness is told about the circumstances of the statement and asked whether he/she made it.

Section 5 relates to previous statements made by the witness in writing – the witness must first be allowed to see those parts which will be used to contradict their evidence (the judge then has a discretion as to whether to let the jury see the entire statement or just those parts).

An advocate should be particularly wary of attempts to introduce multiple hearsay (where the information has passed through more than one person before it is recorded). Section 121 of the Criminal Justice Act states that multiple hearsay is only admissible if it is hearsay evidence relating to business or criminal investigation documents (s. 117) or previous inconsistent statements (s. 119) or previous consistent statements (s. 120) or all parties agree (s. 114(1)(c)) or the court is satisfied that it should be admitted in the interests of justice (s. 114(1)(d)).

Even if hearsay evidence is admitted it is subject to additional safeguards under ss. 123 and 124 of the 2003 Act. Hearsay evidence is not admissible, according to s. 123, unless the person making or supplying the statement would have had the capability to give evidence under the normal principles of witness competency (see discussion in 4.5.1 below). Section 124 provides that the other party may ask the court to take into account any evidence as to the credibility of the maker or supplier of the statement. In addition, if after the prosecution evidence has closed, the hearsay evidence is considered to be so unconvincing that it would render a conviction unsafe then the trial can be stopped (s. 125). This involves an appraisal of the case as a whole including looking at the reliability of the hearsay evidence and its importance in the context of other evidence in the case. It therefore has the same function as a 'submission of no case to answer' but with a different test applied.

# Admission of Evidence

## 5.3 Character and Similar Fact Evidence

We will now go on to look at another type of evidence which will usually be admitted in documentary form, namely previous convictions and other evidence relating to the misconduct of a defendant or non-defendant witnesses. This can include evidence of previous conduct that is similar to the conduct in question if it is relevant to show a pattern of behaviour or a tendency to act in a certain way ('similar fact evidence'). Similar fact evidence is evidence of what can be regarded as 'signature behaviour' by a defendant in the past which is the same or similar to the behaviour alleged in the present case. The rules of admission for character evidence are so wide that it is often argued that this type of evidence is an inclusionary rather than an exclusionary rule.

### 5.3.1 Criminal Justice Act Provisions on Character Evidence

Unlike civil proceedings there is a statutory framework for the admission of character evidence and this is found in ss. 100 (see Chapter 3) and 101 of the Criminal Justice Act 2003. These rules provide for admissibility of character evidence in seven situations and these are often referred to as the 'seven gateways'. An advocate who wishes to use evidence of the bad character of a defendant or a non-defendant witness should follow the procedure in CrimPR Part 21.2 and make a formal application following the additional procedure in Part 21.3 (non-defendants) or Part 21.4 (defendants) and serve the application on the court and the other party.

Bad character evidence is defined by s. 98 of the Criminal Justice Act 2003 as meaning "a disposition towards misconduct" and "misconduct" is in turn defined under s. 112(1) as "the commission of an offence or other reprehensible behaviour".

The previous convictions of a defendant are admissible at trial to prove a defendant committed the offences mentioned in the record of convictions (see Police and Criminal Evidence Act 1984, s. 74). However, they can also be used to show that there is a likelihood that the defendant might have also committed the offences for which he is charged (known as 'propensity').

Cases have confirmed that 'reprehensible behaviour' can include membership of a violent gang, allegations that do not lead to a formal charge and excessive drinking or drug taking. The evidence is not proof of guilt but can be used to challenge the defendant's credibility and the truthfulness of the defendant's evidence and/ or show the defendant has an inclination ('propensity') to commit offences. Certain gateways such as the one found under s. 101(1)(g) can only go towards the credibility of the defendant based on the fact the defendant has attacked another person's character (see *R v Singh (James Paul)* [2007] EWCA Crim 2140). The admission of bad character evidence does not rely on the defendant actually giving evidence at trial. An 'attack' can, for example, be made by a defendant's advocate and so it is important to consider whether any accusations are made against a prosecution witness when an advocate poses their questions. Questions that elicit evidence of misbehaviour by a witness may be regarded as an 'attack'.

Under s. 109 of the 2003 Act there is a rebuttable presumption of truth when assessing the relevance or probative value of bad character evidence.

The definition of bad character evidence excludes evidence which forms part of the central facts or evidence in the trial itself (see s. 98(a)). Such evidence would still be admissible at the trial but would be subject to the 'relevancy test.'

If a judge decides to admit bad character evidence during the course of the trial then under s. 110 he/she must give reasons in open court (but in the absence of the jury) for admitting or excluding this type of evidence (see CrimPR Part 21.5). Since bad character evidence can be damaging to a defendant's case it is incumbent on a judge to give a clear warning to the jury during the summing-up not to place undue reliance on evidence of a defendant's previous convictions. This was confirmed in *R v Hanson* [2005] EWCA Crim 824. In addition, a judge should direct the jury as to whether the admitted evidence can be used as evidence towards credibility or propensity or both – see *R v Highton and Others* [2005] EWCA Crim 1985.

## 5.3.1.1 *Gateways to Admitting Bad Character Evidence of a Defendant*

The seven gateways are as set out in this section's useful reference table.

| Method of Admissibility | Relevant Statutory Provision of the Criminal Justice Act ('CJA') 2003 | Who Can Use the Gateway? | Power to Exclude |
|---|---|---|---|
| All parties agree to its admission | S. 101(1)(a) | Prosecution, defence, co-defendants | Ss. 78 and 82(3) PACE 1984 by virtue of s. 112(3)(c) CJA 2003 |
| The defendant raises his own bad character in evidence | S. 101(1)(b) | Defence | Ss. 78 and 82(3) PACE 1984 by virtue of s. 112(3)(c) CJA 2003 |
| The evidence is 'important explanatory evidence' | S. 101(1)(c) – read in conjunction with s. 102 | Prosecution, defence, co-defendants | Ss. 78 and 82(3) PACE 1984 by virtue of s. 112(3)(c) CJA 2003 |
| The evidence is relevant to an 'important matter in issue' between the defendant and the prosecution as to whether a defendant has a propensity to commit the offence or has a propensity for untruthfulness | S. 101(1)(d) – read in conjunction with s. 103 | Prosecution only – see s. 103(6) CJA 2003 | Ss. 101(3) and 103(3) CJA 2003 |
| The evidence has 'substantial probative value' to an important matter in issue between the defence and a co-defendant | S.101(1)(e) – read in conjunction with s. 104 | Co-defendants – see s. 104(2) | None – see *R v Musone* [2007] EWCA Crim 1237 |
| The evidence is to be used to correct a false impression that has been given by the defendant | S.101(1)(f) – read in conjunction with s. 105 | Prosecution only – see s. 105(7) CJA 2003 | Ss. 78 and 82(3) PACE 1984 by virtue of s. 112(3)(c) CJA 2003 |
| The evidence is admissible because the defendant has made an attack on another person's character | S. 101(1)(g) – read in conjunction with s. 106 | Prosecution only – see s. 106(3) CJA 2003 | S. 101(3) CJA 2003 |

## 5.3.1.2 Evidence of Motive

In *Stanton v R* [2021] EWCA Crim 1075 the Court of Appeal confirmed that evidence of recent past behaviour that tended to show a motive could be automatically admissible under s. 98(a) as evidence to do with the alleged facts of the offence. This would avoid the need to prove admissibility under s. 101. However, the court also concluded that motive evidence could in any event fall into s. 101(1)(d) as evidence that goes towards a matter in issue between the prosecution and the defence.

The facts of the appeal in *Stanton* were that a co-defendant appealed the admission of bad character evidence at his trial which the judge had admitted under s. 101(1)(c), (d) and (e). The evidence related to a mix of a previous charge and allegations relating to that charge. The defendant (Stanton) was charged with offences related to obtaining money over a period of time from an elderly man (Mr Spinks) whom the defendant had subjected to threats and violence. Stanton was a self-confessed drug user and the evidence was that he had stolen the money from Mr Spinks to fund his drug use. The matter was reported to the police and so fell within the definition of bad character under s. 98 ('reprehensible behaviour'). The allegation thereafter was that because the defendant no longer had access to Mr Spinks's money he targeted another vulnerable man (Mr Butt) whom he murdered during a burglary with his co-defendant (Mr McKay). The murder of Mr Butt was the subject of the original trial but the Court of Appeal held that the Spinks allegations were probative in establishing a motive by the defendant to "commit an acquisitive offence" to fund his drug use.

It is interesting that in this case the Court of Appeal did not think that the allegations relating to Mr Spinks could be admissible under s. 101(1)(c) as 'important explanatory evidence'. Cases such as *R v Lee (Peter Bruce)* [2012] EWCA Crim 316 have established that important explanatory evidence must be more than just background evidence that fills the picture. It must be an important part of the overall picture without which a judge or jury could not understand the other evidence in the case (see s. 102 of the CJA 2003).

## 5.3.1.3 Evidence of Propensity

The gateway that is by far the most complex route to the admission of bad character evidence for a defendant is s. 101(1)(d). This requires the prosecution to show that the defendant has either (1) a propensity to commit offences or (2) a propensity for untruthfulness. Propensity is therefore "a matter in issue between the prosecution and the defendant". On its own, propensity cannot establish guilt, it is only part of the picture that emerges about a defendant's guilt.

It is important to note that s. 103(1) provides the definition of "matters in issue" with reference to the two types of propensity mentioned earlier but preceded the definition with the word "includes". For this reason, gateway (d) has also been used to admit 'similar fact' evidence.

The first type of propensity (propensity to commit an offence) can be established either by showing the defendant has committed an offence of the same description or one that is in the same 'category'. These categories have now been set by the Secretary of State – see the Criminal Justice Act 2003 (Categories of Offences) Order 2004. The categories are offences under the Theft Act (e.g. theft robbery, burglary, handling stolen goods, etc) and sexual offences against a person under 16. This also includes 'inchoate offences' under these categories (aiding, abetting, counselling or procuring the commission of one of the offences in the categories).

It is important to note that s. 103(2) of the Criminal Justice Act 2003 states that a defendant's propensity is not restricted to using previous convictions "of the same description" or "same category" and can be proved in other ways and so could stem from conduct which is not criminal but is reprehensible in some other way. For example, in *R v Chopra* [2007] EWCA Crim 2133 the court found that there was sufficient connection (e.g. common features) between the facts in several allegations made against the defendant that could show propensity to commit the offence. The facts of this case involved several allegations by patients that the defendant, a dentist, had squeezed their breasts during a dental examination. These allegations were ruled to have been correctly admitted by the trial judge under s. 101(1)(d). During the defendant's trial for indecent assault convictions involving similar allegations of indecent assault by the defendant were admitted even though two had resulted in acquittals.

Where a defendant is charged with more than one offence s. 112(2) of the 2003 Act provides that each charge will be regarded as separate proceedings for the purpose of deciding the issue of bad character evidence. Therefore, the prosecution can apply for permission to refer to those other charges in the separate proceedings by making an application under s. 101(1)(d). This will be an application for 'cross-admissibility'.

The question of whether a standard of proof is attached to proving propensity was considered in *R v Mitchell* [2016] UKSC 55 – this case was a referral from the Court of Appeal in relation to equivalent Northern Ireland legislation on bad character evidence. The defendant was accused of stabbing her partner and there was previous bad character evidence that she had a propensity to use knives and it was sought to admit bad character under the equivalent gateways of (c), (d) and (f). The court held that neither the CJA 2003 nor the Northern Ireland equivalent legislation gave any indication as to whether bad character evidence must meet the standard of proof before it can be accepted. The Supreme Court followed the decision in *R v Ngyuen* [2008] EWCA Crim 585 that the criminal standard of proof should be met. However, the Supreme Court clarified that this does not mean that in cases where there are several instances of misconduct, all tending to show a propensity, the jury must be convinced of the truth and accuracy of all aspects of each of those. The jury is entitled to, and should, consider the evidence about propensity in the round. Also, this does not mean the jury must be unanimous on the question of whether it exists. The jury should be directed that, if it is to take propensity into account, it should be sure that it has been proved. In its deliberations as to whether propensity has been proved, the jury should consider the evidence on the subject as a whole rather than in individual compartments. The case of *R v Gabanna* [2020] EWCA Crim 1473 has confirmed the criminal standard of proof applies to all gateways, not just the ones considered in the case of *Mitchell*.

Propensity is a question of judgment to be exercised by the judge and as *Hanson* and *R v Renda* [2006] EWCA Crim 2826 confirmed, an appeal court will be reluctant to interfere unless the judge has applied that judgment incorrectly.

To show propensity to commit offences based on past convictions, the prosecution does not have to admit a minimum number of offences. However, *R v Hanson* [2005] EWCA Crim 824 confirms that to show propensity a single conviction will usually not be enough unless the conviction shows "a tendency to unusual behaviour or where its circumstances demonstrate probative force in relation to the offence charged" [9].

The Court of Appeal in *Hanson* provided some guidance on the exercise of judicial judgment about whether or not to admit evidence of previous convictions under gateway (d). A judge will usually consider three questions:

1) does the history of conviction(s) establish a propensity to commit the offences charged? 2) does that propensity make it more likely that the defendant committed the offence charged? 3) Is it unjust to rely on the convictions of the same description or category, and in any event, will the proceedings be unfair if admitted?

[7]

Old convictions may be far more prejudicial if admitted into evidence at trial because it does not then allow for the fact that a convicted person can be rehabilitated. Section 103(3) of the 2003 Act states that gateway (d) does not apply if the court is satisfied, by reason of the length of time since the conviction or for any other reason that it would be unjust to apply it. The court will look at factors such as the degree of similarity, gravity of past offences, strength of prosecution case, date of commission of the offence, sentence passed and whether the past events are disputed.

The Criminal Practice Directions 2015 Division V 21A.3 states that reference should not be made to a 'spent' conviction without leave of the court and the judge should only grant permission if the interests of justice so require.

According to cases such as *R v Lafayette* [2009] EWCA Crim 3238 where non-conviction evidence is being relied on to establish propensity and the evidence is disputed, the jury must be directed not to rely on it unless it is sure of its truth.

On the question of the second type of propensity (propensity to untruthfulness) the case of *Hanson* confirms that this does not mean the same as merely a propensity to dishonesty. It should relate to the defendant's behaviour or lies told by the defendant which impact the offence. The Explanatory Notes to the 2003 Act suggest that the propensity for untruthfulness gateway should be confined to previous convictions for such offences as fraud and perjury. Dishonesty offences might be relevant if truth is in issue at the trial, for example, whether the defendant gave a truthful account during a police interview or where the defendant is alleged to have made false representations.

In *R v Ellis* [2010] EWCA Crim 163 the court accepted that deception offences could be relevant in showing a defendant's willingness to be untruthful in certain circumstances but, given the possible prejudicial effect, a warning should be given to the jury that the deception offences do not prove that the defendant is being untruthful in his current testimony. However, it is important to note that whilst a single conviction for deception can show propensity for untruthfulness (unlike propensity to commit an offence), only offences such as perjury can be strong enough to show that the defendant is actually lying in his/her testimony.

The case of *R v Highton* [2005] EWCA Crim 1985 suggests that a distinction needs to be drawn between the basis for admitting the evidence and the use which may be made of it once admitted. For this reason, the judge will generally have to give the jury a 'clear warning' during his/her summing-up 'against placing undue reliance' on the evidence and explain why it has been admitted and the ways in which it is relevant.

Due to the complex nature of gateway (d) it may not be easy for the prosecution to admit bad character evidence under this section. However, if during the trial, the defendant makes an attack on, for example, the credibility of a prosecution witness, then the prosecution may use gateway (g) to admit the bad character evidence instead. This occurred in *R v Edwards* [2005] EWCA Crim 3244, where previous convictions for robbery and burglary dating back to 1992 were not admitted under s. 101(1)(d) because they were considered to be too old but were allowed in under gateway (g) when the defendant made an attack on a prosecution witness.

The bad character evidence of a witness can also be admissible at trial in certain circumstances, and we have considered this already in the section on rules on questioning witnesses in Chapter 3.

## 5.4  Defendant's Good Character

In the seminal conjoined appeal cases of *R v Vye; R v Wise; R v Stephenson* [1993] 97 Cr App R 134 the Court of Appeal held that where a defendant has a good character and relies upon exculpatory statements made in or out of court, he/she is entitled to a good character direction that has two limbs. The first is known as the 'credibility limb' which allows the jury to take the lack of previous convictions into account when assessing whether they believe the defendant's evidence. However, the defendant must have given evidence either directly at trial or in a pre-trial statement of some kind. The second limb is known as the 'propensity limb' which allows the jury to take into account the defendant's lack of previous convictions when deciding whether he/she has the propensity to commit the offence for which they are charged. The propensity limb can be given regardless of whether a defendant has testified or made a pre-trial statement.

It is important that the judge directs the jury as to the way in which it might treat the fact that the defendant has no previous convictions. However, the judge must also remind the jury that good character is not a defence and it is for the jury to decide how much weight to give to its importance (if at any).

Following the case of *Vye*, a number of subsequent cases appeared to confuse when a *Vye* direction could be given and if it could be given when there were no previous convictions but there was evidence of reprehensible behaviour (which would still be classed as bad character evidence under s. 98 of the CJA 2003). Or indeed whether minor convictions could be overlooked and the *Vye* direction given. There was a danger of the judge giving conflicting directions to the jury about the same defendant where the weight of bad character evidence suggested propensity and the weight of good character evidence suggested a lack of propensity. This could as Lord Steyn noted in *R v Aziz* [1996] AC 41 lead to "absurdity". It was left to the Court of Appeal in *R v Hunter and Others* [2015] EWCA Crim 631 to give some clear guidance on the different ways in which it might be possible to give a *Vye* direction to the jury and this is set out in the two flow diagrams (Figures 5.1 and 5.2).

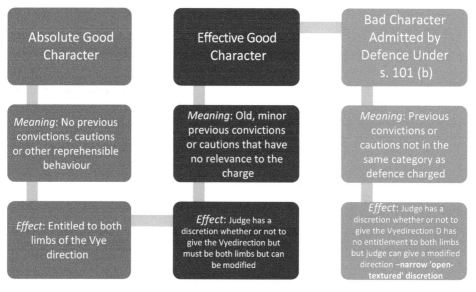

**Figure 5.1** *Hunter* Good Character Guidance.

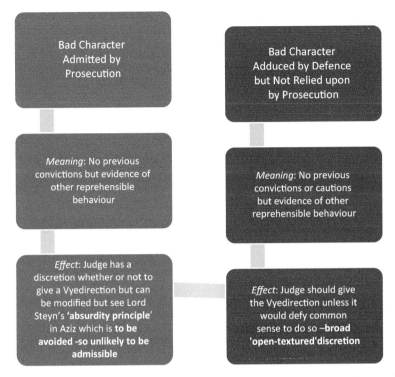

**Figure 5.2** *Hunter* Good Character Guidance *Contd.*

# Refusing to Answer Questions or Disclose Material

## 5.5  Silence at the Police Station

Silence can be used as evidence against a defendant. Whilst a defendant has a right to remain silent when questioned at a police station, under s. 34 of the Criminal Justice and Public Order Act ('CJPOA') 1994, a judge or jury can draw an adverse inference when told about this silence at the trial. It is for the jury to decide whether or not to draw the adverse inference. In addition, s. 38(3) of the 1994 Act provides that an adverse inference alone will not be enough for a finding of guilt against a defendant.

Before an adverse inference can be drawn by the jury at trial, three conditions must apply:

1) the defendant was questioned by the police at any time before and on being charged. This also includes after charge in the case of terrorism offences – see s. 34(1)(c) as amended by s. 22 of the Counter-Terrorism Act 2008, and

2) the defendant was questioned under caution (this is a requirement under Code C PACE 1984, para 10.5), and
3) during the questioning the defendant failed to mention any fact which is later relied upon in his/her defence and which he/she could reasonably have been expected to mention.

It is important to note that for the purposes of s. 34, silence does not mean merely saying nothing at all. It means a failure to mention a material fact. This can either be orally during questioning or if a defendant submits a written statement and omits facts he/she later relies on (see *R v Knight* [2003] EWCA Crim 1977). According to *R v Webber* [2004] UKHL 1 "a fact" should be given a broad meaning and should cover any alleged fact which is in dispute between the prosecution and the defence. The fact must also be one the defendant later relies on at trial (for example as part of their defence).

The question of whether it was reasonable to expect the defendant to have mentioned a fact is one for the jury to decide. The case of *R v Argent* [1996] EWCA Crim 1728 provides some helpful guidance as to circumstances that might affect whether it was reasonable for a defendant to mention a relevant fact when at the police station. These circumstances include:

1. A defendant's age – child defendants are unlikely to recognise what might be an important fact in their case and may forget to reveal important information to the police during questioning.
2. Whether the defendant has experience of the criminal justice system – an experienced defendant is more likely to appreciate what facts are relevant and likely to be disputed at trial.
3. Defendant's mental capacity – a defendant who lacks mental capacity may find questioning confusing and fail to appreciate what are important facts to tell the police about their case.
4. The defendant's state of health whilst at the police station – a defendant who is ill might have difficulties concentrating and recalling information. This is also true for a defendant who is tired (due to lack of sleep).
5. Whether or not the defendant was sober during questioning – drugs or alcohol will affect a defendant's concentration, memory and communication.
6. The level of the defendant's knowledge – it may be that the police have not made the nature of the allegations clear to the defendant during questioning.
7. Whether a defendant was given access to legal advice (see s. 34(2A) of the CJPOA 1994 as inserted by s. 58 of the Youth Justice and Criminal Evidence Act 1999) or was given legal advice to remain silent (a 'no comment interview'). In the case of advice to give a 'no comment interview' cases such as *R v Hoare & Pierce* [2004] EWCA Crim 784 and *R v Beckles (no 2)* [2004] EWCA Crim 2766 state that the accused must genuinely rely on his/her solicitor's advice and it must also have been reasonable for him/her to do so. A defendant can waive their right of access

to legal advice and the right to access can also be temporarily delayed by the police.

If the jury cannot draw an adverse inference because the conditions under s. 34 are not met or it would not be reasonable to draw such inferences (taking account of the *Argent* principles), the judge must actively direct the jury that it cannot draw an adverse inference – see *R v McGarry* [1998] EWCA Crim 2364.

If the jury can draw an adverse inference the judge should still warn the jury of the need to be careful in making a link to guilt by reminding the jury the defendant has a right of silence and that there must still be a *'prima facie'* (on first impressions) case against a defendant before they can be found guilty. This is known as a 'Condron direction' from the case of *Condron and Condron v UK* [2000] ECHR 191.

## 5.5.1 Silence at the Trial

A defendant can also choose to exercise their right of silence at trial by not going into the witness box or failing to answer questions. However, the jury can draw an adverse inference if the defendant does not have a good reason for the silence (see Criminal Justice and Public Order 1999, s. 35). A good reason is either (1) that the accused's guilt is not in issue – see s. 35(1)(a) or (2) that the physical or mental condition of the accused makes it undesirable for them to give evidence – see s. 35(1)(b). In *R v Friend* (No 2) [2004] EWCA Crim 2661, the Court of Appeal held that a defendant suffering from "attention deficit and hyperactivity disorder" would have good cause to remain silent at trial.

When the trial reaches the half-way point at which the defendant would be expected to be called as the first defence witness, the judge should ask the defendant whether he intends to give evidence. If the answer is "no" then the judge must be satisfied that the implications of silence have been explained to the defendant and if necessary explain this to the defendant. This obligation is set out in CrimPR Part 25.9(2)(f).

Before a jury draws an adverse inference, the court must direct the jury (known as a 'Cowan direction' – see *R v Cowan* [1995] EWCA Crim 8). Again, the judge should remind the jury that a defendant has a right of silence as well as reminding them that the burden of proof at the trial remains with the prosecution and the jury must be satisfied that the prosecution has established a case to answer. The jury must also be satisfied that the silence at trial can only be attributed to the fact that the defendant has either no answer to the case against them or none that would stand up to cross-examination. As with s. 34, the jury cannot use an adverse inference as the sole basis for deciding on guilt (see s. 38(3)).

## 5.5.2 Silence on Arrest

Other circumstances where a jury may draw an adverse inference from silence during the trial is where the silence has occurred on the defendant being arrested and the defendant fails to account for any object, substance or mark found on them (s. 36) or fails to account for their presence at a particular place at the time of the offence (s. 37). In both these circumstances the defendant must have been cautioned on arrest. There is a special wording for this caution (see Code C PACE 1984 para 10.11). The drawing of an adverse inference is also subject to s. 38(3) in terms of not being used as the sole basis for deciding on the defendant's guilt.

### 5.5.3 Other Examples of Silence as Evidence

Other circumstances in which the jury may draw an adverse inference from silence are to be found (1) under s. 11(5) of the Criminal Procedure and Investigation Act 1996 (where a defendant who is required to file a defence statement in the Crown Court fails to do so) and (2) where a defendant fails to consent to an intimate sample being taken at a police station (e.g. blood, semen) without good cause (see Police and Criminal Evidence Act 1984, s. 62(10) and Code D of PACE 1984, para 5A).

### 5.5.4 Privilege Against Self-Incrimination

As with civil proceedings, in criminal proceedings a witness may rely on the privilege against self-incrimination and refuse to answer questions or provide documents or information. For a defendant, the right of silence means that it is not necessary to rely on an additional privilege against self-incrimination. There are however certain statutes that require a witness to answer questions or face criminal prosecution. However, under the Youth Justice and Criminal Evidence Act 1999, s. 59 where a statute requires a defendant to answer questions (such as the Companies Act 1985, s. 434) the answers given cannot be used in a later criminal trial if the answer was given as part of non-judicial investigations.

## 5.6 Pre-Trial Applications

As is the case in civil proceedings, criminal judges have a broad range of case management powers (see CrimPR Part 3). They can determine pre-trial issues at pre-trial hearings such as case management conferences, plea before venue hearings. This enables the judge to, for example, set a timetable for the progression of the case including fixing a grounds rule hearing, determining points of law, deciding on the admissibility of specific pieces of evidence or establishing the number of witnesses and the order in which they should be called and their needs.

Some pre-trial applications can be made without the other party being notified and, in their absence ('without notice' applications) and these include, for example, applications to notify the court of the existence of material which the prosecutor does not wish to disclose due to a real risk of serious prejudice to an important public interest.

In the Crown Court the first hearing that will be take place is usually the 'Plea and Trial Preparation Hearing ('PTPH'). During this process the defendant is 'arraigned' which means that they are called and the charges against them are formally read out in court. They are then asked to enter a plea of 'guilty' or 'not guilty'. At these hearings a judge can set the timetable and also make pre-trial rulings. Section 39(1) of the Criminal Procedure and Investigations Act 1996 states that any hearing that takes place either after the accused has been sent for trial from the Magistrates' Court to the Crown Court or before the start of the trial will be regarded as a pre-trial hearing. Section 40 of the 1996 Act further states that a pre-trial ruling can be made on the application of any party. A judge can also decide that a pre-trial ruling on a matter is necessary. Such rulings have binding effect until the trial (see s. 40(3)).

In the Magistrates' Court CrimPR Part 3.16 provides for pre-trial hearings to take preparatory steps for trial. Under ss. 8A and 8B of the Magistrates' Court Act 1980 pre-trial rulings on the admissibility of evidence or other questions of law will be binding unless it is in the interests of justice for the ruling to be varied or discharged.

# 5.7 The Criminal Case Study

In this section you will find documentation relating to three pre-trial applications in the fictional case of *R v Vermont*. Each application is preceded by a memorandum explaining the task (see Memorandums A, B and C). You should assume that all dates given are current dates. Where it is indicated in italics that a document is 'not supplied', assume that it has been correctly served and does not include any procedural irregularities and can be ignored for the purposes of the fact pattern. Each memorandum will give an indication of the criminal procedure rule that is relevant as well as some relevant case law and legislation. However, you should read the accompanying documents as they may lead you to consider further procedural rules and cases. You should also make use of the tables on procedural rules and evidential rules found at Appendix A and B. You may also find it helpful to re-read Chapters 2 and 3 for a reminder of legal research, case strategy and argument construction techniques.

You will find suggested guidance on possible arguments that can be advanced in support of each application in section C. You should however try to work through the exercises first and prepare your own arguments drawing on some of the skills learnt in the chapters in Part A.

You might approach the criminal exercises in the following way:

1.  Read all documents through once.
2.  Read through all documents a second time but this time highlight any key words or sentences that you think are important.
3.  Read any criminal procedure rules mentioned in the documentation.
4.  Consider any additional rules that might be relevant (refer to Appendix A).
5.  Read any cases mentioned in the documentation.

6.  Consider whether any other cases might be relevant – for example, do the cases referred to in the documentation lead you to a research trail of other cases/ legislation?
7.  Start to construct possible arguments – you might want to use a 'strengths and weaknesses' table similar to the table discussed in Chapter 2.
8.  Practice making your submissions aloud without heavy reliance on a script (cue or prompt cards are acceptable).

## 5.7.1  Exercise 1 (Bail)

The following exercise relates to a bail application. You act for the defence and will be seeking to persuade the court to grant bail under the Bail Act 1976 after the pros- ecution have made submissions as to why bail should not be granted. Memorandum A sets out what grounds of the Bail Act the prosecution will rely on and you should assume that they have made submissions based on those grounds at the hearing that you will attend.

Bail under the Bail Act 1976 refers to the process of release from custody for a defend- ant who is under arrest. Release is temporary until the trial takes place, or bail is revoked. A defendant can be released with conditions attached to bail or be granted unconditional bail. Both the Magistrates' Court and the Crown Court can grant bail and the procedure is set out in CrimPR Part 14 and the Bail Act 1976 as amended by the Legal Aid, Sentencing and Punishment of Offenders Act 2012.

The prosecution advocate will start by giving a summary of the case and explain why bail is opposed and what part(s) of the Bail Act is/are relied upon (see CrimPR Part 14.5). The prosecution should also anticipate what the defence might say in response and deal with the possible counter arguments. When the prosecution has made all its submissions the defence will then respond to the points made by the prosecution and explain why the exceptions to the right to bail should not apply. The defence can offer suggestions about what bail conditions the defendant might accept – see CrimPR Part 14.11–15 and Bail Act 1976, s. 3.

The Bail Act, s. 4 (and its subsequent amendments) gives a right to bail except in cer- tain circumstances. The exceptions to the right to bail are set out in Schedule 1 Part 1, 1A and 2 of the Bail Act. If a defendant does not pose a risk as outlined above, then they should be granted unconditional bail. If there is evidence that the defendant is a bail risk, the court should consider whether attaching conditions to bail would allevi- ate that risk. If not, the defendant should not be granted bail.

The Bail Act 1976 is a complex piece of legislation and it is good to practice to read legislation of this nature in order to decide which provisions apply, or do not apply to your client. The Act has been subject to a number of amendments by other pieces of legislation and so it may be necessary to trace some of those amendments back to their original source to fully understand the intention behind each ground. The various grounds/exceptions have been set out below for ease of reference.

The presumption of a right to bail can be rebutted where there are substantial grounds for believing that if a defendant were to be released on bail, they would act in ways contrary to the Bail Act 1976, Schedule 1 Part 1, 1A or 2.

### Imprisonable Offences/Extradition Offences (see Schedule 1, Part 1 paras 2–7 of the 1976 Act as amended)

a) Fail to surrender to custody, or
b) Commit an offence while on bail, or
c) Interfere with witnesses or otherwise obstruct the course of justice, whether in relation to himself or any other person (para 2), or
d) The defendant would engage in conduct that would or is likely to cause physical or mental injury to an 'associated person' or cause them to fear physical (para 2ZA). An 'associated person' means those in relationships of marriage, cohabitation or personal intimate relationships see s. 62(3) of the Family Law Act 1996,
e) The offence is an indictable or either-way offence and it appears to the court that the defendant was already on bail at the date of committing the offence (para 2A), or
f) In the case of extradition offences, the offence in question would have been an offence if carried out in England and Wales and it appears to the court that the defendant was on bail on the date of the offence (para 2B), or
g) The court is satisfied that the defendant should be kept in custody for his own protection, or if the defendant is a child, that they should be kept in custody for their own welfare (para 3), or
h) The defendant is in custody as a result of a sentence imposed under the Armed Forces Act 2006 (para 4), or
i) The court is satisfied that it has not been practicable to obtain sufficient information for the purposes of taking decisions about bail because of lack of time (para 5), or
j) The defendant was previously granted bail and has been arrested for failing to surrender to bail (para 6), or
k) The defendant has been charged with murder and there is significant risk of the defendant committing an offence whilst on bail that would be likely to cause physical or mental injury to a person other than the defendant or cause that person to fear physical or mental injury (para 6ZA), or
l) In certain courts where the Secretary of Secretary of State has confirmed that relevant assessment and follow-up provisions are available, the defendant who is aged over 18 is a Class A drug user and there is a significant risk of him committing an offence whilst on bail (para 6A, 6B and 6C), or

m)  The defendant's case has been adjourned for inquiries or a report and the court is of the view it would be impracticable to complete those inquiries or report without keeping the defendant in custody (para 7).

## Imprisonable Offences Under Criminal Justice and Public Order Act 1994, s. 25

a)  The defendant has previously been charged with or convicted of one of the offences under the Criminal Justice and Public Order Act 1994, s. 25(2) (murder, attempted murder, rape or specified sexual offences) and there are no exceptional circumstances to justify bail.

## Imprisonable Offences Tried Summarily or Low Value Either Way Imprisonable Offences/Extradition Offences (see Schedule 1, Part 1A paras 2–9 of the 1976 Act as amended)

a)  The defendant appears to have previously failed to surrender to custody when previously granted bail and the court believes in view of this that the defendant would fail to surrender to custody again if released on bail (para 2), or

b)  At the date the offence was committed the defendant was already on bail in criminal proceedings and the court is satisfied that there are substantial grounds for believing that if released on bail the defendant would go on to commit an offence again while on bail (para 3), or

c)  The court is satisfied that there are substantial grounds for believing the defendant would commit an offence whilst on bail that would be likely to cause physical or mental injury to an associated person' or cause that person to fear physical or mental injury (para 6). An 'associated person' has the same definition as under Schedule 1 Part 1 from s. 62 (3) of the Family Law Act 1996.

d)  The court is satisfied that the defendant should be kept in custody for his own protection, or if the defendant is a child, that they should be kept in custody for their own welfare (para 5), or

e)  The defendant is in custody as a result of a sentence imposed under the Armed Forces Act 2006 (para 6), or

f)  The defendant was previously granted bail and has been arrested for failing to surrender to bail and the court is satisfied if released would (1) fail to surrender to custody, or (2) commit an offence while on bail or (3) interfere with witnesses or otherwise obstruct the course of justice, whether in relation to himself or any other person (para 7), or

g)  The court is satisfied that it has not been practicable to obtain sufficient information for the purposes of taking decisions about bail because of lack of time (para 8), or

h)  In certain courts where the Secretary of Secretary of State has confirmed that relevant assessment and follow-up provisions are available, the defendant who is aged over 18 is a Class A drug user and there is a significant risk of him committing an offence whilst on bail (para 9 & Schedule 1 Part 1A para 6A, 6B and 6C).

**Non-Imprisonable Offences (see Schedule 1, Part 2 paras 2–6 of the 1976 Act as amended)**

a) The defendant is a child/young person or a defendant who has been convicted in the proceedings of an offence and it appears to the court that he failed to surrender to bail when previously granted bail in criminal proceedings and the court believes that because of this the defendant would fail to surrender to bail again (para 2), or

b) The court is satisfied that the defendant should be kept in custody for his own protection or if the defendant is a child that they should be kept in custody for their own welfare (para 3).

c) The defendant is in custody as a result of a sentence imposed under the Armed Forces Act 2006 (para 4), or

d) The defendant is a child/young person or a defendant who has been convicted in the proceedings of an offence and was previously granted bail and has been arrested for failing to surrender to bail and the court is satisfied if released would (1) fail to surrender to custody, or (2) commit an offence while on bail or (3) interfere with witnesses or otherwise obstruct the course of justice, whether in relation to himself or any other person (para 5), or

e) Having previously been released on bail the defendant has been arrested for failure to surrender to bail and the court is satisfied that if released on bail there are substantial grounds for believing the defendant would commit an offence whilst on bail that would be likely to cause physical or mental injury to an associated person' or cause that person to fear physical or mental injury (para 6). An 'associated person' has the same definition as under Schedule 1 Part 1 from s. 62(3) of the Family Law Act 1996.

When structuring a reply to each ground relied upon by the prosecution, the defence advocate should follow the schedule1, Part 1 para 9 factors from the Bail Act and address the following in their submissions:

1. Nature and seriousness of the offence (including the likely sentence).
2. Defendant's character, antecedents, associations and community ties.
3. The defendant's previous record of fulfilling any obligations on previously being granted bail.
4. The strength of the evidence against the defendant (except where a defendant's case has been adjourned for inquiries or a report).
5. If the court considers there is a bail risk, whether the risk would be by engaging in conduct that would, or is likely to, cause physical or mental injury to a person other than the defendant.
6. If the defendant is a child who has failed to surrender to bail at an appointed time whether the child defendant had reasonable cause for that failure and whether they surrendered for bail as soon as reasonably practicable after the appointed time,
7. Any other factors that appear relevant.

## Criminal Case Study – R v Vermont

### Memorandum A – Defendant

From: Assiah Proctor (Supervising Solicitor)

Date: 9 January (year)

I attended Anytown police station a few days ago to represent a client who we picked up through the police station representation scheme. The client is Mr Grant Vermont and you will see from the charge sheet that he has been charged with a number of offences. Mr Vermont is a company director who also has an OBE. We have acted for him in the past on company matters. I must say, I am surprised at the charges that he faces. All the offences are imprisonable offences and so fall under Schedule 1 Part 1 of the Bail Act 1976. Given the seriousness of the allegations, the offences will all be tried on indictment in the crown court.

I managed to speak to Mr Vermont at the police station after questioning and charge and we have been instructed to apply for bail on his behalf. Could you read the attached documents and make a bail application.

I have spoken to a representative from the Crown Prosecution Service ('CPS') and they have indicated that the right to bail does not exist because there is a charge of attempted murder and they will be relying on the Criminal Justice and Public Order Act 1994, s. 25(2)(b). Mr Vermont tells me however that he does not have any previous convictions for attempted murder or any other offences. I have repeatedly asked the CPS for a copy of Mr Vermont's criminal records from the Police National Computer, but the CPS have not responded.

The CPS have in any event arranged for the magistrates' court to commit the defendant to be sent to the crown court and for the bail application to be heard by a crown court judge under s. 115 of the Coroners and Justice Act 2009. This has caused a delay of five days in the bail hearing being fixed due to a backlog of cases in the crown court.

I anticipate that if the CPS does not succeed on the s. 25 ground under the Criminal Justice and Public Order Act 1994 that they will try the following grounds as alternatives:

Bail Act 1976, Schedule 1 Part 1, para 2 (all grounds)
Bail Act 1976, Schedule 1 Part 1, para 2ZA

Could you appear at Mr Vermont's bail application tomorrow to make an application for bail?

In case the court has reservations about granting bail, Mr Vermont has indicated that he would accept one or more of the conditions set out in CrimPR Part 14.11 and 14.14 including leaving the matrimonial home at 41 Tennyson Avenue and residing at his mother's address. Mr Vermont has indicated that he will consider the imposition of conditions relating to electronic monitoring tags (see CrimPR Part 14.12) but only as a last resort. He attends charity functions and other important events and doesn't want to be seen in public wearing a tag. Can you decide which conditions you think would be suitable based on the information in PC Parker's report?

If bail is refused don't forget to ask the judge for reasons under s. 5 of the 1976 Act and CrimPR Part 14.4(b).

You may find the following case helpful:

1.　*O (FC) v Crown Court at Harrow* [2006] UKHL 42

You should also consider the following legislation when preparing your submissions:

1.　Bail Act 1976, s. 4, s. 5 and Schedule 1 Part 1
2.　Coroners and Justice Act 2009, s. 115(1) & 115(3)
3.　Criminal Justice and Public Order Act 1994, s. 25
4.　Family Law Act 1996, s. 62(3)

You may also want to think about trying an application for costs under the Prosecution of Offences Act 1985, s. 19(2) and s. 19A(2)(a).

## Document 2

### Initial Details of the Prosecution Case ('IDPC')

Criminal Procedure Rules, Part 15
PTI URN: 53809

### R v Vermont

Anytown Magistrates Court
Case No. AM7321/2000

Date: 6 January (current year)

ANTICIPATED PLEA - NOT GUILTY ('NGAP')

(Tick if document attached)

| | |
|---|---|
| ✓ | MG04 Charge Sheet |
| ✓ | MG05 Police Report |
| ✓ | MG06 Case File Evidence and Information |
| ✓ | MG08 Breach of Bail Conditions Form (*not supplied*) |
| ✓ | MG09 List of Witnesses |
| ✓ | MG10 Witness Non-availability |

| ✓ | MG11 Key Witness Statements |
| ✓ | MG15 Interview Record (*not supplied*) |
| ✓ | MG16 Bad Character/Dangerous Offender |
| ✓ | MG18 Offences Taken Into Consideration ('TIC') |

## Document 3

**MG04**

**Charge Sheet**

**Anytown Police Station**

| **To:** | **Grant Vermont** |
| **Address:** | **41 Tennyson Avenue, Anytown** |
| **Date of Birth:** | **11 September 2000** |

You are charged with the offence(s) shown below. You do not have to say anything, but it may harm your defence if you do not mention now, something which you later rely on in court, anything you do say may be given in evidence.

1. Grant Vermont on the 4th day of January (current year), having entered a building as a trespasser, namely the Moonrise Guest House, Anytown you then caused grievous bodily harm to June Vermont contrary to section 9(1)(b) of the Theft Act 1968.
2. Grant Vermont on the 4th day of January (current year), you did, without lawful excuse, cause damage or destruction to property belonging to another, namely the door and furnishings in room 101 of the Moonrise Guest House contrary to section 1 of the Criminal Damage Act 1971.
3. Grant Vermont on the 4th day of January (current year), you did cause wounding with intent contrary to section 18 of the Offences Against the Person Act 1861 by stabbing June Vermont 5 times in different parts of her body causing injuries to the right side of her chest and to her right arm.
4. Grant Vermont on the 4th day of January (current year) you attempted to murder June Vermont at the Moonrise Guest House, Anytown.
5. Grant Vermont on the 4th day of January (current year) you stole property belonging to the Moonrise Guest House, namely the sum of £500 contrary to section 1 of the Theft Act 1968.

| Time & date charged: | 4.15 am | 5 January (current year) |

Anticipated Plea:       Not Guilty

Defendant's Comments on Grounds for Detention and Account of Arrest: None

Linked Defendant(s):       None

**PC 214 Parker**
Officer in the case

Officer charging
**DC 217 Hamilton**

**PC 551 Omari**
Officer accepting charge

I have received a copy of this document and written notice of my rights under paragraph 3.2 of Code C of the Police and Criminal Evidence Act 1984.................

*Grant Vermont*..........................................................

Bailed to appear at.........Anytown Magistrates Court
At...9a.m.... 6 January (current year)

## Document 4

**MG05**

### Police Report

Case Name:           R v Vermont
Reporting Officer:   PC 214 Parker
Date:                5 January (current year)
Prepared By:         PC 214 Parker

### Details of Incident

On the 4th day of January at approximately 10.30pm PC Omari and I responded to an emergency call made by the manager of the Moonrise Guest House Anytown. We arrived at the Guest House at approximately 10.45pm. At this time there was already an ambulance crew and paramedics at the Guest House attending to an injured women who we now know to be Mrs June Vermont. We met with the manager, a Mr Callum Proustin. Mr Proustin reported that a guest had been injured by a suspect who was believed to be the victim's husband. The suspect had fled before our arrival. Mr Proustin explained that he was on night duty when a gentleman came to the Guest House at approximately 10.15pm. The gentleman, whom he described as being approximately 6ft 5 inches tall with red hair and a beard and black- rimmed glasses, appeared agitated. The suspect was wearing a green hooded sweatshirt and blue jeans. He asked to see his wife. Mr Proustin asked for the gentleman's name and the name of his wife so that he could check the guest register. However, the gentleman simply ran upstairs and began knocking on rooms on the first floor of the guest house shouting, the following words, to the best of Mr Proustin's recollection: "June, I know you are here. I need to talk to you, I am begging you, please don't do this, you will ruin us". Mr Proustin followed the gentleman upstairs and says that he found the door of room 101 open and that it had clearly been forced open as there was damage to the doorframe. When he entered he found Mrs June

Vermont lying on the floor covered in blood. He could not see the man (believed to be Mr Vermont) in the room. He was able to recall that furniture had been thrown across the room and that the curtains had been ripped from the railings. Mrs Vermont appeared to be unconscious and Mr Proustin checked Mrs Vermont's pulse before running back down to the reception area to call for an ambulance. It was at this point that Mr Proustin discovered that a cash register at the reception front desk was open. Mr Proustin reported that £500 was missing from the cash register.

## Actions Taken

PC Omari took a full statement from Mr Proustin while I drove to the hospital that Mrs June Vermont had been taken to by the ambulance crew. I was able to interview Mrs Vermont at Anytown NHS Hospital. I was told by the nurse attending to Mrs Vermont that she had suffered knife wounds to her right chest and right arm and that she also had some facial bruising. Her injuries were not life threatening but would leave some permanent scarring. At 12.05am I was permitted to speak with Mrs Vermont who was now conscious. I took a witness statement from her. I was able to observe Mrs Vermont's injuries during this time. I returned to the Moonrise Guest House at approximately 1.00am where a forensic team and detectives were conducting a full search and crime scene analysis. I asked if any weapon had been found, possibly a knife, given Mrs Vermont's injuries. I was told no weapons had been found in the room or at the guesthouse. A warrant was eventually obtained for Mr Vermont's arrest and PC Omari and I went to arrest him and he was found by us at the matrimonial home, 41 Tennyson Avenue, Anytown, Landshire at 1.30am. He did not resist arrest but gave the following reply: "she did it to herself". The premises were searched under section 32 of PACE 1984 but no weapon was found but a green hooded sweatshirt with blood stains was found at the premises. Mr Vermont was taken to Anytown police station and interviewed at 2.30am after all forensic analysis and searches had been completed. He was charged at 4.15am and bailed to appear the following morning at Anytown Magistrates' Court. Fingerprint and other DNA evidence (blood) were taken from Mr Vermont during his detention.

## Evidence and Potentially Disclosable Material

Forensic evidence – Fingerprints and blood
Clothing – Green hooded sweatshirt with blood stains
Photographic Evidence – Suite 101 Moonrise Guest House
Photographic Evidence – Injuries sustained by Mrs June Vermont
Mobile Telephone – Belonging to Mr Grant Vermont

Witness Statement of Mr Simon Callum Proustin

*Investigating Officer Certification*: To the best of my knowledge and belief, no information has been withheld from disclosure, which would assist the accused in the preparation of the defence case, including the making of a bail application.

*Disclosure Officer's Certification*: I certify that any relevant unused material has been recorded and retained in accordance with the CPIA 1996 Code of Practice (as amended) and that such material as is non-sensitive is shown on the schedule above (where applicable) and that to the best of my knowledge and belief the item [mobile telephone records of Mr Grant Vernon and witness statement of Mr Simon Montiana] in the schedule might reasonably undermine the prosecution case, or assist the defence with the early preparation of their case or at a bail hearing because it corroborates part of the defendant's case.

Investigating Officer's Name: PC Lerovian Parker

Signature: Lerovian Parker

Disclosure Officer's Name: PC Margaret Delaware

Signature: Margaret Delaware

## 5.7.2 Exercise 2 (Specific Disclosure)
In this exercise you will continue in the role of defence advocate and be asked to make an application for specific disclosure. The application is made by following the procedure in CrimPR Part 15.5. This rule provides that once the defence has filed a defence statement in the Crown Court, it may apply for further disclosure from the prosecution, but any application must:

a)   Describe the material that the defendant wants the prosecutor to disclose;
b)   Explain why the defendant thinks there is reasonable cause to believe that
    i.   The prosecutor has that material, and
    ii.  It is material that the Criminal Procedure and Investigations Act 1996 requires the prosecutor to disclose; and
c)   Ask for a hearing, if the defendant wants one, and explain why it is needed.

The Criminal Procedure and Investigations Act 1996 is therefore important to this application as it is the main legislation governing disclosure and an advocate should ensure that he/she is familiar with its provisions.

## Document 5

### Memorandum B – Prosecution

From: Assiah Proctor (Supervising Solicitor)

Date: 12 March (year)

You will recall applying for a bail application for the client Mr Grant Vernon which was fortunately successful. I have received advance disclosure from the Crown Prosecution Service (CPS) that includes the witness statements of their key prosecution witnesses. However, their MG05 form (*see document 4*) shows that they also had a witness statement from a Mr Simon Montiana. I requested and have now received a copy of this witness statement. Reading the contents, I believe that the CPS may have further documents that are relevant to this case, namely any documents regarding the company owned by our client, June Vermont and Mr Montiana. In particular, I believe there may be documents that incriminate Mrs Vermont by showing that she has falsified documents relating to the company. This is important evidence as it may damage her credibility as a witness.

We served a Defence Statement on our client's behalf in accordance with the time limits set out in the CPIA, s. 12.

A Plea and Trial Preparation Hearing ('PTPH') has been fixed for tomorrow. I have already served an application for specific disclosure on the CPS and have followed the procedure in CrimPR Part 15.5. This application is due to be heard tomorrow too. Could you attend to make representations on our client's behalf to obtain an order for specific disclosure please?

You will need to read the case file and also consider CrimPR Part 15.5 and the Attorney-General's Guidelines on Disclosure (Attorney-General's Office, December 2013) para 6. You may also find the following legislation helpful:

1. Criminal Procedure and Investigations Act 1996, s. 3, s. 7A, s. 8 and s. 23.
2. Criminal Procedure and Investigations Act Code of Practice 2015, para 5.1–5.8.

You may also find the following case helpful:

1. *R v H and C* [2004] UKHL 3 [14].

## Document 6

**MG09**

**List of Prosecution Witnesses**

1. **PC Christopher Omari**
2. **PC Lerovian Parker**
3. **Mr Callum Proustin**
4. **Mrs June Vermont**

## Document 7

**MG11**

**Key Witness Statements**

1. **Mr Callum Proustin**
2. **Mrs June Vermont**

See s. 9 witness statements attached

### WITNESS STATEMENT

(CJ Act 1967, s. 9; MC Act 1980, s. 5A(3)(a) and s. 5B; MC Rules 1981, r. 70)

STATEMENT OF:          Callum Proustin

AGE OF WITNESS:       Over 18

ADDRESS:                     Supplied

OCCUPATION:             Hotel Manager

This statement (consisting of 2 pages signed by me) is true to the best of my knowledge and belief and I make it knowing that if it is introduced in evidence then it would be an offence if I have wilfully stated in it anything that I know to be false or do not believe to be true.

DATED: 4 January (current year)                    Signed: Callum Proustin

---

I am the Manager of the Moonrise Guest House, Anytown, Landshire. On 4 January (current year) I was working in the guesthouse and had started my shift at 8.00pm. The guesthouse had 50% occupancy that evening and a new guest, Mrs June Vernon, had checked into the guesthouse at approximately 8.30pm on that day.

At approximately 10pm that evening, a gentleman who I now know to be Mr Grant Vermont, entered the guesthouse and approached me. I greeted him and asked if he wanted to make a reservation. He appeared to be agitated and kept looking around the reception area as if he was expecting to see someone. He asked where the guestrooms were located and I told him that they were on the first floor. He asked if his wife was staying at the guesthouse. I said that I could not give details of the names of our guests but that if he gave me his name and details of who he was looking for and could confirm that they were expecting him, then I could telephone through to their room. He responded by saying "forget it!" and ran upstairs before I could stop him. I quickly went into our restaurant, which, is located next to the reception area and asked a member of staff, Sue Burnley, to take over on the reception desk. I then ran after the gentleman. At first, I could not see him as the corridor divides into two separate corridors where the guestrooms are located. I then heard a noise, which sounded like somebody kicking a door and this was followed by the sound of a woman screaming. I followed the sound and came to room 101.

Room 101 is occupied by Mrs June Vermont. The door was open but with signs of damage to the lock and the door frame. I found Mrs Vermont lying on the floor in a pool of blood in the middle of the room. I could also see that furniture had been disturbed, a table lamp overturned, and curtains pulled from the curtain rail. I called her name, but she did not appear to be conscious. I ran back downstairs to the reception area and asked Sue to call the police. I then ran outside to see if I could see where the man had gone but no one was outside. The police arrived at around 10.30pm.

I would describe the gentleman in question as a white male in his mid-thirties with dark short curly hair and a beard and glasses wearing a green hooded sweatshirt. He was approximately 6ft tall and he was wearing blue jeans and trainers.

I am willing to come to court to give evidence.

**WITNESS STATEMENT**

(CJ Act 1967, s. 9; MC Act 1980, s. 5A(3)(a) and s. 5B; MC Rules 1981, r. 70)

STATEMENT OF:          June Vermont

AGE OF WITNESS:       Over 18

ADDRESS:                    Supplied

OCCUPATION:             Company Director

This statement (consisting of 2 pages signed by me) is true to the best of my knowledge and belief and I make it knowing that if it is introduced in evidence then it would be an offence if I have wilfully stated in it anything that I know to be false or do not believe to be true.

DATED: 4 January (current year)                    Signed: June Vermont

I left the matrimonial home at 41 Tennyson Avenue, Anytown on the afternoon of 4 January after we had a heated argument during which I accused my husband, Grant Vermont of defrauding large sums of money from our company. I had just returned from a meeting with our accountants who had discovered irregular accounting entries in relation to an investment fund that that I owned with my husband and a third partner, Mr Simon Montiana called 'Global Ethical Trading'. My husband denied that he had been involved in any wrongdoing but said that he suspected Simon. I said that I did not believe him because Simon was unlikely to do anything of that nature as he is the most honest person that I know.

My husband accused me of always sticking up for Simon and demanded to know if we were having an affair. This is something that my husband has accused me of in the past. The allegation is untrue, my husband is a very jealous man with a temper and I was worried that the argument could turn violent now that he was accusing me of infidelity. I went upstairs to the bedroom and started to pack an overnight bag. I told my husband that I was going to stay at a hotel for the night as we were both upset and it would help to calm things between us and we could talk the next day. I then ran out of the house and drove to the Moonrise Guest House.

I arrived at about 8.00pm and checked into my room. My husband and I have used this local guesthouse in the past when we have had guests and needed somewhere for them to stay. At about 9.00pm my husband rang me on my mobile phone to ask me where I was. I said that I was safe and at a local hotel. He must have guessed from this conversation that I was at the Moonrise. He said he wanted to come to talk to me but I told him to leave me alone as I needed time and space to think. I told him that I would call him in the morning. I then got ready to go to bed. I remember being woken by a noise in the corridor of someone shouting my name. I got out of bed and at this point I realised it was my husband in the corridor. I shouted at him to go away. I was angry that he had ignored my request to be left alone. I realise now that this was a mistake because it alerted him to what room I was in. He started kicking at the door a number of times and I was worried he might wake the other guests and so I let him in. However, I immediately backed away from him as he was carrying a knife. He said, "I have spoken to Simon and he has admitted the affair you liar" and he then started stabbing me. That is all that I remember before I passed out. I am convinced that if my husband had not been disturbed by other people coming to see what all the commotion was about, he would have killed me – there was so much rage in his eyes.

I am willing to come to court to give evidence.

## Document 8

**MG06**

**Unused Material**

1.  **Mr Simon Montiana**

See s. 9 witness statement attached

**WITNESS STATEMENT**

(CJ Act 1967, s. 9; MC Act 1980, s. 5A(3)(a) and s. 5B; MC Rules 1981, r. 70)

| | |
|---|---|
| STATEMENT OF: | Simon Montiana |
| AGE OF WITNESS: | Over 18 |
| ADDRESS: | Supplied |
| OCCUPATION: | Company Director |

This statement (consisting of 2 pages signed by me) is true to the best of my knowledge and belief and I make it knowing that if it is introduced in evidence then it would be an offence if I have wilfully stated in it anything that I know to be false or do not believe to be true.

DATED: 5 January (current year)                    Signed: Simon Montiana

---

I have known June and Grant Vermont for over 20 years, we were all at university together. About 10 years ago, I started an investment company with them called 'Global Ethical Trading'. The company traded in ethical stocks and shares. Previously I had been working as a stockbroker and June and Grant had both worked in the City for insurance companies. We felt we had spotted a gap in the market, and we wanted an investment fund that was easily accessible and attractive to young professionals starting their career who wanted better returns on their investments than the average pension fund. In truth, the fund had been underperforming for the last 5 years.

June and Grant had also been having problems in their relationship for the past two years and June and I had started an affair approximately six months ago and she was planning to leave her husband. We had talked about how we would tell Grant. June decided that we should first try to sort out the company, possibly attempt to sell it as a going concern to another investment company owned by a friend she knew. She seemed confident that she could persuade the accountant to hide some of the losses and value the company for more than it was worth. I was not happy about being part of this kind of fraudulent deception and told her as much. I felt that I was seeing another side to June that I had not seen before and that I did not like. I told her that I thought that we should end our relationship. I told her this during a dinner date with her on the evening of 3rd January.

I did not hear from either Grant or June until I received a telephone call on 5 January from PC Parker asking to interview me and explaining that June was in hospital and that Grant had been charged with her attempted murder.

I don't know whether any of the allegations are true. All I can say about Grant and June is that they have a destructive relationship and it is very hard sometimes to tell who is lying and who is telling the truth. I do know that June had prepared some false accounts for the company that she wanted me to look at as she mentioned this over dinner. I am surprised the police did not find this when they searched her apartment.

I am willing to come to court to give evidence.

## 5.7.3 Exercise 3 (Hearsay and Character Evidence)

The final exercise in this chapter relates to an application to admit hearsay and character evidence. This time you will take on the role of prosecution advocate. You should read the relevant sections of this chapter on character and hearsay to refresh your memory before attempting the exercise. Remember that there are limitations placed on the admission of both types of evidence. Even if the evidence would be admissible under the relevant provisions of the Criminal Justice Act 2003, the judge has an discretion to exclude the evidence. In the case of hearsay evidence, the judge also has an inclusionary discretion to be found under s. 114(1)(d).

---

### Document 9

**MEMORANDUM C – PROSECUTION**

From Crown Prosecution Service

To:                       Prosecution Advocate

Date:                    12 March (current year)

Many thanks for taking this case on once again.

A Plea and Trial Preparation Hearing ('PTPH') has been fixed for tomorrow. The defence has already served an application for specific disclosure on us and plan to seek specific disclosure under CrimPR Part 15.5.

We intend to make a counter application to admit hearsay and character evidence. One of the prosecution witnesses (Mr Callum Proustin) is unable to attend the trial as he is leaving the country to take up new employment and we would like to admit his witness statement as hearsay evidence under the Criminal Justice Act 2003 s. 116 (2) (c) and CrimPR Part 20. We have served a witness summons on him to compel him to attend court, but we suspect he will not attend. We could, I guess also look into the possibility of him giving his evidence by video link. I think this is permissible under the Criminal Justice Act 2003, s. 51.

We also plan to adduce the criminal convictions of a witness that the defence may call, Mr Simon Montiana. We intend to produce this under the provisions of the Criminal Justice Act 2003, s. 100 (1) (b) and CrimPR Part 21. We would like to use the evidence of Mr Montiana's previous convictions to discredit him during cross-examination.

Could you attend to make representations to admit these two pieces of evidence please?

You may find the following cases helpful:

*R v Castillo* [1996] 1 Cr App R 438
*R v Gyima (Edward)* [2007] EWCA Crim 429
*Riat and Others v R* [2012] EWCA Crim 1509
*Brewster and Cromwell v R* [2010] EWCA Crim 1194

You may find the following legislation helpful:

Criminal Justice Act 2003, ss. 51, 98, s. 100(1)(b), s. 100(3), s. 112, s. 116(2)(c)

## Document 10

**MG10**

### Details of Witnesses' Non-Availability

1.  Mr Callum Proustin

### Details

Mr Proustin will be moving to New Zealand on 1st April this year to take up employment as a manager at Dreamland Hotels in Dunedin.

## Document 11

**MG16**

### Previous Convictions

**Division**                    **Station**

ACRO Criminal Records Office

**Previous Convictions in respect of** Simon Montiana

Date of Birth: 2/08/1988

**PNC No** **MS 4652**

| 2 Date | 3 Court | 4 Offences | 5 Result |
|--------|---------|------------|----------|
| 1/6/2010 | Anytown Crown Court | Fraud (Insurance) | One year Sentence (suspended) |
| 4/10/2020 | Anytown Magistrates' Court | Speeding | Disqualified six months |

When you have completed all three exercises, go to Part C to find suggested approaches and solutions to all three exercises.

# Self-Reflection Checklist

| | | | |
|---|---|---|---|
| What **three** important things have you learnt from this chapter? | 1 | 2 | 3 |
| Set out **three** additional steps that you need to take to learn the skills in this chapter in more detail | 1 | 2 | 3 |

# References

## Cases

*Alec John Smith v R* [2020] EWCA 777.
*Al Khawaja and Tahery v United Kingdom* (2011) 54 EHRR 23.
*Brewster and Cromwell v R* [2010] EWCA Crim 1194.
*Condron and Condron v UK* [2000] ECHR 191.
*Khan v UK* (2000) 31 EHRR 45.
*O (FC) v Crown Court at Harrow* [2006] UKHL 42.
*R v Andrews* [1987] AC 281.
*R v Argent* [1996] EWCA Crim 1728.
*R v Aziz* [1996] AC 41.
*R v Beckles (no 2)* [2004] EWCA Crim 2766.
*R v Castillo* [1996] 1 Cr App R 438.
*R v Chopra* [2007] EWCA Crim 2133.

## Legislation

s. 117(1), s. 117(4), s. 117(6), s.117(7), s. 118, s. 118(1)–(8), s. 118, s. 119, s. 120, s. 120(1)–(7), s. 121, s. 123, s. 124, s. 125, s. 126, s. 126(2), s. 139.
The Criminal Justice Act 2003 (Categories of Offences) Order 2004.
Criminal Justice and Public Order Act 1994, s. 25, s. 25(2)(b), s. 34, s. 34(1)(c), s. 35, s. 35(1)(a), s. 35(1)(b), s. 36, s. 37, s. 38(3).
Criminal Procedure Act 1865, s. 4, s. 5.
Criminal Procedure and Investigation Act 1996, s. 11(5), s. 39(1), s. 40, s. 40(3).
Family Law Reform Act 1996, s. 62(3).
Police and Criminal Evidence Act 1984, s. 56, s. 58, s. 62(10), s. 74, s. 76(2), s. 76(2)(a), s. 76(2)(b), s. 76(4), s. 76(4)(a), s. 76(4)(b), s. 76A, s. 77, s. 78, s. 82(1), s. 82(3).
Code B of the Police and Criminal Evidence Act 1984.
Code C of the Police and Criminal Evidence Act 1984, para 10.5, 10.11.
Code D of the Police and Criminal Evidence Act 1984.
European Convention on Human Rights 1950, Article 6(3)(d).
Legal Aid, Sentencing and Punishment of Offenders Act 2012.
Magistrates' Court Act 1980, s. 8A and s. 8B.
Youth Justice and Criminal Evidence Act 1999, s. 34(2A), s. 58, s. 59.

## Procedure Rules and Directions
Criminal Practice Directions 2015 21A.3.
Criminal Procedure Rules Part 3, 3.16.
Criminal Procedure Rules, Part 14, 14.4 (b), 14.11–14.
Criminal Procedure Rules Part 20.
Criminal Procedure Rules Parts 21.2, 21.3, 21.4, 21.5.
Criminal Procedure Rules Parts 24.4(3), 24.5(3).
Criminal Procedure Rules Parts 25.9(2)(f), 25.11(3), 25.12(3).

## Codes of Conduct and Guidance
Crown Court Compendium.

## Reports
Law Commission 'Evidence in Criminal Proceedings: Hearsay' (Cmnd No.245, Law Com 1997).

## Websites
www.ballll.org
www.gov.uk
www.legislation.gov.uk
www.nationalarchives.gov.uk

# 6 An Introduction to Civil Litigation

## 6.1 Introduction

In this chapter we will focus on (1) the civil rules of evidence and (2) how to make interim applications. At the end of this chapter, we will work through a case study that will provide an example of three types of interim applications, namely setting aside a default judgment, applying for summary judgment and applying for an interim payment.

## Rules on the Admissibility of Evidence

## 6.2 Excluding Evidence

In Chapter 2 we considered the various forms that evidence could take (real, oral, documentary and circumstantial). In this section we will discuss when and how such evidence is 'admissible' or can be 'excluded'. It is often the oral testimony and documentary evidence that present the most admissibility difficulties in terms of ensuring the correct balance between relevance and fair admission of the evidence at the trial.

DOI: 10.4324/9781003134770-9

The basic principle of most court hearings is that all relevant evidence is admissible unless it breaches (1) a specific rule of law contained in legislation or (2) a common law exclusionary rule of evidence or (3) the judge exercises his/her discretion to exclude the evidence under the principles of fairness. In civil proceedings the discretion is found under CPR Part 32.1 (2) and this rule can be used to exclude different types of evidence.

## 6.2.1  Illegally or Improperly Obtained Evidence

There is not a general rule of exclusion in civil proceedings for improperly or illegally obtained evidence or evidence that has been tainted in some way. However, the civil procedure rules do contain mechanisms to make it more difficult for such evidence to be admitted. For example, under CPR Part 31.20 a privileged document which has been 'inadvertently' produced for inspection may not be relied upon by the opposing party unless the judge permits it. The court can of course use its discretion under CPR Part 32.1(2) to exclude any evidence including improperly obtained evidence.

The civil procedure rules promote transparency and obligations of disclosure of evidence by a party. This includes evidence that may be adverse to their own case or that of the other party. In *Jones v University of Warwick* [2003] EWCA Civ 151 the court had to consider whether to admit covertly recorded video evidence of a claimant in personal injury proceedings. This evidence had been obtained without her knowledge. It was argued by the defendants that the evidence was relevant to show that the claimant did not have a continuing significant disability to her right hand as a result of being injured during an accident, despite claims made in her evidence. The claimant asked the court to exercise its discretion to exclude the evidence. Whilst accepting that privacy issues under Article 8 of the European Convention on Human Rights 1950 might be engaged, the court also had to balance this with the court's overriding duty under CPR Part 1 to deal with cases justly. The court accepted that whilst the conduct of the insurers in commissioning the secret video footage was improper and unjustified, the conduct was not so outrageous that it would impede the progress of the trial and the proper administration of justice. The court remarked in its judgment that "[e]xcluding the evidence is not, moreover, the only weapon in the court's armoury. The court has other steps it can take to discourage conduct of the type of which complaint is made. In particular it can reflect its disapproval in the order for costs which it makes" [30]. As such, civil proceedings arguably take a more inclusive approach to unfairly obtained evidence than criminal proceedings.

## 6.2.2  Character and Similar Fact Evidence

A party may wish to use evidence of the bad character of an opponent such as the fact that they have previous convictions or there is evidence of other misconduct. A party may also want to use as evidence the fact that a defendant has behaved in a similar way before as this might suggest a tendency towards repeated misconduct or negligence (known as 'similar fact evidence'). However, because of its prejudicial nature the opposing party would want the judge to exclude such evidence.

Unlike the criminal procedure, there is not a formalised structure for the exclusion of such evidence in the civil courts and the court will instead use its wide discretion under CPR Part 32.1 to consider whether such evidence is relevant to the proceedings. The case of *O'Brien v Chief Constable of South Wales Police* [2005] UKHL 26 was the first case to consider the use of character evidence within civil proceedings and examined the existing criminal framework for some guidance. The House of Lords decided that whilst the use of similar fact evidence had been a contentious issue in criminal proceedings, it could be important and decisive to issues and therefore the principle of relevance would determine its admissibility. Ultimately it will be a matter of discretion for the trial judge to decide on admissibility.

The case law that has evolved in the area of bad character in civil proceedings has therefore largely been in relation to similar fact evidence. For example, in *Mitchell v News Group Newspapers* [2014] EWHC 3590 (QB) the court allowed 'similar fact evidence' that tended to show that the MP Andrew Mitchell had previously acted in a rude and confrontational manner towards police officers in earlier incidents. It was argued that this gave some weight to the question of whether he had behaved in a similar way towards police officers as alleged in a news story by the News Group Newspapers Ltd that was the subject of the civil proceedings. In *Alleyne v Commissioner of Police for the Metropolis* [2012] EWHC 4406 (QB) similar fact evidence of previous allegations of police misconduct by two police officers was admitted on the basis that these were probative to the question of whether the same police officers had injured the claimant during a search of his premises. In *Laughton v Shalaby* [2014] EWCA Civ 1450, the court was asked to consider whether evidence of complaints of incompetence made against a defendant surgeon could be admissible under the same *O'Brien* principle. The court held that complaints are not probative because they have not been proven and cannot therefore be said to amount to similar fact evidence.

The Civil Evidence Act 1968 also provides a route for the defendant's criminal conviction to be used as evidence in civil proceedings. Under s. 11 such convictions can be used to prove that the defendant committed the offence. This may be important evidence, for example, in a civil trial for personal injuries arising from a road traffic accident. The defendant might have already been convicted in the criminal court for a road traffic offence relating to the accident, e.g. speeding. The claimant can then use this conviction as proof that the defendant was indeed speeding when producing evidence in the civil trial. A similar provision exists to use previous criminal convictions in defamation cases (see s. 13). Findings of adultery or paternity in the family courts can also be used in civil proceedings (see s. 12 of the 1968 Act).

## 6.3  Admitting Evidence into the Proceedings

In civil proceedings the courts take a more inclusive approach to evidence as long as it is relevant to the matters involved in the case. Evidence will still have to follow procedural rules in terms of format and providing notice to the opposing party before the evidence can be admitted. The court's power to admit and control evidence is found in CPR Part 32. CPR Part 32.1 provides that:

1) The court may control evidence by giving directions as to –
   a) the issues on which it requires evidence;
   b) the nature of the evidence which it requires to decide those issues; and
   c) the way in which the evidence is to be placed before the court.

## 6.3.1 Hearsay

The Civil Evidence Act 1995, s. 1(2) and the CPR Part 33.1 define hearsay in a similar way to the criminal definition as, "a statement made, otherwise than by a person while giving oral evidence in proceedings, which is tendered as evidence of the matters stated". Like criminal hearsay, it applies to statements (both oral, written and in pictorial form) that are made out of court, but the intention is to produce the evidence in court as proof that the information contained within the statement is true. It is the purpose for which the out of court evidence is to be used that categorises it as hearsay.

In civil proceedings all hearsay evidence is admissible as long as it is relevant to the proceedings. As we have seen in Chapter 5, the opposite is true in criminal proceedings. The Civil Evidence Act 1995, s. 1(1) states that evidence shall not be excluded on the grounds that it is hearsay.

Whilst as a general rule, hearsay evidence is admissible in the civil courts, there is still a procedure for admissibility that must be observed. Under s. 2 of the 1995 Act advance notice must be given to the other side of an intention to produce hearsay evidence. There is not a prescribed format for the notice. However, where a party fails to give notice, this may be taken into account as a matter adversely affecting the weight (value) to be given to the evidence. The court can also make other sanctions such as cost orders.

Section 3 of the Civil Evidence Act 1995 states that where a party has admitted hearsay evidence and refuses to call the witness, then the other party can, with the permission of the court, call and cross-examine the witness.

Section 4 of the 1995 Act deals with the question of what happens to the hearsay evidence once admitted. It is essentially for the court to decide how much weight to attach to the evidence. In deciding on the weight to attach to the hearsay evidence the court can look at matters such as:

- Whether it would have been reasonable and practicable for the party adducing the evidence to have called the witness.

- Whether the original statement was made contemporaneously with the matters stated.
- Whether it is multiple hearsay.
- Whether any person had a motive to conceal or misrepresent matters.
- Whether the original statement was an edited account or made in collaboration with another for a particular purpose.
- Whether the circumstances in which the hearsay evidence was introduced suggest there was an attempt to prevent its weight being properly assessed.

There are additional safeguards to be found under s. 5 of the 1995 Act, which stipulates that the maker of the statement must be competent as a witness and any evidence which could have been called to attack the credibility of the witness (if he had been called) is still admissible.

Under s. 6 of the Act the previous statements of a person called as a witness require the permission of the court unless they are used for the purpose of rebutting a suggestion that the witness's evidence is fabricated. Such statements are subject to the notice and weight provisions. Section 6(3) also preserves the admissibility of previous inconsistent statements and these can be used to cross-examine a witness.

There is of course the option for the court to exclude the hearsay evidence under CPR Part 32.1(2); however these powers are subject to the overriding objective of ensuring cases are dealt with justly and at proportionate cost.

## 6.3.2 Admissions

In civil proceedings admissions are generally admissible (unless obtained by torture). The procedure is set out in CPR Part 14 and PD 14. An admission should be made in writing (see CPR Part 14.1(2)). A written admission will need to be contained in the hearing/trial bundle and may take the form of letter, email or statement of case.

Under CPR Part 32.18 a party can serve a notice on another party requiring them to admit facts or to admit part of the case. However, this cannot be served later than 21 days before the trial. If the other party makes the admission, then it can be used against the party in the proceedings although the court has the power to allow a party to amend or withdraw their admission.

If an admission is made before proceedings have begun, then it can be withdrawn before any proceedings are issued as long as the other party agrees (see CPR Part 14.1A). However, if an admission has been made after proceedings are issued then it can only be withdrawn with either the consent of the other party or, failing that, the permission of the court.

In deciding whether to give permission, the court will consider the factors set out in CPR PD 14 para 7.2. These factors include whether new evidence has come to light, the conduct of the parties, any prejudice that would be caused, how promptly the application to withdraw was made and the prospects of success of the claim.

In *Woodland v Stopford* [2012] EWCA Civ 266 the Court of Appeal held that a judge has to carefully balance these relevant factors and that they need not be considered in a hierarchical order. As such one factor does not have greater weight than another. The para 7.2 factors are matters for a judge's discretion and the case of *Woodland* confirmed that an appeal court would not interfere with that discretion unless the judge had made an error in taking into account a factor that he/she was not entitled to consider.

Where an admission remains and has not been withdrawn by a party, the other party can then seek to enter judgment based on that admission. However, the authenticity of an admission might be challenged. For example, an admission may have been obtained improperly, for example, by torture. The court has a wide discretion to exclude such evidence under CPR Part 32.1 (2). In *Shagang Shipping Company Ltd v HNA Group Company Ltd* [2020] UKSC 34 the Supreme Court held that before deciding the question of admissibility, the court should first decide the question of weight of the evidence. This is an important first step because it may be that the evidence is not of great importance in the final decision the court must reach and so can be admitted for the time being. By side stepping the question of admissibility, the judge can decide what weight to attach to the evidence at a later date if it continues to remain a contentious issue between the parties and this decision can take into account any arguments about the fairness of its admission.

## Refusing to Answer Questions or Disclose Material

## 6.4 Privilege Against Self-Incrimination

There may be circumstances in which a witness (including a defendant) can refuse to answer questions or provide disclosure of relevant material in civil proceedings. This is where a witness relies on the privilege against self-incrimination. This privilege is set out in the Civil Evidence Act 1968, s. 14 and entitles a person "to refuse to answer any question or produce any document or thing if to do so would tend to expose that person to criminal proceedings for an offence or for the recovery of a penalty". The privilege does not apply to protection from civil suits. The criminal proceedings or penalty must be one under UK law. However, the court does have a discretion to extend this privilege to cover offences and penalties abroad. The right also extends to the witness's spouse or civil partner also refusing to answer questions/produce material if it would incriminate that witness. In *Blunt v Park Lane Hotel Ltd* [1942] 2 KB 253 it was held that the risk of exposure to proceedings for an offence or a penalty must be reasonably likely.

In *Versailles Trade Finance Ltd (in administrative receivership) v Clough* [2001] EWCA Civ 1509 the Court of Appeal held that the privilege against self-incrimination could not be used as a defence to prevent an application for summary judgment going ahead. We will discuss summary judgment applications later in this chapter.

In addition, some statutes such as the Fraud Act 2006, s. 13 and the Theft Act 1968, s. 31 provide exceptions to the privilege against self-incrimination in civil proceedings relating to the recovery or administration of property or the execution of a trust or for an account of any property or dealings.

## 6.5  Interim Applications

An interim application is one that is made before trial. The application is made using an application notice (form N244) and will seek a particular order or direction to resolve a preliminary issue(s) in the case. This might include disposing of the case without trial because of its weakness or applying for an interim payment to help the claimant manage financially before the trial date. Generally, witnesses will not be called during an interim hearing and the hearing itself will usually take place 'in chambers' (a private room with the parties' representatives and the judge present). The parties will be seated when speaking. The judge will also usually reach a decision at the end of the hearing rather than reserving judgment for a later date.

Some interim applications can be made without notifying the other party and these are known as 'without notice' applications. Examples include urgent injunctions.

Interim applications are made using an application notice form with a supporting statement (witness statement or in some cases an affidavit). The procedure for making such applications is set out in CPR Part 23. You can find a template form for an application notice and all other court forms by visiting www.gov.uk.

The procedure under CPR Part 23 PD 23A should be read and followed in conjunction with the specific rule that applies to the type of application being made. For example, setting aside a default judgment requires an additional process set out in CPR 13. For summary judgments the relevant CPR is Part 24 and for interim payments it is CPR Part 25. These must all be read in conjunction with CPR Part 23 PD 23A.

In addition to following CPR Part 23 and the relevant rule and practice direction for the specific type of application, it is important to note that some types of actions have their own specific rules and practice directions that may also be relevant. For example, CPR Part 53 and PD 53B cover media and communication claims, CPR Part 54 and PD 54A cover judicial reviews, CPR Part 55 and PD 55 A & B cover possession claims in landlord and tenant disputes claims, and CPR Part 63 and PD 63 cover intellectual property claims.

The nature of the advocacy involved in an interim application is different from a trial because the arguments focus on the criteria and requirements to be met for making the application rather than attempting to prove the factual matters in dispute within the case itself.

An interim application can be made by either the claimant or the defendant. Whoever makes the application will be termed 'applicant' on the documentation and the opposing party will be known as the 'respondent'.

## 6.5.1 Applicants

The applicant will always speak first and introduce themselves and their opponent. Applicants should also ideally:

- Ask the judge if he/she has had a chance to read the papers.
- If the opponent has made a cross-application, then the applicant will need to explain to the court that there are two applications and explain in which order they will deal with the applications – this will usually be the applicant's own application first.
- Explain the nature of the application by reference to the relevant CPR and the precise section(s) of the rules and practice directions.
- Refer the judge to the relevant application documents; these will usually be in a pre-prepared court bundle and, for example, include witness statements but may also include medical reports or a schedule of losses (for personal injury/clinical negligence cases).
- Set out the nature of the order sought and the reasons why – this will involve referring to relevant facts, the relevant law and the procedural rules.
- If any procedural irregularities have been identified in the applicant's application, find the relevant rule that will allow the court to cure the defect or allow the application to proceed regardless of procedural breaches. This can usually be found within CPR Part 3 which relates to the courts' case management powers.
- Refer to the overriding objective under CPR Part 1 to help the court arrive at a decision that supports the client's case, for example, "by putting the parties on an equal footing" or by "ensuring the case is dealt with expeditiously and fairly".
- Explain what orders/directions the court should make.
- In the case of successful applications, make an order for summary assessment of costs. These are costs related to the work for the interim application that is assessed on the day of the hearing rather than waiting until after the trial for a final assessment of the costs of the whole case.

## 6.5.2 Respondents

The respondent will speak after the applicant has made their submissions. However, if there is a counter application it may be appropriate for the respondent to speak first, and this will be decided and agreed with the judge. The respondent should:

- Make clear that the application is opposed and why.
- Use both the facts, relevant authorities (law) and procedural rules to support the contention that the applicant's application should be dismissed.
- Use the court bundles (the respondent will prepare their own) and refer to any factual weaknesses in the applicant's application.
- Make the judge aware of any procedural irregularities (if any) with the applicant's application and explain if and where there has been a failure to follow a particular procedural rule.
- Refer to the overriding objective under CPR Part 1 to help the court arrive at a decision that supports the client's case, for example, by "dealing with the case in a way that is proportionate to costs" or "saving expense".
- Ask the court to dismiss the applicant's application and make an order for summary assessment of costs.
- If successful and the applicant's application is dismissed, make an order for summary assessment of costs. If unsuccessful, challenge the amount that the applicant seeks on a summary assessment of costs.

As we have discussed in Chapter 4, some types of action have their own pre-action protocol. This is a process that must be followed before court proceedings can be issued. Go to the www.gov.uk website and see if you can find out how many pre-action protocols currently exist.

Each pre-action protocol must be read in conjunction with the Practice Direction on Pre-action Conduct and Protocols. If no pre-action protocol exists for a particular type of action, then this practice direction alone is followed. If a pre-action protocol does exist, then the practice direction must still be followed but only part of it will apply (see para 6 of the Practice Direction). Failure to follow the practice direction can lead to the court making sanctions such as costs orders with or without a penalty applied and deprivation of entitlement to interest on the claim (see paras 15 and 16).

A judge can decide to grant or refuse an application and make a directions order setting out what further steps are to be taken in the case. The directions might include disclosure of documents by mutually or sequentially exchanging a list of documents or serving further witness statements or expert evidence.

## 6.6 The Civil Case Studies

In this section you will find documentation relating to three interim applications in the fictional case of *Landice and Landice v Wheeler*. Each application is preceded by a memorandum explaining the task (see Memorandums A, B and C). You should assume that all dates given are current dates. Where it is indicated in italics that a document is 'not supplied', assume that it has been correctly served and does not include any procedural irregularities and can be ignored for the purposes of the fact pattern. Each memorandum will give an indication of the civil procedure rule that is relevant as well as some relevant case law (you can find the civil procedure rules at www.gov.uk). You should also read the accompanying documents as they may lead you to consider further procedural rules and cases. You should also make use of the helpful tables on procedural rules and evidential rules found in Appendix A and B. You may also find it helpful to re-read Chapters 2 and 3 for a reminder of legal research, case strategy and argument construction techniques.

You will find suggested guidance on possible arguments that can be advanced in support of each application in Part C. You should however try to work through the exercises first and prepare your own arguments drawing on some of the skills learnt in Part A.

You might approach the exercises in the following way:

- Read all documents through once.
- Read through all documents a second time but this time highlight any key words or sentences that you think are important.
- Read any civil procedure rules mentioned in the documentation.
- Consider any additional rules that might be relevant (refer to Appendix A).
- Read any cases mentioned in the documentation.
- Consider whether any other cases might be relevant – for example, ask yourself, do the cases that are referred to in the documentation lead you to a research trail of other cases/legislation?
- Start to construct possible arguments – you might want to use a 'strengths and weaknesses' table similar to the Table discussed in Chapter 2.
- Practice making your submissions aloud without heavy reliance on a script (cue or prompt cards are acceptable).

## 6.6.1  Exercise 1 (Setting Aside Default Judgment)
The following exercise relates to an application to set aside a default judgment. A default judgment can be entered by a claimant when a defendant has failed to file either an acknowledgement of service ('AOS') or a defence within the prescribed period of time under the civil procedure rules. The AOS is a standard court form that is completed to confirm that the defendant has received the claimant's claim form and particulars of claim. The defence sets out the defendant's reasons for opposing the claim.

Once a default judgment has been entered against a defendant, it is still possible for the defendant to apply to set aside the default judgment if one of the grounds set out in CPR Part 13 applies.

You will notice throughout the exercises that the main case documents will show the parties' status as either 'claimant' or 'defendant' but that the documents relevant to the interim application itself will include additional status titles of 'applicant' and 'respondent'. This is standard practice for interim applications.

The second claimant, Rose Landice, is under 18 years of age and is therefore a minor and so special procedural rules apply. Rose is suing through her 'litigation friend' who is her father, and CPR Part 21 covers children and protected parties and is worth reading in advance of the exercise. You can assume that the litigation friend requirements under CPR Part 21.5 have been followed but it is worth familiarising yourself with these requirements.

Read CPR Part 13 (setting aside a default judgment) and construct arguments to make the following interim application after reading documents 1–5. The applicant in this exercise is the defendant.

### Civil Case Study – Landice and Landice v Wheeler

## Document 1

### Memorandum A – Applicant/Defendant

From: Margrit Munsted (Supervising Solicitor)
Date: 16 December (year)

We have been instructed by Mr Lupin Wheeler to set aside the judgment in default order dated 17 November.

Mr Wheeler instructs me that he was very surprised to receive a copy of the order as he had not previously received a copy of the Particulars of Claim. Mr Wheeler says that he did receive an initial letter of claim, but it was sent to his neighbour's home address. He also received the judgment in default order which was sent to the same address. He thinks that the Particulars of Claim may also have been posted to the neighbour's address by mistake but unlike the other documents, the neighbour did not pass that document on to him.

Mr Wheeler explained that he lives in a house which bears the address 11 Roam Way, but he sublets the house, and he lives in the basement which is separately addressed as 11A Roam Way. His tenants are therefore his neighbours. He believes the Particulars of Claim may have been wrongly posted to the 11 Roam Way address (the house). Usually, the occupants of 11 Roam Way pass on any mail posted to that address that bears his name. Unfortunately, the tenants left on 10 November. They left owing rent and so Mr Wheeler says it is unlikely they would have volunteered that they were holding mail addressed to him after the beginning of October as they were not on speaking terms by then. He did however find a copy of the default judgment whilst clearing out the house to let it to new tenants.

I have telephoned the court office which says that they are not able to substantiate when the Particulars of Claim was posted by the claimants because the claimants have not yet filed a Certificate of Service.

I have made an application to set aside the default judgment under Part 13 of the Civil Procedure Rules. I served the application notice (*not supplied*) together with the supporting witness statement on the claimants' solicitors LegalWays LLP and so have complied with CPR Part 23.

The hearing is tomorrow but unfortunately, I am involved in a trial at the local county court that has over run. Could you attend the hearing on behalf of Mr Wheeler please?

I would be grateful if you would consider the relevant civil procedure rules to identify the grounds for the application as well as considering any cases that may assist us. I am particularly concerned that the claimants' solicitors commenced proceedings too quickly without following the relevant pre-action protocol for personal injury claims. Could you investigate this as well together with any other possible rule breaches? I think CPR Part 1 and 6 may also be relevant as well as possibly CPR Part 35. Also look at the Pre-Action Protocol for Personal Injury and the Practice Direction on Pre-Action Conduct and Protocols.

I have opened a new case file for Mr Wheeler and have entered the relevant details on our case management system.

I asked our trainee to do some preliminary research and she tells me that the following cases may be relevant so please read these as it may help you to put forward arguments in support of the application or pre-empt arguments that may be put in opposition by the other side:

1. *Core-Export Spa v Yang Ming Marine Transportation Corporation* [2020] EWHC 425 (comm)
2. *Cranfield and Another v Bridgegrove Ltd* [2003] EWCA Civ 656
3. *Denton and Others v TH White Ltd and Others* [2014] EWCA Civ 906
4. *Henriksen v Pires* [2011] EWCA Civ 1720

## Document 2

IN THE HIGH COURT OF JUSTICE            No. HC/CD/0921
QUEENS BENCH DIVISION
BETWEEN:

|  |  |
|---|---|
| Clarissa Landice | First Claimant |
| -and- | |
| Rose Landice | Second Claimant |
| **(a child by Mario Landice, her litigation friend)** | |
| Lupin Wheeler | Defendant |

### PARTICULARS OF CLAIM

1. On the 18 September (year) the first claimant was driving her Nissan Leaf motor vehicle registration number GB20YEA along Slodan Road, AnyTown when an Audi A3 Volvo V40 registration number GB70NAY driven by the defendant emerged from a side road known as Pocket Place and collided with the claimant's motor vehicle.
2. At all material times the second claimant was a rear passenger in the first claimant's vehicle.
3. The above accident was caused wholly by the negligence of the defendant.

### Detailed Allegations of Negligence of the Defendant

a) Failing to give sufficient consideration to other traffic on the road
b) Emerging and driving onto the junction when it was not safe to do so
c) Driving above the official speed limit for the road
d) Failing to stop at a designated stop sign
e) Failing to notice, observe or respond in time to the signs, markings and layout of the junction
f) Failing to give priority to the claimant's motor vehicle
g) Failing to stop, slow down, swerve or manage or control his car in a way that would have avoided the accident

On the 30 October (year) at the AnyTown Magistrates Court the defendant was convicted of the offence of driving without due care and attention. This conviction is relevant to the question of proof of negligence in this matter and the claimants intend to rely upon the conviction as evidence within this action.

4. As a result of the defendant's negligence, the first and second claimants have suffered injury, loss and damage

### Details of Consequential Loss

See attached Schedule of Loss (*not supplied*). Further the claimant claims interest upon such damages pursuant to section 35A of the Senior Court Act 1981

## Details Of Injury

The first claimant was born 16 June 1980 and suffered pain, suffering and loss of amenity (see attached medical record – *not supplied*). The second claimant was born 2 November 2011 and suffered pain, suffering and loss of amenity (see attached medical record – *not supplied*).

## Details Of the Basis of the Claim for Interest

Interest is claimed under section 35A of the Senior Court Act 1981.

### *Special Damages*

Interest is claimed upon each, and every item of consequential loss incurred from the date such loss occurred to be assessed at half the full special account rate prescribed under the provisions of the Court Fund Rules 1987 as amended.

### *General Damages*

The claimant claims interest on general damages at the rate of 2% from the date of service of the claim form in this case until the date of judgment.

AND the claimants claim:

1.  Damages exceeding £50,000
2.  Interest pursuant to section 35A of the Senior Court Act 1981

### *STATEMENT OF TRUTH*

The claimant believes that the facts stated in this particulars of claim are true. The claimant understands that proceedings for contempt of court may be brought against anyone who makes, or causes to be made, a false statement in a document verified by a statement of truth without an honest belief in its truth.

Signed on behalf of the claimant Assiah Proctor

Dated this 13th day of October (year)

> LegalWays LLP
> Rising Hill
> AnyTown
> Landshire
> Solicitors for the claimants who will accept service of proceedings at the above address

## Document 3

IN THE HIGH COURT OF JUSTICE
QUEENS BENCH DIVISION                                    No. HC/CD/0921
BEFORE MASTER RODEAN
BETWEEN:

Clarissa Landice          First Claimant
-and-
Rose Landice          Second Claimant
**(a child by Mario Landice, her litigation friend)**
Lupin Wheeler Defendant
ORDER

---

**UPON** the application of the first and second Claimants

**AND UPON** hearing Solicitors for the first and second Claimants

**AND UPON** reading the Court file

**IT IS ORDERED THAT:**

1.  there be judgment in default for the first and second claimants' claim and for damages to be assessed.
2.  The court to list a hearing for the assessment of damages to take place within 6 weeks.
3.  the costs of the claim, to be assessed, to be paid to the first and second claimants by the defendant.

Dated
17 November (year)

## DOCUMENT 4

IN THE HIGH COURT OF JUSTICE        No. HC/CD/0921
QUEENS BENCH DIVISION        Defendant
        M Munsted
        First Witness Statement
BETWEEN:        20 November (last year)

    Clarissa Landice    First Claimant/Respondent
        -and-
    Rose Landice    Second Claimant/Respondent
    **(a child by Mario Landice her litigation friend)**
    Lupin Wheeler Defendant/Applicant

**WITNESS STATEMENT OF MARGRIT MUNSTED**

I Margrit Munsted, born on 5 July 1970, senior partner of Messrs Munsted and Partners of Value Street, AnyTown, Landshire **WILL SAY** as follows:

1. I act for the defendant Mr Lupin Wheeler. Except where otherwise expressly stated, I make this witness statement from matters within my own knowledge, information and belief.
2. This witness statement is made in support of an application under CPR Part 13.3(1)(a) and (b) to set aside a default judgment entered by the court dated 17 November. It is asserted that the defendant has a real prospect of successfully defending the claim and that there are also good reasons why the court should set aside the judgment.
3. The defendant did not receive the original claim form and particulars of claim despite the claimants' assertion that these were posted to the defendant's address at 11 Roam Way. The defendant's address is in fact divided into two properties.
4. The defendant was served with the claim form and particulars of claim by postal service effected by the claimants' solicitors. However, this was sent to the wrong address, namely 11 Roam Way, AnyTown, Landshire. Whilst the defendant is the legal owner of this property, he in fact lives in the basement flat at number 11A Roam Way.
5. In addition, no certificate of service was filed at court by the claimants' solicitors as required by CPR Part 6.17(2)(a).
6. The defendant has a real prospect of successfully defending the action because it is alleged that the first claimant made admissions of liability at the scene of the accident when she stated, "I just turned to settle my daughter into her seatbelt for one second and none of this would have happened if I had seen you".
7. The defendant seeks an order setting aside the judgment in default and asks the court to make directions for the progression of this case.

## Statement of Truth

I believe the facts stated in this witness statement are true. I understand that proceedings for contempt of court may be brought against anyone who makes, or causes to be made, a false statement in a document verified by a statement of truth without honest belief in its truth.

Margrit Munsted
Solicitor for and on behalf of the Defendant/Applicant
Dated 20 November (year)

> Messrs Munsted and Partners
> Value Street
> AnyTown
> Landshire
> Solicitors for the defendants who will accept service of proceedings at the above address

---

## Document 5

| | |
|---|---|
| IN THE HIGH COURT OF JUSTICE | No. HC/CD/0921 |
| QUEENS BENCH DIVISION | First and Second Claimants |
| | A Proctor |
| | First Witness Statement |
| BETWEEN: | 30 November (last year) |

| | |
|---|---|
| Clarissa Landice | First Claimant/Respondent |
| -and- | |
| Rose Landice | Second Claimant/Respondent |
| **(a child by Mario Landice her litigation friend)** | |
| Lupin Wheeler | Defendant/Applicant |

### WITNESS STATEMENT OF ASSIAH PROCTOR

I Assiah Proctor, born on 23 December 1966, senior partner of Messrs LegalWays LLP of Rising Hill, AnyTown, Landshire **WILL SAY** as follows:

1. I act for the first and second claimants, Ms Clarissa Landice and Ms Rose Landice. Except where otherwise expressly stated, I make this witness statement from matters within my own knowledge, information and belief.
2. The first claimant and her daughter, the second claimant were involved in a car accident at approximately 12.00pm on 18 September (year). On

20 September the first claimant and the second claimant's litigation friend instructed my firm to act on their behalf. We were satisfied that there was not a conflict of interest because the first claimant informed us that the defendant admitted liability at the roadside with the words "I didn't see you, it all happened so fast, I should have been more careful".

3.  On 27 September we sent a Letter of Claim dated 24 September to the defendant's address at 11 Roam Way, AnyTown, Landshire. We also sent a copy of the letter to the defendant's insurance company.

4.  The defendant did not respond to the letter of claim and so on 13 October we issued proceedings. The claim form and particulars of claim were posted to 11 Roam Way on 13 October together with a response pack in accordance with CPR Part 7.8. Under the provisions of CPR Part 6.14 deemed service occurred on the second business day after that date.

5.  No Acknowledgement of Service was received by the defendant within the 14-day period specified under CPR Part 10.3 and no defence was filed within the 14-day period specified under CPR Part 15.4.

6.  In the circumstances an application was made for judgment in default on 17 November under CPR Part 12.3 and the court granted judgment with damages to be assessed at a further hearing.

7.  The judgment has been properly entered and we oppose the defendant's application to set aside the default judgment.

### Statement of Truth

I believe the facts stated in this witness statement are true. I understand that proceedings for contempt of court may be brought against anyone who makes, or causes to be made, a false statement in a document verified by a statement of truth without honest belief in its truth.

Assiah Proctor

Solicitor for and on behalf of the Claimant/Respondent

Dated 30 November (last year)

> LegalWays LLP
> Rising Hill
> AnyTown
> Landshire
> Solicitors for the claimants who will accept service of proceedings at the above address

## 6.6.2 Exercise 2 (Summary Judgment)

The next exercise involves an application by the claimant for summary judgment. Unlike a default judgment, a summary judgment application, if made against a defendant, is made after the defence has been filed and on the basis that the defence does not have a reasonable prospect of succeeding at trial. However, a summary judgment can also be sought against the claimant on the basis that their claim does not have a reasonable prospect of succeeding at trial. In addition, for both types of application, there must not be any "other compelling reason why the case or issue should be disposed of at trial".

In this exercise the claimant is making the summary judgment application against the defendant. The claimant is therefore the applicant.

Read CPR Part 24 and construct arguments for the following interim application after reading documents 6–8.

Remember to follow the guidance at the beginning of this chapter on how best to approach your case strategy for constructing arguments. You might also refer to Part A, in particular Chapter 2 for a reminder of communication skills.

### Document 6

#### Memorandum B – Applicant/Claimant

From: Assiah Proctor (Supervising Solicitor)
Date: 20 January (year)

Could you take on this file for me please? I have been dealing with a claim made on behalf of Clarissa and Rose Landice arising out of a road traffic accident which occurred on 18 September. We issued proceedings on 13 October and obtained a judgment in default on 17 November. This has been set aside by the court following a successful application by the defendant at a recent hearing.

The court made an order that the defendant file a defence within 14 days. We have now received a copy of the defence and quite frankly it is not in the least bit convincing. It amounts to no more than a bare denial and makes no mention of the admission which our client says was made by the defendant at the roadside.

The defence has been signed by the defendant and so I can only assume that he is now acting in person. I have made an application for summary judgment under CPR Part 24 by serving an application notice and supporting witness statement as required by CPR Part 23. I prepared the witness statement in a rush so could you please check that it complies with the procedural requirements. There is always CPR Part 3 that can be used if you run into difficulties.

The hearing has been listed for tomorrow. Could you attend the hearing on behalf of the claimants please to argue for summary judgment? Please read the witness statement that I prepared and consider any relevant procedural rules and supporting cases. You will see that I have also asked the court to consider a strike out application under CPR 3.3, just as an alternative measure.

Could you also make an application for costs? Ensure that you take a Schedule of Costs form with you with calculations of your perusal and preparation time and attendance at court. You should base this on your hourly rate of £186.

You may also find it helpful to read the following cases as they all give a helpful perspective on the nature of summary judgment applications:

1.  *Swain v Hillman and Others* [1999] EWCA civ 3053
2.  *Royal Brompton Hospital v Hammond (no 5)* [2001] EWCA Civ 550
3.  *Three Rivers District Council v Governor and Company of the Bank of England* [2001] UKHL 16
4.  *ED & F Man Liquid Products v Patel* [2003] EWCA Civ 472
5.  *Arsenal Football Club Plc v Elite Sports Distribution Limited* [2002] EWHC 3057
6.  *Doncaster Pharmaceuticals Group Ltd v Bolton Pharmaceutical Co 100 Ltd* [2007] FSR 63

I believe that the defendant may be appearing as a litigant-in-person at this hearing as there is currently some dispute with his insurance company about his motor insurance cover. This may make the hearing a little trickier so you may want to read the case of *Barton v Wright Hassall LLP* [2018] UKSC 12 for guidance.

---

## Document 7

IN THE HIGH COURT OF JUSTICE                                No. HC/CD/0921

QUEENS BENCH DIVISION

BETWEEN:

|                     |                  |
|---------------------|------------------|
| Clarissa Landice    | First Claimant   |
| -and-               |                  |
| Rose Landice        | Second Claimant  |

**(a child by Mario Landice, her litigation friend)**

Lupin Wheeler Defendant

**DEFENCE**

1.  Paragraph 1 and 2 of the particulars of claim are admitted.

2. It is admitted that the first and second claimant suffered injury, but this was because of the first claimant's negligence.
3. In the circumstances the first and second claimants are not entitled to the sums claimed in the particulars of claim or any sum from the defendant.
4. The defendant denies each and every element of the claim.

### Statement of Truth

I believe the facts stated in this witness statement are true.

*Lupin Wheeler*

30 December (year)

---

## Document 8

---

| | |
|---|---|
| IN THE HIGH COURT OF JUSTICE | No. HC/CD/0921 |
| QUEENS BENCH DIVISION | First and Second Claimants |
| BEFORE MASTER RODEAN | A Proctor |
| | Second Witness Statement |
| BETWEEN: | 4 January (year) |

Clarissa Landice     First Claimant/Applicant
-and-
Rose Landice     Second Claimant/Applicant
**(a child by Mario Landice, her litigation friend)**
Lupin Wheeler Defendant/Respondent

### WITNESS STATEMENT OF ASSIAH PROCTOR

I Assiah Proctor, born on 23 December 1966, senior partner of Messrs LegalWays LLP of Rising Hill, AnyTown, Landshire **WILL SAY** as follows:

1. I act for the first and second claimants, Ms Clarissa Landice and Ms Rose Landice. Except where otherwise expressly stated, I make this witness statement from matters within my own knowledge, information, and belief.
2. This witness statement is made in support of an application for summary judgment under CPR Part 24.2(a)(ii) on the basis that the defendant does not have any real prospects of successfully defending the claim and CPR Part 24.2(b) that there are no other compelling reasons why this action should be disposed of at trial.
3. On 17 December (year) Master Rodean made an order setting aside a default judgment that had been entered against the defendant on 17 November and instead gave directions that the defendant should file a

defence within 14 days. The defendant filed a defence dated 30 December within the 14-day time period but the defence amounts to no more than a bare denial and is inconsistent and unconvincing. Alternatively, the court is invited to use its powers under CPR Part 3.4(2)(a) and (c) to strike out the defence on the basis that the defence discloses no reasonable ground for bringing or defending the claim and that there has been a failure to comply with a rule, practice direction or court order.

### Statement of Truth

I believe the facts stated in this witness statement are true. I understand that proceedings for contempt of court may be brought against anyone who makes, or causes to be made, a false statement in a document verified by a statement of truth without honest belief in its truth.

Assiah Proctor

Solicitor for and on behalf of the Claimant/Applicant

4. Dated 4 January (year)

> LegalWays LLP
> Rising Hill
> AnyTown
> Landshire
> Solicitors for the claimants who will accept service of proceedings at the above address

## 6.6.3 Exercise 3 (Interim Payment)

The final exercise in this chapter relates to an application for an interim payment on behalf of a child (the second claimant Rose Landice). The second claimant is the applicant for the purposes of this exercise.

An application for an interim payment allows a claimant to apply for an early payment of the damages they expect to win at trial. However, in order to do this, they must satisfy the criteria under CPR Part 25.7. Interim payments are a type of interim remedy, and the court has general powers to make any interim remedies (including interim payments and injunctions) under CPR 3.1(2).

The application in this exercise is made on the criterion under CPR Part 25.7.1(c), that if the matter went to trial, on the evidence, Rose Landice would obtain judgment for a substantial amount of money.

## Memorandum C – Applicant/Claimant

From: Assiah Proctor (Supervising Solicitor)
Date: 23 February (year)

You will recall that we made a summary judgment application in this case last month which was unsuccessful. We are, however, starting to make some progress in this case as the defendant seems prepared to acknowledge some responsibility on his part for the accident. You will see that we have obtained a medical report relating to Rose's injuries.

I have issued an application for an interim payment under CPR Part 25.6 with the relevant supporting evidence (*not supplied*). As Rose is a minor any interim payment has to be approved by the court in accordance with CPR Part 21.10(1) in any event. The court will have to make directions as to how the money is to be applied. We would ask that it is simply paid out to Rose's Litigation Friend Mario Landice (who is of course Rose's father). The court can make this direction under CPR PD 21 para 8.1(2).

Could you attend the hearing before Master Hempton tomorrow and make the necessary submissions to obtain the interim payment please? You will see from the medical report that an estimate has been made regarding Rose's accommodation needs. This is the only valuation that we have at present.

The respondent has not served any witness statement in reply and so I am assuming he does not intend to rely on written evidence. His solicitors have however sent me their counsel's skeleton arguments. I am not sure why they need counsel on an interim application such as this, but could you attend and put our side of the case please.

You will see from the defendant's skeleton arguments that they will be relying on specific cases. Could you read those cases so that you have a clear idea of the potential arguments that the defendants might raise and then be prepared to respond to those arguments.

We have previously filed a schedule of loss (*not included*) in which a claim for pain suffering and loss of amenity is made of £105,000 and past losses of £26,000. In terms of future losses, we took an actuarial evaluation based on appropriate multipliers and calculated this to be £1.5 million (including future loss of earnings). The defendants have been served with a copy of our schedule of loss. We are therefore asking for interim payments that represent, very roughly, about 10% of the total amount that we calculate Rose would receive at trial.

It has become clear that Rose was not wearing a seatbelt at the time of the accident. I am sure the defendants will try to make something of this at the hearing. You might therefore want to review the case of *Froom v Butcher* [1975] EWCA Civ 6 again so that you are clear on the guidelines.

Don't forget to refer to the overriding objective under CPR Part 1 if you need to!

## Document 10

**MEDICAL REPORT**

Date of Report: 24 January (current year)

Author of Report: Mrs L Agiare

Prepared For: The Court (on instructions from LegalWays LLP)

Subject: Rose Landice

I refer to my CV which is attached to this report, and which details my qualifications (*not supplied*).

I have been instructed by LegalWays LLP to advise in relation to the injuries sustained by their client Rose Landice on 18 September (*last year*) following a car accident. Rose was a rear passenger in a vehicle driven by her mother Clarissa Landice. The mother was driving on a dual carriageway in AnyTown when a car emerged from a turning on her right, failed to give way or stop at a stop sign and the vehicles collided.

In preparing this report I have had access to copies of Rose's hospital and GP records. I have also had the benefit of conducting a physical examination of Rose on 17 January and taking x-rays.

Rose suffered multiple injuries, the most severe of which was the fracture to her hip and pelvis resulting in long term difficulties in movement. She underwent surgery on 18 September immediately following the accident, which was partially successful, but Rose has some restrictions in her movement.

A hip fracture manifests in a crack or break in the hip bone. This often occurs in the upper part of the femur (the femoral neck) or the pelvic bone. In Rose's case the fracture was at the pelvic bone in which the pelvis was broken at both the front and the back. These types of fractures are more complex because the pelvis is made up of a series of bones that form a ring and a fracture of one will usually lead to a fracture of another. This is commonly known as an 'unstable fracture'. Rose would have been in severe pain and shock given the degree of her injuries and her medical records show that she was unconscious for a period of approximately 30 minutes and also lost a lot of blood. She received an epidural anaesthetic to stabilise the pain. Surgery involved external fixation using metal plates and screws.

I have been instructed to give my opinion as to the prognosis and what long term effect the injuries will have upon Rose's recovery. Rose has been undergoing physiotherapy since her surgery and uses crutches as a walking aid. It is likely to be a further 3 months before Rose can walk without support.

Early x-rays suggest that there has been some extensive nerve damage which is one of the risks of this type of surgery. This will cause Rose some continued difficulties in mobility for the foreseeable future and she is also at greater risk of osteoporosis.

Rose currently lives in a two-bedroom house with her parents. Both bedrooms are on the first floor. Rose has difficulties managing stairs and is temporarily sleeping on a mattress on the living room floor. Rose's parents would like to build a ground floor extension with a bedroom and separate bathroom with an adapted shower and toilet for Rose. The cost of this is likely to be extensive and based on previous patients who have undertaken similar adjustments at their property it is likely to be in the region of £70,000–£100,000.

I have arranged to review Rose again in three months' time.

### Statement of Truth

I confirm that I have made clear which facts and matters referred to in this report are within my own knowledge and which are not. Those that are within my own knowledge I confirm to be true. The opinions I have expressed represent my true and complete professional opinions on the matters to which they refer.

I understand that proceedings for contempt of court may be brought against anyone who makes, or causes to be made, a false statement in a document verified by a statement of truth without an honest belief in its truth.

Signed

Mrs. L. Agiare F.R.C.S. CCST

Consultant Orthopaedic Surgeon

## Document 11

IN THE HIGH COURT OF JUSTICE                    No. HC/CD/0921
QUEENS BENCH DIVISION
BEFORE MASTER HEMPTON
BETWEEN:

|                |                        |
|----------------|------------------------|
| Clarissa Landice | First Claimant       |
| -and-          |                        |
| Rose Landice   | Second Claimant/Applicant |

**(a child by Mario Landice, her litigation friend)**
Lupin Wheeler Defendant/Respondent

### SKELETON ARGUMENTS OF THE DEFENDANT/RESPONDENT

#### *INTRODUCTION*

1. This is an application made on behalf of the applicant for an interim payment of damages arising from a road traffic accident which occurred on 18 September at the junction of Slodan Road and Pocket Place, AnyTown, Landshire. The application is opposed by the respondent.

#### *ISSUES*

2. The first issue is whether the application is premature.
3. The second issue is whether the capital sum likely to be awarded at trial would be more than the amount of the interim payments that is claimed in the application.
4. The second issue is whether the award of an interim payment of £105,000 would be a reasonable award to make in all the circumstances.
5. Further or alternatively, it is submitted that the applicants have not demonstrated a need for the adaptation in question.

#### *RELEVANT FACTS*

6. The applicant was born on 2 November 2011 and is the second claimant in proceedings for negligence arising from a road traffic accident. The applicant was travelling in the first claimant's car as a rear passenger and sustained injuries.
7. The respondent is the defendant in the proceedings and was driving the car and who in turn is alleged to have caused the applicant's injuries.
8. As a result of the accident the applicant claims that she has suffered pain, injury and loss of amenity and has been unable to enjoy normal activities. Details of the applicant's injuries are set out in a medical report dated 24 January (year).

9.  The claim is defended on the basis that the negligence was wholly or partly contributed to by the failure of the applicant to wear a seatbelt.
10. The applicant seeks an interim payment to the cost of £105,000 to adapt the applicant's current accommodation at her parent's home.

### RELEVANT LAW

11. The power to grant an interim payment arises from the Civil Procedure Rules ('CPR') Part 25.6, 25.7(1)(c) and Practice Direction 25B.
12. The respondent's opposition to the application relies on the principle from the decision in *Cobham Hire Services Ltd v Eeles* [2009] EWCA Civ 204 that where the court is asked to take into account additional factors other than those pleaded in the schedule of loss, the applicant must establish a need for the interim payment.
13. The respondent will argue that in accordance with the CPR Part 25.7(4) the court is unable to make an interim payment that is more than a reasonable proportion of the amount likely to be awarded at trial.
14. For the purposes of CPR 25.7(1)(c) the respondent will rely on the definition of 'a substantial sum of money' given in the case of *Test Claimants in Franked Investment Income Group Litigation v Revenue & Customs Commissioners (No 2)* [2012] EWCA Civ 57.
15. The threshold for the civil standard of proof on an interim payments application is as stated in *Heidelberg Graphic Equipment Ltd v R & C Commissioners* [2009] EWHC 870 (Ch).

### SUBMISSIONS

16. It is submitted on behalf of the respondent that the applicant would not succeed in her claim if the matter went to trial.
17. Consequently, it is submitted that the applicant would not obtain a substantial amount of money.

### CONCLUSION

The respondent asks the court to dismiss the applicant's application for interim payments.

Changeling Chambers
Echo Street
AnyTown
Date: 21 February (year)

**When you have completed all three exercises, go to Part C to find suggested approaches and solutions to all three exercises.**

# Self-Reflection Checklist

| What **three** important things have you learnt from this chapter? | 1 | 2 | 3 |
|---|---|---|---|
| Set out **three** additional steps that you need to take to learn the skills in this chapter in more detail | 1 | 2 | 3 |

# References

## Cases

*Alleyne v Commissioner of Police for the Metropolis* [2012] EWHC 4406 (QB) *Arsenal Football Club Plc v Elite Sports Distribution Limited* [2002] EWHC 3057.

*Barton v Wright Hassall LLP* [2018] UKSC 12.

*Blunt v Park Lane Hotel Ltd* [1942] 2 KB 253.

*Cobham Hire Services Ltd v Eeles* [2009] EWCA Civ 2.

*Core-Export Spa v Yang Ming Marine Transportation Corporation* [2020] EWHC 425 (comm).

*Cranfield and Another v Bridgegrove Ltd* [2003] EWCA Civ 656.

*Customs Commissioners (No 2)* [2012] EWCA Civ 57.

*Denton and Others v TH White Ltd and Others* [2014] EWCA Civ 906.

*Doncaster Pharmaceuticals Group Ltd v Bolton Pharmaceutical Co 100 Ltd* [2007] FSR 63.

*ED & F Man Liquid Products v Patel* [2003] EWCA Civ 472.

*Froom v Butcher* [1975] EWCA Civ 6.

*Heidelberg Graphic Equipment Ltd v R & C Commissioners* [2009] EWHC 870 (Ch).

*Henriksen v Pires* [2011] EWCA Civ 1720.

*Jones v University of Warwick* [2003] EWCA Civ 151.

*Laughton v Shalaby* [2014] EWCA Civ 1450.

*Mitchell v News Group Newspapers* [2014] EWHC 3590 (QB).

*O'Brien v Chief Constable of South Wales Police* [2005] UKHL 26.

*Royal Brompton Hospital v Hammond (no 5)* [2001] EWCA Civ 550.

*Shagang Shipping Company Ltd v HNA Group Company Ltd* [2020] UKSC 34.

*Swain v Hillman and Others* [1999] EWCA civ 30.

*Test Claimants in Franked Investment Income Group Litigation v Revenue & Customs Commissioners (No 2)* [2012] EWCA Civ 57.

*Three Rivers District Council v Governor and Company of the Bank of England* [2001] UKHL 16.

*Versailles Trade Finance Ltd (in administrative receivership) v Clough* [2001] EWCA Civ 1509.

*Woodland v Stopford* [2012] EWCA Civ 266.

# Legislation
Civil Evidence Act 1968, ss. 11–14, s. 16.
Limitation Act 1980.

# Procedure Rules
Civil Procedure Rules Part 1, 1.2(a), (b), (d), (f).
Civil Procedure Rules Part 3, 3.1(m), 3.1A(2), 3.3, 3.4.
Civil Procedure Rules Part 6, 6.17(2)(a), 6.17(2)(b).
Civil Procedure Rules Part 13, 13.3.
Civil Procedure Rules Part 14.
Civil Procedure Rules Part 22, 22.1(a), 22.1(b), 22.2, 22.4.
Civil Procedure Rules Part 23.
Civil Procedure Rules Part 24, 24.6.
Civil Procedure Rules Part 25, 25.6, 25.7(1)(c), 25.7(4).
Civil Procedure Rules Part 32, 32.1(2), 32.6, 32.8.
Civil Procedure Rules Part 31.20.
Civil Procedure Rules Part 35, 35.4.

# Practice Directions
Civil Procedure Rules Practice Direction 22, para 2.1.
Civil Procedure Rules Practice Direction 25B.
Civil Procedure Rules Practice Direction 32, paras 17–28, para 20.2.
Civil Procedure Rules Practice Direction 3A para 1.6(1).
Practice Direction on Pre-Action Conduct and Protocols.

# Pre-Action Protocols
Pre-Action Protocol for Personal Injury Claims.

# Other
Civil Justice Council Costs Committee Guidelines 2010.
SRA Standards and Regulations, 6.

# Websites
www.bailii.org
www.gov.uk
www.legislation.gov.uk
www.nationalarchives.gov.uk

# 7

# An Introduction to Trials and Appeals

- The burden and standard of proof starts with the prosecution (criminal) or claimant (civil) but can reverse on to the opposing party.
- The prosecution bears an evidential burden to produce enough evidence to ensure that there is a case to answer. Failure to do this could lead to the defence making a 'submission of no case to answer'.
- It is important to always adhere to procedural rules and court processes in relation to the preparation of documents and bundles for trial.
- Criminal advocates should be familiar with the sentencing guidelines of the Sentencing Council.
- Civil advocates should be familiar with the different remedies and enforcement powers of the court.
- The rules of appeals differ in criminal and civil proceedings.

## 7.1 Introduction

In this chapter we will focus on evidence in trials and appeals including the procedural rules of evidence that govern these types of hearings

In Chapters 5 and 6 we discussed the admission of certain types of evidence. We now turn to consider how evidence may be useful in proving or disproving issues between the parties ('probative'). In a trial there will be a responsibility on a party to prove the facts which will lead to a conviction in a criminal case or a judgment in a civil case. This duty or responsibility to prove the facts of a case is known as the burden of proof and we will discuss this later in this chapter.

# The Probative Value of Evidence

## 7.2 An Introduction to Trials

The trial will involve the use of the different forms of evidence, real, oral, documentary and circumstantial. Witnesses will be called and will have to swear on oath or

DOI: 10.4324/9781003134770-10

affirm before giving evidence (see Oaths Act 1978). At the end of a trial the trial judge will normally start his/her summing-up by explaining to the jury where the burden of proof lies and the correct standard of proof.

The procedure for conducting a criminal trial is contained in CrimPR Parts 24 (Magistrates' Court) and 25 (Crown Court). Civil trial procedure is contained in CPR Part 32.

## 7.2.1 Burden of Proof

The prosecution (criminal) or claimant (civil) usually bears an obligation (sometimes known as the 'legal' or 'persuasive burden') to prove each and every fact in issue and an 'ultimate burden' to prove the case as a whole. For example, in a murder trial in the criminal courts there may be multiple issues to be proved such as: (1) did the defendant know the victim? (2) Did the defendant have a motive? (3) Was the defendant at the location of the murder? (4) Did the defendant have access to the murder weapon? (5) Did the defendant have an accomplice? These are facts in issue to be proved or disproved by the prosecution.

The prosecution or claimant will also have to produce enough evidence to prove those facts. This is known as the 'evidential burden'. There is not however a standard of proof attached to an evidential burden (see the comments made by Lord Devlin in *Jaysena v R* [1970] AC 618).

The evidential burden rests initially with the party that bears the legal burden (usually the prosecution/claimant) and then there is a 'tactical shift' to the other party (usually the defence/defendant at the half-way point of the trial). When the evidential burden shifts onto the defendant it is usually a matter for them as to whether they take up the evidential burden and adduce evidence to counter the allegations made against them or simply sit back and let the other party establish their case. In most circumstances, it would be dangerous and foolhardy for a defendant in a criminal trial not to produce evidence, for example, if they are relying on a defence of self-defence and the prosecution is seeking to disprove the defence.

An evidential burden is also important where a presumption applies. This is where a state of affairs is assumed to exist. Some presumptions can be rebutted by producing evidence to establish the contrary. For example, the presumption of death applies where a person has been missing for seven years. This presumption can be rebutted by, for example, producing evidence of a sighting of the missing person. However, there are also some presumptions that are irrebuttable such as the presumption of innocence until proven guilty. Presumptions can also apply to admissible evidence. For example, in criminal proceedings, there is a legal presumption that an Evidential Breath Machine ('EBM') that is used to read levels of alcohol consumption is working properly and that the results are therefore correct. This is an example of the common law 'presumption of regularity'. This is however a rebuttable presumption. This means that there is an evidential burden on the defendant to produce evidence to challenge this presumption. However, the burden of proof remains on the prosecution to prove that the machine was operating correctly, and the results are reliable and this is to be proved to the criminal standard of proof (see *Cracknell v Willis* [1988] AC 450).

The prosecution's obligation to discharge the evidential burden is an important one because if at the close of the prosecution's case the evidence they have produced is considered weak or unconvincing, it can lead to the defence making a 'submission of no case to answer'. We will consider this later in this section.

### 7.2.1.1 Burden and Standard of Proof in Civil Proceedings

In civil cases the burden of proof will rest with the claimant because the general principle is whoever brings the claim must prove it and there is not usually a burden on the other party even when the mechanisms of the claim are expressed in a negative way. For example, in a civil action for damages for negligence the claimant will have to prove that the defendant acted without care and disprove any defences raised.

In *Joseph Constantine Steamship Line v Imperial Smelting Corporation* [1942] AC 154 Lord Maugham described the civil burden of proof as a rule, "founded on considerations of good sense [which] should not be departed from without strong reasons" [174]. However, there are some exceptions, e.g. a defendant must prove contributory negligence when raising it as a partial defence, if in a contract D asserts his/her breach is covered by an exemption clause he/she will need to prove why he/she comes within the exemption clause.

The standard of proof in civil proceedings is 'on a balance of probabilities'. According to Lord Denning in *Miller v Minister of Pensions* [1947] 2 All ER 372 this means it carries a reasonable degree of probability that might be expressed as 'more probable than not'. However, in civil cases which have a quasi-criminal element the standard of proof can change from 'on a balance of probabilities' to 'beyond reasonable doubt' – see the decision in *R v Briggs-Price* [2009] UKHL 19 where the House of Lords held that a judge in confiscation proceedings who is considering whether the order should apply because a convicted person has benefited from a specific drug trafficking offence, should decide this based on the criminal standard of proof.

### 7.2.1.2 Burden and Standard of Proof in Criminal Trials

When a defendant appears in the criminal court for trial, the prosecution will present its case against the defendant before the defence makes its case. The legal burden of proof is therefore usually on the prosecution. The standard of proof is 'beyond reasonable doubt' which has been expressed by Lord Goddard in *R v Summers* (1952) 3 Cr App R 14 as the jury members asking themselves whether they are satisfied so that they are sure. This has become known as 'the sure test'. The case of *R v Miah* [2018] EWCA Crim 563 confirms that the use of the word 'sure' is sufficient, but no particular words are needed.

Circumstantial evidence may be enough to satisfy proof but in *R v Masih* [2015] EWCA Crim 477 Pitchford LJ stated that if a jury is being asked to draw an inference of guilt from circumstantial evidence then the jury must be able to "exclude all realistic possibilities consistent with the defendant's innocence" [3] in order to be sure of guilt.

Despite Viscount Sankey LC describing the burden of proof as the "one golden thread" of the "web of the English criminal law" in *Woolmington v DPP* [1935] AC 462, he also recognised that sometimes the burden of proof can rest with the defendant. This is known as a 'reverse burden'. When this happens the burden of proof never leaves the prosecution or claimant but temporarily reverses to the other party. However, the prosecution will still have to prove the elements of the crime itself. Viscount Sankey identified three circumstances when a reversal would occur (1) plea of insanity, (2) where a statute expressly provides for a reversal of the burden of proof and (3) where there is the necessary implication that the burden will be reversed.

Examples of statutes that specifically reverse the burden of proof include s. 2(2) of the Homicide Act 1957 (as amended by s. 52 of the Coroners and Justice Act 2009) which places the burden of proving a defence of diminished responsibility upon the defendant. However, not all statutes expressly make clear whether a reverse burden applies and so s. 101 of the Magistrates' Court Act 1980 provides some clarification by stating that wherever a defendant relies on an exception, exemption, proviso, excuse or qualification in a statute as his/her defence then the defendant has the burden of proving he/she comes under the exception, exemption, etc. An example of this can be seen in s. 137 of the Highways Act 1980 which does not expressly state where the burden of proof lies but states that a person will be guilty of obstructing the highway if they do not have lawful authority or excuse. It therefore includes a qualification as to when an offence will not occur. It would therefore be for a defendant who has a lawful authority or excuse to prove this.

An advocate should always read the provisions of a criminal statute carefully to determine whether a reverse burden exists. However, in certain situations, the court has intervened to remove reverse burdens where they have existed in statute but are regarded as unfair. For example, in *R v Lambert* [2001] UKHL 37 the House of Lords read down the words "for the accused to prove" in s. 28(2) of the Misuse of Drugs Act 1971 as imposing only an evidential burden on the defendant with the prosecution being obliged to prove the accused's culpable state of mind beyond reasonable doubt. This means that s. 28(2) is altered by the decision in *Lambert* in terms of where the burden lies for proving lack of knowledge for offences to which the section applies. In *R v Johnstone* [2003] UKHL 28 the House of Lords gave guidance on the factors a judge should take into account when deciding whether or not to uphold a reverse burden. These include a consideration of the nature, extent and importance of the facts to be proved and whether they are matters within the defendant's knowledge that he/she has ready access to prove.

When the burden of proof reverses on to a defendant in criminal proceedings the standard of proof becomes the civil standard of 'on a balance of probabilities' – see *R v Carr-Briant* [1943] 1 KB 607.

# 7.3  A Submission of 'No Case to Answer'

Whilst there is no standard of proof attached to the evidential burden, the prosecution/claimant still needs to produce enough evidence for the tribunal of fact (judge or jury) to reach a finding.

In criminal cases, if the prosecution has not produced enough evidence the defence can make a 'submission of no case to answer' at the half-way point of the trial. In essence the defence will allege that the case has not been proven due to insufficient evidence. A 'submission of no case to answer' can also be made at a pre-trial hearing after the prosecution has disclosed its evidence to the defence.

In *R v Galbraith* [1981] 73 Cr App R 124 Lord Lane CJ gave some guidance on when a judge should grant an application.

An application should be granted:

> Where the Judge comes to the conclusion that the prosecution evidence, taken at its highest, is such that a Jury properly directed could not properly convict on it, it is his duty, upon a submission being made, to stop the case.
>
> *[127]*

An application should be refused and the trial allowed to continue:

> Where however the prosecution evidence is such that its strength or weakness depends on the view to be taken of a witness's reliability, or other matters which are generally speaking within the province of the Jury and where on one possible view of the facts there is evidence upon which a Jury could properly come to the conclusion that the defendant is guilty, then the Judge should allow the matter to be tried by the Jury.
>
> *[127]*

Whilst the *Galbraith* guidance comes from a criminal case, submissions of no case to answer can also be made in the civil courts. The court will use the same principles to consider whether the case has any real prospects of success. However, the defendant must first be offered a right of election as to whether they will call further evidence before a judge dismisses a case based on a defendant's 'submission of no case to answer' (see *Boyce v Wyatt Engineering and Others* [2001] EWCA Civ 692). As the majority of civil cases take place before a single judge rather than a jury, the case of *Bentham Ltd v Kythira Investments Ltd* [2003] EWCA Civ 1794 reminds courts of the need to exercise caution where a 'submission of no case to answer' is made before a judge sitting alone and the judge has not heard all the evidence.

The powers of the court to stop a trial altogether can be found in CrimPR Part 25.3 for criminal proceedings and in CPR Part 32.1 in civil proceedings.

# Preparation of Trial Documents

## 7.4 Trial Bundles

Both parties will rely upon documentation at a trial and these should be included in a paginated file known as a trial bundle (in some courts these may be provided electronically). The bundle should include all statements of case, a case summary and chronology to assist the court, all witness statements/summaries and expert reports, any notice of intention to adduce evidence at trial (e.g. hearsay notices) and the response to these as well as any relevant orders such as orders made at interim hearings. Copies of the trial bundles should be made available to the court and each party.

In civil proceedings the claimant is responsible for preparing, filing and serving the trial bundle and this should be done not more than seven days and not less than three days before the trial (see CPR 39.5(2)). In criminal proceedings trial documentation will usually consist of the prosecution evidence that has been served in advance as part of the disclosure process – see for example, CrimPR Parts 24.8(2) and 24.9(2).

In cases in the High Court, as well as in both the lower civil and criminal courts, the claimant/appellant must also lodge a 'reading list' agreed by the advocates of the material that the judge should read in advance of the hearing. Skeleton arguments are also required for a trial in most courts.

# The Order of Speeches

## 7.5 Speeches

As we have discussed in Chapter 3, effective speaking is very important to an advocate's success and so spending time writing a good speech that gets your points across is worthwhile and can be beneficial when it comes to presenting your case in court. As we will see, good speeches matter.

### 7.5.1 Opening Speeches

An opening speech will describe details of the offence for the judge/jury the offence (criminal cases) or the nature of the claim (civil cases) and identify the agreed and disputed facts and any issues to be proved at trial. It is usual to use the trial bundles to refer to some of the documentary evidence during the opening speech.

In a criminal trial the prosecution will make an opening speech. However, if the defence is calling witnesses of fact (apart from the defendant) it also has a right to make an opening speech. The defence can set out its own case and draw the jury's attention to weaknesses in the prosecution's case. In civil proceedings the claimant is responsible for making the opening speech, but this is usually not required if the judge has read the file in full.

After the opening speech by the advocate representing the prosecution or claimant they will then call their witnesses and present their evidence. Questioning will follow the order of examination-in-chief, cross-examination and re-examination (see Chapter 3, section 3.6). The defence/defendant will call their evidence after the prosecution/claimant have called all their witnesses. This is sometimes referred to as the 'half-way' point of the trial. The defendant will then take their witnesses through the three stages of questioning.

## 7.5.2 Closing Speeches

The defence (criminal cases) and defendant (civil cases) will make the closing speech. The speech will focus on how the judge/jury should interpret the evidence that they have heard and also comment on the weight of the evidence that has been put before the court.

Where a defendant is unrepresented and did not call evidence, the prosecution in a criminal trial does not have an automatic right to a closing speech. After the prosecution closing speech, the defence has a right to summarise its case for the jury before the judge's summing-up.

## 7.5.3 The Judge's Summing-Up (Jury Trials only)

The judge is responsible for the summing-up at the end of the trial. The judge will explain to the jury members their function and obligations and summarise the evidence both for and against a defendant. In *R v Marr* (1990) 90 Cr App R 154, Lord Lane explained the obligation of a judge to sum-up in a way that is fair to a defendant:

> It is an inherent principle of our system of trial that however distasteful the offence, however repulsive the defendant, however laughable his defence, he is nevertheless entitled to have his case fairly presented to the jury by both counsel and the judge. Where the cards seem most heavily stacked against the defendant, the judge should be most scrupulous to ensure that nothing takes place which might exacerbate the defendant's difficulties.
>
> *[156]*

The trial judge should also remind the jury about the purpose for which a piece of evidence has been admitted (e.g. credibility or propensity). Certain types of evidence may require a warning to the jury to exercise caution in how they treat the evidence. Whilst these directions are usually given in the summing-up, judges can decide to give some or all of the directions much earlier in the trial (including before the evidence is called) and indeed this is encouraged by the Crown Court Compendium. The case of *R v ABCD* [2010] EWCA Crim 1622 also encourages the use of written directions to assist the jury and this is set out in the Criminal Practice Direction PD VI 39K. Written directions should be discussed (and where possible agreed) between the judge and the advocates before being put to the jury.

This section includes a table of the most common judicial directions or warnings to the jury.

| Clarification for the Jury in Judge's Summing-Up | Name of Judicial Warning/Direction | Nature of Judicial Warning/Direction |
|---|---|---|
| Burden and standard of proof | Woolmington v DPP Direction – see *Woolmington v DPP* [1935] AC 462 | That the burden is on the prosecution which has to make the jury 'sure' of guilt through the evidence it presents including proving the issues in dispute and disproving the defence's case including any defences. Explain that the defendant does not have to prove anything. However, where the defence does bear a burden of proof explain this will be to the civil standard of proof |
| Pre-Trial silence (s. 34 of the Criminal Justice and Public Order Act 1994) | Condron Direction – see *Condron and Condron v UK* [2000] ECHR 191 | Remind the jury that the defendant has a right of silence and that there must still be a *prima facie* case against a defendant before he/she can be found guilty and the jury must be sure the defendant failed to mention a relevant fact and it was reasonable for the defendant to have mentioned the fact |
| Silence at trial (s. 35 of the Criminal Justice and Public Order Act 1994) | Cowan Direction – see *R v Cowan* [1995] EWCA Crim 8 | Remind the jury that a defendant has a right of silence as well as reminding it that the burden of proof at the trial remains with the prosecution and that the jury must be satisfied the prosecution has established a case to answer. The jury must also be satisfied that the silence at trial can only be attributed to the fact that the defendant has either no answer to the case against them or none that would stand up to cross-examination |
| Not drawing an adverse inference | McGarry Direction – see *R v McGarry* [1998] EWCA Crim 2364 | Where there have been serious breaches of Code C in relation to the questioning of a witness or where the defendant could not reasonably have been expected to mention a fact during questioning, the jury should be told that it cannot draw an adverse inference from the defendant's silence |
| Bad character evidence | Highton Direction – see *R v Highton and Others* [2005] EWCA Crim 1985 | Explain the purpose for which the bad character evidence has been admitted (credibility or propensity of the defendant or both) and that it may be relevant but warn against the prejudicial nature of the evidence |

*(Continued)*

(Continued)

| Clarification for the Jury in Judge's Summing-Up | Name of Judicial Warning/Direction | Nature of Judicial Warning/Direction |
|---|---|---|
| Good character direction | Vye/Hunter Direction – see *R v Vye; R v Wise; R v Stephenson* [1993] 97 Cr App R 134 and *R v Hunter and Others* [2015] EWCA Crim 631 | That the jury can take into account the fact that the defendant has no previous convictions in deciding whether it believes the defendant's evidence ('credibility limb') and/or whether it makes it less likely that he/she committed the offence ('propensity limb') |
| Lies of the defendant | Lucas Direction – see *R v Lucas* [1981] QB 720 | This direction is only required where the lie is relied upon by the prosecution as evidence of the defendant's guilt. In addition, four circumstances as set out in *R v Burge and Pegg* [1996] 1 Cr App R 163 must be established. If these circumstances apply then where the lie of the defendant has been shown by other evidence to be a deliberate lie and material to the issues or made out of realisation of guilt and fear of the truth, the jury can note the lie but must be reminded that there may be other reasons for the lie other than guilt (e.g. concealing other non-criminal behaviour that the defendant is ashamed of). Only if the jury is sure the defendant did not lie for an innocent reason can it use the lie as support for the prosecution's case |
| An unreliable lying witness | Makanjuola Warning – see *R v Makanjuola* [1995] All ER 730 | This is a discretionary warning which a judge can decide to give and essentially warns the jury to be cautious about relying on the evidence it has heard from a particular witness and/or look for other evidence to support what the witness has said. If the jury is advised to look for supporting evidence the judge should identify which evidence is capable of supporting the witness's evidence. This warning only occurs if there is some evidence to suggest that the witness is unreliable (e.g. a witness who has been discovered to have lied or has a motive to lie). Unlike a defendant's non-innocent lie, a witness's lie goes to credibility only. The direction can be custom-built in the case of a non-defendant's lies (see *Pitcher v R* [2021] EWCA Crim 1013) |

(Continued)

| Clarification for the Jury in Judge's Summing-Up | Name of Judicial Warning/Direction | Nature of Judicial Warning/Direction |
|---|---|---|
| Unreliability of admissible hearsay evidence | Riat Direction – see *Riat and Others v R* [2012] EWCA Crim 1509 | Identify the source of the hearsay evidence and whether the hearsay evidence is disputed and why. Explain that if the prosecution is producing the hearsay evidence it bears the burden of proof still. Identify the limitations generally of hearsay evidence and if it is oral hearsay identify evidence that exists about the witness's credibility |
| Special measures | Section 32 Warning (Youth Justice and Criminal Evidence Act 1999) | Explain the purpose of presenting the evidence using special measures (e.g. to put a witness at ease) and that this should not prejudice the jury's view of the defendant's innocence or guilt or its view of the witness's evidence |
| Visual identification | Turnbull Warning – see *R v Turnbull* [1977] QB 224 | Take the jury through an assessment of the quality of the visual ID evidence, tell the jury of the need for special caution if the case depends wholly or substantially on the ID evidence. Explain why the warning is needed as a witness can be an honest and convincing witness but may be a mistaken witness and there is a need for caution to avoid an injustice occurring. Direct the jury to look carefully at the circumstances in which the identification was made and identify any discrepancies between the identification and the defendant's actual appearance |

For more details of these directions and others, refer to the Crown Court Compendium.

## 7.6  Verdicts and Judgments

In the civil courts a statement of claim can be struck out or judgment entered against the absent party. A judgment may be entered for a sum of money plus interest (damages), or be made to set off claims and counterclaims, resolve disputed issues between the parties, order a party to take a particular step or desist from taking certain action, approve terms of settlement already reached by the parties or stay proceedings on the basis that agreed action will be taken by one of the parties (this is known as a 'Tomlin Order').

Deductions may be made from damages, for example, as a result of contributory negligence or to off-set the receipt of state benefits for an injury (this occurs in personal injury claims (see the Social Security (Recovery of Benefits) Act 1997).

In civil proceedings all judgments and orders are sealed by the court (bear the court seal) and include the name and title of the judge making the order. Judgments can be 'reserved' to be given at a later date in open court.

In a criminal trial in the Crown Court, a jury will make a finding of guilt or innocence. To help the jury arrive at a decision the trial judge can give the jury a document known as 'Routes to Verdict'. This can take the form of a list of questions, which, if the jury is satisfied have been answered, would lead it towards the path of a verdict of 'guilty' or 'not guilty'. The questions should be confined to the evidence in the trial and the facts in issue. A trial judge can decide to put the 'Route to Verdict' document in pictorial format.

In a non-jury trial in criminal proceedings, the judge will be responsible for deciding the ultimate issue of guilt or innocence and noting the nature of warnings related to various types of evidence.

## 7.6.1  Newton Hearings (Criminal Cases)

If after a verdict of guilt has been reached, there are still issues to be determined in order for the judge to decide the correct level of sentence to impose, a 'Newton hearing' can be held (see *R v Newton* (1982) 77 Cr App R 13). An example is if the defendant is one of several defendants tried and it is alleged that the defendant's involvement in the offence was significantly less than the other co-defendants. If true, this would be a mitigating factor towards reduction of the sentence and therefore the position may be important to establish the position in a Newton hearing. Alternatively, it might be argued that a defendant murdered his/her victim for financial gain. This might be disputed and if proved would amount to an aggravating factor that would increase the sentence. A Newton hearing might be needed in such circumstances.

## 7.6.2  Sentencing (Criminal Cases)

When sentencing a defendant, the judge must apply the criteria set out in the Sentencing Act 2020 (this Act is also known as the 'sentencing code') and interpret these in line with the appropriate sentencing guidelines. Section 59 of the 2020 Act imposes a duty on judges to follow the sentencing guidelines when passing sentence on a defendant.

As most offences include sentences that are in a range of possibilities, the Sentencing Council has issued guidelines as to the factors (both aggravating and mitigating) to be taken into account when deciding on the level of sentence to apply. You will find the guidelines at https://www.sentencingcouncil.org.uk/.

All advocates should ensure that they are aware of the provisions of the 'Sentencing General Guideline: Overarching Principles' as well as the guidelines that apply to the particular offence in question. These are all published on the Sentencing Council's website.

If a defendant is found guilty in a criminal trial, then the proceedings move towards sentencing. The sentencing powers of the criminal court vary between the Magistrates' Court and the Crown Court. However, when sentencing adults, the court should be mindful of the purposes of sentencing as set out in s. 57(2) of the Sentencing Act 2020 as:

a) the punishment of offenders,
b) the reduction of crime (including its reduction by deterrence),
c) the reform and rehabilitation of offenders,
d) the protection of the public, and
e) the making of reparations by offenders to persons affected by their offences.

In the case of offenders under 18, the court should be mindful of the principal aim of the youth justice system which is to prevent offending (or re-offending) and to have regard to the offender's welfare – see Sentencing Act 2020, s. 58. Under s. 25 of the 2020 Act, children who are tried in an adult court must have their case sent back to the Youth Court for sentencing (unless the offence is a homicide).

The court should also consider the seriousness of the offence with reference to the offender's culpability (blameworthiness) and any harm caused that was intentional or foreseeable – see Sentencing Act 2020, s. 63.

In addition, the judge can take into account certain mitigating factors that might reduce the sentence (see ss. 73–75 of the 2020 Act) as well as aggravating factors that would increase the likely sentence (see ss. 64–72 of the 2020 Act).

The judge will adjourn proceedings to obtain pre-sentence reports. This is a requirement if an offender is 18 or over (see Sentencing Act 2020, s. 30) unless the court considers that such reports are unnecessary. It is also a requirement if an offender is under 18 unless there exists a previous pre-sentence report on the defendant and the court considers, given the circumstances of the case and the information in the previous report(s), that another pre-sentence report is unnecessary (see s. 30(3)).

Pre-sentence reports are reports about the offender's circumstances and may include medical or psychiatric evaluation as well as any welfare concerns. For adult offenders these are prepared by the probation service and for offenders under 13 these will be prepared by a local authority social worker. For minors aged 13–17 the report may involve the participation of both the probation service, the local authority social serves and/or the youth offending team ('YOT').

The different types of sentences include imprisonment, detention in a young offender's institution (in the case of minors), fines, community sentences and conditional discharge (see the Powers of the Criminal Courts (Sentencing) Act 2000). The Sentencing Act 2020 introduced further types of sentencing as well as adjustments to existing sentences. These include 'criminal behaviour orders' (ss. 330–342), 'sexual harm prevention orders' (ss. 343–358) and 'parenting orders' (ss. 365–375), including 'binding over' a parent or guardian (ss. 376–378).

Where an offence carries a custodial sentence a judge in most cases has a discretion as to whether to impose a custodial sentence (unless the offence carries a mandatory custodial sentence, e.g. murder). Under s. 230(2) of the Sentencing Act 2020, the court must not pass a custodial sentence unless the court is of the opinion that the offence (or a combination of the offence and one or more offences associated with it) is so serious that neither a fine alone nor a community sentence can be justified for the offence (known at 'the custody threshold').

Section 204 of the 2020 Act states that the court must not make a community order unless the court is of the opinion that the offence (or a combination of the offence and one or more offences associated with it) is serious enough to justify the making of an order (known as 'the community order threshold').

The court can make an order deferring the passing of sentence (a 'deferment order') until a later date specified in the order (see Sentencing Act 2020, s. 3). Such orders are made to enable the court to review the defendant's conduct after conviction or to take account of changes in the defendant's circumstances. Such orders can impose certain requirements on a defendant about their residence or contain restorative justice requirements (the defendant takes part in an activity to maximise their awareness of the impact of their offence). Such an order has the effect of merely adjourning the trial and a defendant can be re-sentenced if he/she breaches the terms of a deferment order.

The court can also suspend a custodial sentence so that it does not take effect unless an event occurs (such as the defendant reoffending) which activates the original custodial sentence (see s. 286). A suspended sentence should be imposed only if a custodial sentence is under consideration. If the court is considering imposing a term of imprisonment between 14 days and two years (either for one sentence or two or more sentences) then it can suspend the sentence for between six months and two years (known as 'the operational period')

Under s. 52 of the 2020 Act a court has a duty to give reasons for the sentence and identify the relevant sentencing guidelines used to inform its decision. In deciding on the length of any sentence for imprisonment, the court can give credit for any time the offender has already spent on remand in prison or on bail but under a curfew (see Sentencing Act 2020, s. 325). We will examine one of the sentencing guidelines in exercise 1 at the end of this chapter.

### 7.6.3 Enforcement of Judgments (Civil Cases)

A civil advocate's duties may not end once the trial is over as further steps may be required to secure the judgment. For example, if a money judgment remains unpaid, it is possible for a party to take a number of additional steps to recover the sums owed by making further applications to the court after the trial.

The various methods of enforcing a judgment are set out in the CPR Parts 71–89. The methods include applying for a 'third party debt order' whereby an order can be obtained that any third party who owes a debt to the judgment creditor should pay that debt to the applicant instead. This might include banks that hold monies for a judgment creditor (see CPR Part 72). Another enforcement method is an attachment of earnings order whereby an order is made that sums are to be deducted from an employed judgment debtor's salary, wages, fees, bonuses, commission or overtime payments to pay the outstanding debt (see Attachment of Earnings Act 1971, s. 6 and CPR Part 89). If the judgment creditor owns a property, then an order can be made to register a charge against the property as security for payment of the debt. This is known as a 'charging order'. The application can be made in two stages, the first to register a charge (interim charging order) and the second to enforce the charge through a sale of the property (final charging order) – see Charging Orders Act 1979 and CPR Part 73.

Certain enforcement procedures can only be granted by a High Court and so it may be necessary to transfer a County Court debt to the High Court for enforcement – see High Court and County Courts Jurisdiction Order 1991. Similarly, a High Court case may have to be transferred to the County Court for enforcement, for example, where a debt of less than £600 is to be enforced through a control of goods order. The County Court does not have powers to make an attachment of earnings order and so such applications would need to be made in the High Court.

As there are so many different methods of enforcement, an advocate will first need to establish the financial situation of a judgment debtor and details of their assets in order to decide on the best method of enforcement. This can be done by first issuing an application for an 'Order to Obtain Information from Judgment Debtors' by following the procedure set out in CPR Part 71.

### 7.6.4 Costs

As discussed in Chapter 2, the court has the power to make civil costs orders at various stages of the proceedings (including trial). Trial costs are calculated after the trial in a process known as 'detailed assessment' (this differs to the summary assessment of costs discussed in earlier chapters). The procedure is set out in CPR Part 47. Costs can be made on both an indemnity and a standard basis.

A costs order in criminal proceedings will usually be made at the end of the trial. A costs order can be made from central funds to pay the defendant's costs or a private prosecutor's costs (see Prosecution of Offences Act 1985, ss. 16 and 17). The court can also make a wasted costs order. Criminal costs are dealt with in CrimPR Part 45. The court must not make a costs order unless each party or anyone else who would be directly affected is present (see CrimPR Part 45.2).

Certain trial costs orders only apply to particular types of civil cases. For example, in personal injury cases the court can make what is known as 'Qualified One-Way Costs Shifting' ('QOCS') orders (see CPR Part 44). This is where the normal rules about a losing claimant bearing the defendant's costs will not arise in certain circumstances. This is to protect claimants who no longer have access to costs insurance from having to pay large costs to defendant insurers. Any QOCS costs order is not to exceed the sum of damages and interest that the claimant would have recovered if they had been successful in the personal injury action.

In *Siddiqui v University of Oxford Chancellor, Masters and Scholars* [2018] EWHC 536 the court indicated that QOCS could still apply even if the personal injury claim included other causes of action such as contract. However, whilst costs can be recovered in such circumstances they will be reduced accordingly at the judge's discretion. The case of *Brown v The Commissioner of Police of the Metropolis (The Equality and Human Rights Commission intervening)* [2019] EWCA Civ 1724 confirms there is no automatic right to a QOCS in a mixed personal injury and non-personal injury case. The protection is therefore subject to judicial discretion.

## 7.6.5 Finality of Litigation

Generally in civil proceedings parties are expected as a matter of public policy to put forward the entirety of their case to the court for resolution in one set of proceedings. This is to avoid parties embarking on piecemeal litigation. This rule was established in *Henderson v Henderson* (1843) 3 Hare 100. Any attempts to relitigate issues that could have been litigated in earlier proceedings could amount to an 'abuse of process' and be struck out by the court. The exception to this is where the issues, although the same, involve different defendants or different legal entities where there are legitimate reasons for not amalgamating the claims (see *Johnson v Gore Wood and Co (a firm) Ltd* [2000] UKHL 65). In *Taylor Goodchild Ltd v Scott Taylor and Another* [2021] EWCA Civ 1135 Newey LJ remarked "[i]t by no means follows that either the public interest in efficiency and economy in litigation or the interests of the parties, including in particular the interests of C, D and E, is or are best served by one action against them all" [51]. However, where the later action can be shown to be 'oppressive' or an abuse of process then it should be struck out according to the *Taylor Goodchild Ltd* case. An advocate should however follow the 'Aldi guidelines' from the case of *Aldi Stores Ltd v WSP Group PLC* [2007] EWCA Civ 1260. This requires the advocate to raise the possibility with the trial judge that separate and subsequent proceedings might be issued. This would then enable the court to express a view about resourcing and the efficient use of court time and whether it would be in the public interest for further litigation to be conducted after one court has already decided some of the issues.

In criminal proceedings a rule exists known as the 'double jeopardy rule' that would ordinarily prevent a person from being charged with the same offence twice. However, the Criminal Justice Act 2003 has created exceptions to this rule for serious offences following recommendations made in the Macpherson Report (1999) after the death of Stephen Lawrence who was killed in a racist attack (see recommendation 38). The qualifying offences are to be found in Part 1 Schedule 5 of the 2003 Act and include murder, kidnapping, rape sexual offences against a minor, class A drug offences, arson, war crimes and terrorism. Under section 77 of the 2003 Act an application can be made to the Court of Appeal to quash the original acquittal of a defendant and order a retrial.

## 7.7  An Introduction to Appeals

Where a judge has made a decision that is considered to be either (1) wrong due to errors of law, fact or the exercise of a discretion or (2) unjust due to a procedural irregularities or other irregularities, then an advocate may wish to appeal that decision.

Appeals due to errors of fact, whilst permissible, do have some restraints placed upon them. This is because it is assumed that the original trial judge or jury will be best placed to decide issues of fact as they will have heard the evidence and been able to make assessments about the truthfulness of each witness's evidence. However, examples of where it may be appropriate to allow an appeal based on errors of fact include where the judge has made an important finding of fact that cannot reasonably be explained on the basis on the evidence, or the judge has fundamentally misunderstood relevant evidence or failed to consider critical or important evidence (see *Henderson v Foxworth Investments Ltd* [2014] UKSC 41).

### 7.7.1  Appeals in Civil Proceedings

The appeal may be based on a wrong decision at or on an interim application or trial. However, there must be proper grounds on which to appeal. An appeal does not involve a retrial and so witnesses will not be recalled. The appeal is conducted by considering the transcript of the evidence at the original trial. The appeal court does however have a discretion to hold a rehearing if it considers that it would be in the interests of justice – see CPR Part 52.21.

Appeals are made using an application notice (e.g. form N161 for cases on the small track). A skeleton argument is required for all appeals and should comply with CPR PD 52A para 5.1. In addition, the appellant should file a chronology of events (see CrimPR PD para 5.2)

Advocates must comply with CPR Part 52 and Practice Directions 52A (general provisions), 52B (appeals in the County Courts and the High Court), PD52C (appeals to the Court of Appeal), 52D (statutory and special appeals) and 52E (appeals by way of case stated). The Supreme Court has its own rules for appeals (the Supreme Court Rules 2009 statutory instrument No 1603) and these relate to both civil and criminal cases and are accompanied by practice directions that are published on the Supreme Court website.

The Access to Justice Act 1999 (Destination of Appeals) Order 2016 specifies the correct appeal route for decisions of judges (according to their status).

For a first appeal to a court (other than the Court of Appeal) the test is found under CPR Part 52.6 and is whether:

1. The court considers that the appeal would have a real prospect of success or
2. There is some compelling reason for the appeal to be heard.

If a second appeal takes place to the Court of Appeal, then the test under CPR Part 52.7 becomes whether:

1. The court considers that the appeal would have a real prospect of success and
2. The appeal raises an important point of principle or practice or
3. There is some compelling reason for the appeal to be heard by the Court of Appeal.

Examples of the route to appeals can be found in Figure 7.1.

An appeal 'by way of case stated' is an appeal from a lower court to a higher court to resolve a point of law. The lower court will set out the particular facts and the relevant legal issues arising from it that require resolution. Once the point of law is resolved, the matter is then referred back to the lower court to continue with the hearing and make the final determination. The procedure is covered by CPR PD 52E.

An appeal that takes the form of 'judicial review' is a challenge to the lawfulness of a decision made by a public body (for example, a local authority, a regulator, etc). There is a pre-action protocol that governs judicial review hearings and the procedure is also set out in CPR Part 54 and CPR PD 54A.

Where permission to appeal is needed this will usually be a paper exercise without the need for a formal hearing but the advocate should follow the procedure in CPR Part 52.4–6 and 52.12–13. The appeal notice must state that the appellant requires permission to appeal if they are applying for permission from the appeal court. Equally they can apply for permission from the original court whose decision is to be appealed – see CPR Part 52.3(2).

Advocates should observe the time limit for filing an appeal notice which is either the time period stipulated by the lower court or 21 days after the date the decision was actually made by the lower court (see CPR Part 52.12). The 21-day time limit runs from the date the decision is formally announced in court (see *Sayers v Clarke Walker* [2002] EWCA Civ 645) and not from the date the decision was drawn up as an order. If the judge reserves judgment, then it will be the date that the judgment is handed down in open court rather than any earlier date, such as, for example, when the judge circulates a draft judgment to counsel for approval (see *Owusu v Jackson* [2002] EWCA Civ 877).

If judgment is handed down in open court in the absence of the parties (because a draft judgment has already been circulated and their attendance has been excused by the judge), it is recognised that there may not be an opportunity for a party to make the application for permission to appeal to the original court in accordance with CPR Part 52.3(2). In those circumstances the case of *McDonald v Rose and Others* [2019] EWCA Civ 4 states that the judge should formally adjourn the hearing after handing down judgment and then the 21-day period to apply for permission will run from then (the application for permission can be made in writing rather than recon-stituting the hearing). Equally if the judge announces their decision but then states they will give reasons for their decision at a later date, the case of *McDonald* confirms the judge should adjourn the hearing and extend the 21-day time period.

The court has the power to vary the appeal time period under CPR Part 52.15 and Part 3.1(2)(a). The advocate will also need to prepare an appeal bundle which will be extensively read by the court to reduce the need for opening speeches.

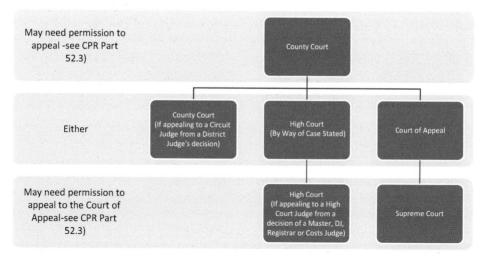

**Figure 7.1** Routes to Appeal in the Civil Courts.

## 7.7.2  Appeals in Criminal Proceedings

In criminal proceedings, appeals are governed by the Criminal Appeal Act 1968 and CrimPR Parts 34–44 as well as the Senior Courts Act 1981 and the Sentencing Act 2020. Appeals are heard in public unless the hearing relates to a public interest ruling.

An appeal from a decision in the Magistrates' Court is made to the Crown Court under CrimPR 34 and can be made in relation to appeals against conviction, sentencing and other orders. Appeals from a Crown Court may be made to the Court of Appeal in relation to conviction, sentence or verdicts and findings of guilt. Crown Court decisions relating to other orders made are usually made on points of law and referred to appeal either 'by way of case stated' (see the procedure in CrimPR Part 35) or by way of judicial review (see Senior Courts Act 1981, s. 29(3)) to the divisional court of the High Court. This procedure can also be used to challenge decisions made in the Magistrates' Court.

Whilst an appeal court will usually focus only on the evidence that was considered at the trial, s. 23 of the Criminal Appeal Act allows the court to receive fresh evidence in limited circumstances if it is in the interests of justice to do so.

When an appeal is heard by the Court of Appeal it must include a panel of at least two judges, and in some circumstances three judges will be required to sit (e.g. appeals against conviction, applications for leave to appeal to the Supreme Court, appeals against findings of fitness to plead – see Senior Courts Act s. 55(2)). Certain limited cases may be heard by a single Court of Appeal judge (e.g. initial applications for leave to appeal to the Court of Appeal and applications for bail pending an appeal). If a case is extremely complex, then more than three judges may sit as long as the number of judges is kept uneven.

The procedure for appeals in the Supreme Court is governed by the Supreme Court Rules which are outside the scope of this book. An appeal can be made to the Supreme Court, either by the Court of Appeal certifying that the appeal involves a point of general importance or the Supreme Court giving leave to appeal because the point of law is considered an important one. The procedure for applying for leave from the Court of Appeal to appeal to the Supreme Court is set out in CrimPR Part 43.

## 7.7.3  Appeal Notice

An appeal notice and response notice should follow the format set out in CrimPR 34.2 and 34.3 (appeals to the Crown Court) or CrimPR Part 39.3 (appeals to the Court of Appeal) and specify details of the conviction or finding of guilt, the sentence or the order to be appealed and summarise the issues giving arise to the appeal.

In the case of an appeal from the Magistrates' Court to the Crown Court, an appellant must serve the notice of appeal on the Magistrates' Court and the opposing party (Crown Prosecution Service). This must be done not more than 15 days after

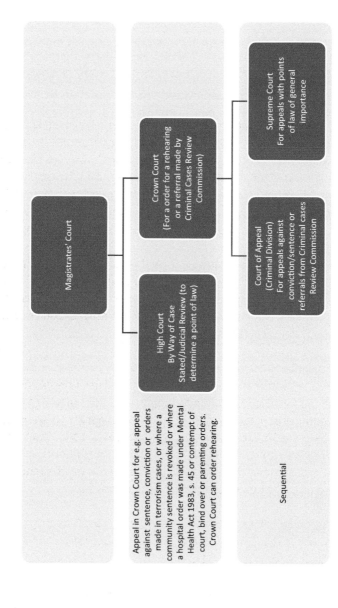

**Figure 7.2** Routes to Appeal in the Criminal Courts.

sentencing (or the date sentence is deferred or the date of committal for sentence) or the making of the relevant order (see CrimPR Part 34.2). An appellant can apply for an extension of the time limit to appeal (CrimPR Part 34.2 (3)). The Magistrates' Court can grant an appellant bail pending an appeal. The respondent serves a response notice not more than 15 days after service of the appeal notice where the appeal is against a conviction or finding of guilt (see CrimPR Part 34.2(5)).

In the case of an appeal from the Crown Court to the Court of Appeal, the time limit for service of the appeal notice is 28 days after the conviction, verdict, finding, sentence or order (see CrimPR Part 39.2). The respondent then has ten business days to file a response (see CrimPR Part 39.6(4)).

Once the relevant court has received a notice of appeal, it will apply for the transcripts from the lower court to determine whether the application shows substantial grounds for appeal. Under s. 20 of the Criminal Appeal Act 1968, if the Registrar (usually a barrister or solicitor of ten years' standing) considers that the grounds of appeal do not show any substantial grounds then he/she can refer the matter to the court for a summary determination. The court can dismiss any appeal applications that it considers to be frivolous or vexatious without the need to hold a hearing.

An appellant is expected to assist the court with its case management functions by helping the court to identify relevant witnesses who gave evidence at trial, detail any special measures arrangements made, detail the issues at trial and how they differ from the issues on appeal and also identify any relevant reports and state how long the original trial lasted (see CrimPR 34.3(c)).

## 7.7.4  Crown Court as an Appeal Court

On an appeal from the Magistrates' Court to the Crown Court, CrimPR Part 34.11 provides that the hearings should be heard by a judge of the level of a High Court Judge, Circuit Judge or Recorder or a qualifying judge advocate together with no more than four justices of the peace. If the appeal is from a decision in the Youth Court, then each justice of the peace must be qualified to sit in a Youth Court. In exceptional circumstances, to avoid a delay in the constitution of an appeal the requirement for four justices of the peace to be present can be reduced to one.

## 7.7.5  Sources of Potential Miscarriages of Justice

One of the bases for an appeal may be that there has been a miscarriage of justice due to judge's failure to conduct a proper summing-up of the evidence for the jury. As we have discussed, the admission of certain pieces of evidence might lead to the jury placing undue weight on their importance and/or reliability. The judge therefore has an obligation to guide the jury on how to treat such evidence and the inherent dangers associated with the evidence. The judge must also remind the jury about the burden and standard of proof. In *R v Lawrence* [1982] AC 510 Lord Hailsham emphasised the importance of the judge's summing-up task:

A direction to a jury should be custom-built to make the jury understand their task in relation to a particular case. Of course, it must include references to the burden of proof and the respective roles of jury and judge. But it should include a succinct but accurate summary of the issues of fact as to which a decision is required, a correct but concise summary of the evidence and arguments on both sides and a correct statement of the inferences which the jury are entitled to draw from their particular conclusions about the primary facts.

*[519]*

Another common area leading to potential miscarriages of justice is the use of visual identification evidence, particularly when this is not supported by a second identification through the more formal process of Code D of the Police and Criminal Evidence Act 1984. Visual identification evidence therefore requires caution when deciding how much weight should be attached to its significance given that sightings can be unreliable, misleading or mistaken. The common law has developed a test to be used for identification evidence taken from the case of *R v Turnbull* [1977] QB 224 known as the 'Turnbull Guidelines'. Where a case relies wholly or substantially on visual identification evidence that is contested the judge should provide a 'Turnbull warning' to the jury of 'a special need for caution'. This warns the jury of the dangers of relying on such evidence because a convincing witness can still make an honest mistake. The judge therefore directs the jury to examine, assess and evaluate the identification evidence as follows:

1. Assess the quality of the evidence – for example, how long did the witness have the defendant under observation? Did the witness get only a 'fleeting glimpse' of the defendant? These and other questions should be asked by the jury when assessing whether the identification is strong or weak.
2. Look at the circumstances that led up to the identification evidence being made – for example, what were the weather conditions? How far away was the witness standing from the defendant at the time of the identification? Was their view of the defendant obstructed or impeded? What were the lighting conditions at the time of the identification? Was it day or night? Had the witness seen the defendant before? These and other questions should be asked when looking at how the identification was made.
3. Consider any discrepancies in the description given by the witness and the defendant's actual description and whether these are material discrepancies.
4. Be reminded of weaknesses in the identification that have been drawn to the jury's attention by the judge.
5. Remember that whilst recognition evidence will usually be good identification evidence, mistakes can still be made.

The guidelines provide that if the quality of the identification is merely a 'fleeting glimpse' it should not be left to the jury to consider it as evidence unless there is other evidence to support the identification. This might be, for example, a positive identification from a witness during a Code D formal identification procedure or another witness who has also identified the defendant in a statement.

The Turnbull guidelines have been developed for use in voice identification and other forms of identification. You can find more details about the guidelines in the Crown Court Compendium (15).

Another potential source of miscarriages of justice is forensic evidence and an advocate should always be prepared to challenge the science where there is a basis for doing so such as DNA evidence that might not have been stored in the correct climate conditions prior to analysis.

## 7.8  The Post-Trial Case Studies

We will now turn to our exercises in this final chapter by considering two case studies. The first relates to sentencing and the second relates to evidential matters on an appeal.

In this section you will find documentation relating to two types of applications that might be made after a criminal trial namely, (1) a 'plea in mitigation' to reduce a sentence that a judge might be thinking of passing and (2) an appeal based on a defective summing-up given by a trial judge. This time, each application is preceded by a set of instructions for each exercise. You should assume that all dates given are current dates. Where it is indicated in italics that a document is 'not supplied', assume that it does not include any procedural irregularities and can be ignored for the purposes of the fact pattern.

You will find suggested guidance on possible arguments that can be advanced in support of each application in section C. You should however try to work through the exercises first and prepare your own arguments drawing on some of the skills learnt in Part A.

You might approach the exercises in the following way:

- Read the documents through once.
- Read through the document a second time but this time highlight any key words or sentences that you think are important.
- Read the criminal evidential rules contained in Chapter 5 and the criminal standard and burden of proof contained in this chapter and details of potential sources of miscarriages of justice (also in this chapter).

Consider any additional evidential rules that might be relevant (refer to the Table in Appendix B).

- Read any cases and legislation mentioned in the documentation.
- Consider whether any other cases might be relevant – for example, do the cases that are referred to in the documentation lead you to a research trail of other cases/legislation?
- Start to construct possible grounds – you might want to use a 'strengths and weaknesses' table similar to the Table discussed in Chapter 2 but this time divide by 'points of law' and 'incorrect factual analysis' arising from the summing-up or 'aggravating factors' and 'mitigating factors' in the case of the sentencing exercise.

## 7.8.1 Exercise 1 (Sentencing)

In this exercise you will play the role of defence advocate. Following a trial, your client Simeon Notte (who is the defendant) has been convicted of violent disorder under the Public Order Act 1986. This exercise requires you to find the correct sentencing guideline for this type of offence to appreciate the range of sentences that the court could make and what matters will be regarded as aggravating factors (that would increase the likely sentence) and mitigating factors (that would reduce the likely sentence). Where an offence has a possible sentence that includes both a custodial sentence and/or a community sentence, it is also important to read and consider the sentencing overarching guidelines 'Imposition of Community and Custodial Sentences', in particular, whether the 'custody threshold' or the 'community order threshold' have been passed to justify imposing such a sentence. It is also important to consider whether the offence allows for other types of sentences to be imposed such as a fine which might be more suitable depending on the level of seriousness of the offence. Finally, any recommendations made in a pre-sentence report should be taken into account in accordance with s. 30 of the Sentencing Act 2020.

### Instructions

You are a solicitor employed by LegalWays LLP and have represented the defendant Simeon Notte at a trial for violent disorder under the Public Order Act 1986 for which he was convicted. You are now appearing before the judge to make a 'plea in mitigation' to persuade the judge to give the minimum rather than the maximum sentence for the offence. You have been asked to read the pre-sentence report that was ordered by the judge (see document one).

Construct your submissions with reference to:

1) the offence (including minimising aggravating factors and emphasising mitigating factors); and
2) the offender (including the offender's personal circumstances as set out in any pre-sentence report); and
3) the offender's conduct; and
4) the offender's capacity to reform; and
5) relevant sections of the pre-sentence report that assist your arguments about the appropriate sentence or that you disagree with.

It may be necessary to disagree with the recommendations made in the pre-sentence report. Those recommendations are not binding on the court and so it may be necessary to persuade the judge against adopting the recommendations if they are adverse to your client.

You may find the following case helpful:

*R v York* [2018] EWCA Crim 2754.

You may also find the following legislation and guidelines helpful:

Sentencing Act 2020, ss. 125, 201, 202, 230(2), 204.
Sentencing Guideline: Violent Disorder – see www.sentencingcouncil.org.uk.
Sentencing Guideline: Overarching Principles – see www.sentencingcouncil.org.uk.
Sentencing Guideline: Overarching Guidelines Imposition of Community. Custodial
    Sentences – see www.sentencingcouncil.org.uk.

## Case Study 1 – Simeon Notte (Sentencing)

### Document One

### *Extracts from Pre-Sentence Report*

### The Offence

Simeon was convicted of violent disorder contrary to s. 2 of the Public Order Act 1986. This offence relates to an altercation which was alleged to have taken place between him, a group of his friends and another rival group. The events took place outside a local cinema. Altogether six men were charged but only four (including Simeon) were convicted.

The prosecution's case was that at the time of the offence Simeon had gone to see a film with his girlfriend (Diane) and as he was leaving the cinema, he said hello to two men he recognised from an estate close to where he lives (Frank and Meko). A group of three men who were also coming out of the cinema then barged past all three of them. One of the men was known locally as a drug dealer who lives on the same housing estate as Frank and Meko (who were also convicted along with Simeon). This man is called Thomas ('Tommy') Lennon and was convicted at a separate trial of wounding contrary to s. 18 of the Offences Against the Person Act 1861 but arising from the same incident. It was accepted at the trial that Tommy made a derogatory comment about Simeon's girlfriend Diane describing her as "a sight for sore eyes". Simeon turned around and challenged Tommy and called him "ignorant". Tommy's friend (who at the trial was referred to as 'Popeye' but is known as Dameon Fellows), then pushed Simeon and told him to "show more respect to my friend Tommy". Simeon responded by saying "look, I don't want any trouble" and started to walk away with his girl-friend Diane. Thomas Lennon then shouted "don't you turn your back on me". At this point the two men, Frank and Meko, intervened to try to calm things down as a crowd of about ten people had now gathered around them all outside the cinema. The man who had been described as Popeye then grabbed Diane's arm and it looked like he was going to try to kiss her. Simeon says Meko tried to pull Diane away and at this point the third man known as Carlos Ferraria, then punched Meko. However, the jury found that Simeon started the fight that then ensued by throwing the first punch. All six men started fighting. During the incident, Diane and a passer-by were injured and the glass door of the cinema was damaged when a stone was thrown at it. Simeon suffered a fractured jaw and the other three men sustained cuts and bruising. Thomas Lennon was con-victed at a separate trial for wounding in relation to both Diane and one of the bystanders known as Ari Fleiss. Simeon, Frank, Meko and Carlos were all found guilty of violent disorder under the Public Order Act 1986 which carries a maxi-mum sentence on indictment of five years or a fine or both.

### The Offender

Mr Notte currently resides at 3 Prince Court, AnyTown, Landshire with his mother and was born on 12 February 1996. Prior to the incident he was employed as a tax consultant with a leading business advisory service but has since lost his job due to the criminal charges that he faced. Mr Notte owns the property at 3 Prince Court and cares for his ageing mother who has Parkinson's disease. He separated from his girlfriend Diane, a few weeks after the offence.

Simeon continues to maintain his innocence in terms of starting the fight but accepts that he was involved in the fighting that ensued and that property damage was caused, and people were injured. He says that the police made the incident look like gang-related violence when in truth it was simply a disagree-ment between men who barely knew each other. It is Thomas Lennon's known links to drug gangs that have made the offence more serious than it was, he believes. Only Thomas Lennon carried a knife that led to wounding Diane and Ari but because they were all present together when the violence occurred, they have all been blamed for serious violence. Simeon says that he is not in a gang and to his knowledge neither are Frank or Meko.

Simeon received a caution following a stop and search last year when the police found a knife on him. He says this was not intended as a weapon as he had bought it for a friend who was going travelling and it was more a multi-tool device. Details of his caution were admitted as evidence at the trial.

**Recommended Sentence**

The court has a range of sentences available to it including a discretionary custodial sentence. This is a defendant with a recent prior record, but it is for a caution which is less serious than a conviction. Mr Notte continues to maintain his innocence in terms of starting the fight and does not accept guilt despite the findings of the jury. The defendant was not found to have had or used weapons during the present offence for which he was found guilty although he did participate in an incident that involved the serious acts of violence in which two members of the public were injured. This is in my view culpability in the midrange of the Sentencing Guidelines for Violent Disorder and the jury did accept evidence that Mr Notte had initially attempted to diffuse the situation before the fight broke out.

## 7.8.2 Exercise 2 (Grounds of Appeal)

In this exercise you are asked to consider an extract from a summing-up in the fictitious case of *R v Greenham* in order to advise on potential grounds for appeal. These will be based on a defective summing-up given by the trial judge. You may find it helpful to re-read the section in this chapter relating to judicial directions and warnings as well as referring to the Crown Court Compendium to consider where errors may have been made in the summing-up.

### Instructions

You are a solicitor employed by Messrs Munsted and Partners and have been asked to draft a notice of appeal based on the summing-up given by the trial judge which is thought to have breached a number of evidential rules.

Consider the following extract from the summing-up. In order to identify the grounds for appeal consider where the summing-up may have been defective by considering the latest edition of the Crown Court Compendium.

You may also find the following cases helpful:

- *R v Turnbull* [1977] QB 224
- *R v Highton* [2005] EWCA Crim 1985
- *R v Hanson* [2005] EWCA Crim 824
- *R v Summers* (1952) 3 Cr App R 14
- *R v Miah* [2018] EWCA Crim 563
- *Derek William Bentley (Deceased)* [1998] EWCA Crim 2516

You may also find the following legislation helpful:

* s. 101(1)(g), 101(3) and 101(4) of the Criminal Justice Act 2003
* Code D of the Police and Criminal Evidence Act 1984

## Case Study 2 – R v Greenham (Appeal)

### Document Three

### *Extract from Summing-up of His Honour Judge Toklein*

The defendant Teresa Greenham has been charged with robbery. Your role as members of the jury is to consider her guilt or innocence. You have heard the prosecution's case that in the early hours of the morning on 9 March (*year*) the defendant attempted to steal from a member of the public, Darren Smith. At first, she approached Mr Smith on compassionate grounds asking for money in order to buy food. When he refused, she then blocked his path so that he could not continue on his way and she then became aggressive and threatened to "cut him" unless he gave her £50. Mr Smith gave her all that he had on his person at the time which was £10.00. He then managed to run away and call the police on his mobile telephone. The police were called to the scene at which time the defendant had fled. Mr Smith described the defendant in terms of colour, height, clothing and distinguishing features all of which matched the defendant. The defendant was later arrested by the police, but Mr Smith failed to correctly identify the defendant Teresa Greenham during a police video identification procedure at the police station under Code D of PACE 1984. At the time of the arrest the defendant had £10.00 on her person.

During the trial, objection was made to the admissibility of the visual identification evidence but I allowed the evidence to be admitted. This is because the prosecution also had supporting evidence from a witness, a Ms Lowden, who claimed to have seen the defendant running from the scene. The defence deny that the defendant has been correctly identified as the perpetrator of the crime. The prosecution however state that Ms Lowden's evidence is recognition evidence. This is because the main prosecution witness Ms Lowden is known to the defendant. She is a shopkeeper and the defendant, who was homeless at the time, had often slept outside her shop. Ms Lowden often threw water over the defendant to get her to move from the shop and they would often argue as a result and one such altercation led to the police being called. Ms Lowden struck me as a truthful witness, one who is to be believed.

You have been permitted to consider evidence of the defendant's previous conviction for theft of a bicycle which took place eight years ago. This evidence was admitted because the defendant made an attack on the truthfulness of Ms

Lowden's evidence during the trial. The evidence of the defendant's previous conviction can be used to decide whether you consider it likely that the defendant committed the present crime.

During the trial the defendant claimed that the £10 was money that she found in the street. She later changed her story and said a friend had given her the £10 but did not produce the friend as a witness to support this story. You may decide that this constitutes a lie that the defendant has been found to have told and this lie may be causative when deciding guilt or innocence.

Your role is an important one. Having heard the evidence, you must now decide on the defendant's guilt or innocence. Remember that it is for the prosecution to convince you of the defendant's guilt and this must be done to a very high standard indeed. You must examine the evidence and decide which evidence you believe based on its credibility and certainty of truth.

**When you have completed both exercises, go to Part C to find suggested approaches and solutions to the exercises.**

## Self-Reflection Checklist

| What **three** important things have you learnt from this chapter? | 1 | 2 | 3 |
|---|---|---|---|
| Set out **three** additional steps that you need to take to learn the skills in this chapter in more detail | 1 | 2 | 3 |

You can now check Part C for further guidance on how to approach the two exercises in this chapter!

# References

## Cases

*Aldi Stores Ltd v WSP Group PLC* [2007] EWCA Civ 1260.
*Bentham Ltd v Kythira Investments Ltd* [2003] EWCA Civ 1794.
*Boyce v Wyatt Engineering and Others* [2001] EWCA Civ 692.
*Cracknell v Willis* [1988] AC 450.
*Brown v The Commissioner of Police of the Metropolis (The Equality and Human Rights Commission intervening)* [2019 EWCA Civ 1724.

*Condron and Condron v UK* [2000] ECHR 191.
*Derek William Bentley (Deceased)* [1998] EWCA Crim 2516.
*Henderson v Foxworth Investments Ltd* [2014] UKSC 41.
*Henderson v Henderson* (1843) 3 Hare 100.
*Jaysena v R* [1970] AC 618.
*Johnson v Gore Wood and Co (a firm) Ltd* [2000] UKHL 65.
*Joseph Constantine Steamship Line v Imperial Smelting Corporation* [1942] AC 154.
*McDonald v Rose and Others* [2019] EWCA Civ 4.
*Miller v Minister of Pensions* [1947] 2 All ER 372.
*Owusu v Jackson* [2002] EWCA Civ 877.
*R v ABCD* [2010] EWCA Crim 1622.
*R v Briggs-Price* [2009] UKHL 19.
*R v Burge and Pegg* [1996] 1 Cr App R 163.
*R v Carr-Briant* [1943] 1 KB 607.
*R v Cowan* [1995] EWCA Crim 8.
*R v Galbraith* [1981] 73 Cr App R 124.
*R v Hanson* [2005] EWCA Crim 824.
*R v Highton* [2005] EWCA Crim 1985.
*R v Hunter and Others* [2015] EWCA Crim 631.
*R v Johnstone* [2003] UKHL 28.
*R v Lambert* [2001] UKHL 37.
*R v Lawrence* [1982] AC 510.
*R v Lucas* [1981] QB 720.
*R v Makanjuola* [1995] All ER 730.
*R v Marr* (1990) 90 Cr App R 154.
*R v McGarry* [1998] EWCA Crim 2364.
*R v Miah* [2018] EWCA Crim 563.
*R v Masih* [2015] EWCA Crim 477.
*R v Newton* (1982) 77 Cr App R 13.
*R v Summers* (1952) 3 Cr App R 14.
*R v Turnbull* [1977] QB 224.
*R v Vye; R v Wise; R v Stephenson* [1993] 97 Cr App R 134.
*R v York* [2018] EWCA Crim 2754.
*Sayers v Clarke Walker* [2002] EWCA Civ 645.
*Siddiqui v University of Oxford Chancellor, Masters and Scholars* [2018] EWHC 536.
*Taylor Goodchild Ltd v Scott Taylor and Another* [2021] EWCA Civ 1135.
*Woolmington v DPP* [1935] AC 462.

## Legislation
Access to Justice Act 1999 (Destination of Appeals) Order 2016.
Attachment of Earnings Act 1971, s. 6.
Charging Orders Act 1979.
Criminal Appeal Act 1968, s. 23.
Criminal Justice Act 2003, s. 101(g), 101(3), 101(4).
Coroners and Justice Act 2009, s. 52.

Highways Act 1980, s. 137.
Homicide Act 1957, s. 2(2).
Magistrates' Court Act 1980, s. 101.
Misuse of Drugs Act 1971, s. 28(2).
Police and Criminal Evidence Act 1984.
Powers of the Criminal Courts (Sentencing) Act 2000.
Prosecution of Offences Act 1985, s. 16, s. 17.
Senior Courts Act 1981, s. 29(3), s. 55(2).
Sentencing Act 2020, s. 3, s. 25, s. 30, s. 52, s. 57(2), s. 58, ss. 63–75, s. 325, ss. 330–342,
    ss. 343–358, ss. 365–375, ss. 376–378.
Social Security (Recovery of Benefits) Act 1997.
The Supreme Court Rules 2009 statutory instrument No. 1603.
Youth Justice and Criminal Evidence Act 1999, s. 32.

## Procedure Rules and Directions
Civil Procedure Rules Part 3.1(2)(a).
Civil Procedure Rules Part 32.
Civil Procedure Rules Part 39.5(2).
Civil Procedure Rules Part 44.
Civil Procedure Rules Part 52, PD 52A–E, 52.3, 52.3(2), 52.4, 52.6, 52.7, 52.12, 52.15.
Civil Procedure Rules Parts 71–89.
Criminal Practice Direction PD VI 39K.
Criminal Procedure Rules Part 24.
Criminal Procedure Rules Part 25, 25.3.
Criminal Procedure Rules Part 34–44.
Criminal Procedure Rules Part 45, 45.2.

## Codes of Conduct and Guidance
Code D Police and Criminal Evidence Act 1984.
Crown Court Compendium Part I.
Cron Court Compendium Part II (Sentencing).
Sentencing Guidelines: Imposition of Community and Custodial Sentences.
Sentencing General Guideline: Overarching Principles.
Sentencing Guidelines: Violent Disorder.

## Reports
The Stephen Lawrence Inquiry: Report of Inquiry by Sir William MacPherson of Cluny
    (Cm 4262-I, Assets Publishing 1999).

## Websites
www.bailii.org
www.gov.uk
www.legislation.gov.uk
www.nationalarchives.gov.uk
www.sentencingcouncil.org.uk

# Appendix A

# Table of Key Procedural Rules

| Steps in Litigation | Criminal Procedure Rules | Civil Procedure Rules | Criminal Practice Directions | Civil Practice Directions |
|---|---|---|---|---|
| *Overriding Objective* | Part 1 | Part 1 | Criminal Practice Direction Division I [2015] EWCA Crim 1567 (as amended), 1A | Practice Direction Part 1A, Practice Direction on Pre-Action Conduct and Protocols |
| *Case Management Powers* | Part 3 | Part 3 | Criminal Practice Direction Division I [2015] EWCA Crim 1567 (as amended), 3A | Practice Direction Part 3A–3G |
| *Starting Proceedings* | Parts 7 & 10 | Part 7 & 8 (Alternative Procedure) | Criminal Practice Direction [2015] Division I 5A (forms) and Criminal Practice Direction Division II [2015] EWCA Crim 1567 (as amended), 9A, 10A & 10B | Practice Direction Part 2F, Practice Direction Part 8, Practice Direction-Pre-Action Conduct and Protocols, Practice Direction on County Court Closures |
| *Service of Proceedings* | Part 3.19 and Part 4, Part 7.4 | Part 6 | None but see Magistrates Court Act 1980, s. 47, Criminal Justice Act 2003, s. 30(5) and Children and Young Persons Act 1933, s. 34A | Practice Direction Part 6A & 6B |
| *Bail* | Part 14 (Bail) | N/A | Criminal Practice Direction [2015] EWCA Crim 1567 (as amended), Division III 14A–H | N/A |
| *Acknowledgment of Service/Proof of Service* | Part 4.12 and Part 5 | Part 10 | Criminal Practice Direction [2015] EWCA Crim 1567 (as amended), Division I 5A | None |
| *Default Judgment/ Trials in Absence* | Part 24.12 & Part 25.2 (b) | Part 12 | Criminal Practice Direction [2015] EWCA Crim 1567 (as amended), Division III 14B, 14E & 14F | None |
| *Setting Aside/Varying Default Judgment/ Conviction* | Parts 28.4 and 44.3 | Part 13 | None but see Magistrates' Courts Act 1980, s.14, s.16E and s.142 | None |

| | | | |
|---|---|---|---|
| *Defence and Reply* | Part 15.4 | Part 15 | Criminal Practice Direction [2015] EWCA Crim 1567 (as amended), Division IV 15A | Practice Direction Part 15 |
| *Statements of Case/ Forms* | Part 5 & 8 | Part 16 | Criminal Practice Direction [2015] EWCA Crim 1567 (as amended), Division I 5A | Practice Direction Part 16 |
| *Request for Further Information/Specific Disclosure* | Part 15.5 | Part 18 | Criminal Practice Direction [2015] EWCA Crim 1567 (as amended), Division IV 15A | Practice Direction Part 18 |
| *Counterclaims and Additional Claims/ Offences* | Part 7.3 | Part 20 | N/A | Practice Direction Part 20 |
| *Amendments* | Part 3.30 | Part 17 | Criminal Practice Direction [2015] EWCA Crim 1567 (as amended), Division I 3A and Division II 10A.10 | Practice Direction Part 17 |
| *Statements/ Declarations of Truth* | Part 16.2 | Part 22 | Criminal Practice Direction [2015] EWCA Crim 1567 (as amended), Division V 16A and 19B | Practice Direction Part 22 |
| *Interim Hearings* | Parts 9, 12, 13 & 14, 3.9, 3.11, 3.16, 3.21, 3.22–3.26, 3.28–3.32 | Part 23 | Criminal Practice Direction [2015] EWCA Crim 1567 (as amended), Division I 3E, Division I 7A and 9A, Division III and Division V 22A | Practice Direction Part 23A & 23B |
| *Summary Judgment* | N/A | Part 24 | N/A | Practice Direction Part 24 |
| *Interim Remedies and Security for Costs* | Part 47 | Part 25 | Criminal Practice Direction [2015] EWCA Crim 1567 (as amended), Division III 14C and 14F | Practice Direction Part 25A & 25B |
| *Allocation/Listing/ Transfer* | Part 9 (Allocation anc sending for trial) | Part 26.7–10 (Allocation) / Part 30 (Transfer) | Criminal Practice Direction [2015] EWCA Crim 1567 (as amended), Division II 9A, Division XIII F, G and E | Practice Direction Part 26 and Part 30 |

*(Continued)*

(Continued)

| Steps in Litigation | Criminal Procedure Rules | Civil Procedure Rules | Criminal Practice Directions | Civil Practice Directions |
|---|---|---|---|---|
| Track System (small, fast and multi) | N/A | Parts 27–29 | Criminal Practice Direction [2015] EWCA Crim 1567 (as amended), Division II 9A | Practice Direction Part 27A & 27B |
| Warrants/Writs | Part 13 | Part 83, 87 | Criminal Practice Direction Division XI [2015] EWCA Crim 1567 (as amended), 47A & 47B | Practice Direction Part 83 |
| Disclosure | Part 8 & 15 | Part 31 | Criminal Practice Direction Division IV [2015] EWCA Crim 1567 (as amended), 15A and Division II 8A | Practice Direction Part 31A, 31B, 31C |
| Evidence | Parts 19–23 | Part 32 and Part 35 | Criminal Practice Direction Division I [2015] EWCA Crim 1567 (as amended), 3B & 3R, 3D–3G, Division V 16A, 16B, 16C, 18A, 18B, 18C, 18D, 18E, 19A, 19B, 19C, 21A, 22A, 23A | Practice Direction Part 32 and Part PD 35 |
| Witnesses and Depositions | Parts 16, 17, 18 and 19 | Part 34 | Criminal Practice Direction Division I [2015] EWCA Crim 1567 (as amended), 3N Division IV 16A, 16C, 18A–18E and 19B–19C | Practice Direction Part 1A, 34 and 57AC |
| Experts | Part 19 | Part 35 | Criminal Practice Direction Division I [2015] EWCA Crim 1567 (as amended), 3P and Criminal Practice Direction [2015] EWCA Crim 1567 (as amended), Division V 19A, 19B & 19C, Division VII R | Practice Direction Part 35 |
| Offers to Settle/ Prosecution Agreements | Part 11 (Prosecution Agreements) | Part 36 (Offers to Settle) | None but see Crime and Courts Act 2013 Schedule 17 | Practice Direction Part 36 |
| Discontinuance | Part 12 | Part 38 | None | None |
| Trial | Parts 24–27 | Part 26.6 & 26.11 | Criminal Practice Direction [2015] EWCA Crim 1567 (as amended), Division III 14E & 14G and Division VI 24A–26Q Division X111F | Practice Direction Part 2B, 2F,40E, 51P, 57AB (shorter and flexible trials schemes) |

| | | | Criminal Practice Direction | Practice Direction |
|---|---|---|---|---|
| *Judgments/ Damages* | Part 24, Part 25 and Part 33 | Parts 40 & 41 | Criminal Practice Direction [2015] EWCA Crim 1567 (as amended), Division VI and Division XIII C–F | Practice Direction Part 40A, 40B, 40D, 40E, 41A & 41B |
| *Fixed Costs* | N/A | Part 45 | N/A | Practice Direction Part 45 |
| *Costs Generally* | Part 45 | Parts 44, 46, 47 & 48 | Criminal Practice Direction Division X [2015] EWCA Crim 1567 (as amended) | Practice Direction Part 44, 46, 47, 48 |
| *Appeals* | Parts 27 & 34–43 | Part 52 | Criminal Practice Direction Division III [2015] EWCA Crim 1567 (as amended), 14H, Criminal Practice Direction Division IX [2015] EWCA Crim 1567 (as amended), 34A–H & 44A | Practice Direction Part 52A, 52B, 52C, 52D, 52E |
| *Enforcement/ Sentencing* | Part 28–32 (Sentencing) | Parts 70–89 (Enforcement) | Criminal Practice Direction Division VIII [2015] EWCA Crim 1567 (as amended), A–R | Practice Direction – Civil Recovery Proceedings, Practice Direction Part 70A, 70B, 71, 72, 73, 74A, 74B, 75, 83, 84 |
| *Contempt of Court* | Part 48 | Part 81 | Criminal Practice Direction Division XI [2015] EWCA Crim 1567 (as amended), 48A | None |
| *Extradition* | Part 50 | N/A | Criminal Practice Direction Division XI [2015] EWCA Crim 1567 (as amended), 50A–50F | N/A |
| *Children and Protected Parties* | Part 9.3 | Part 21 & Part 26.6B | Criminal Practice Direction Division I [2015] EWCA Crim 1567 (as amended), 3D, 3E, 3F & 3G and Criminal Practice Direction Division V [2015] EWCA Crim 1567 (as amended), 17A | Practice Direction Part 1A, Practice Direction Part 21 |

# Appendix B

# Table of Evidential Rules

| Trial Evidence | Criminal Legislation and Rules | Civil Legislation and Rules | Criminal 'Synopsis Case' | Civil 'Synopsis Case' |
|---|---|---|---|---|
| *Privilege* | Police and Criminal Evidence Act 1984, s. 10 | Civil Evidence Act 1968, s. 14 & ss. 16–17, Senior Courts Act 1981, s. 72 and Civil Procedure Rules Part 31.20 and PD 31A para 6.1 & 6.2 | *R v Seaton* [2010] EWCA Crim 1980 | *Civil Aviation Authority v R (on the application of Jet2.com Ltd)* [2020] EWCA Civ 35 |
| *Public Interest Immunity* | Criminal Procedure and Investigation Act 1996, s. 3(6), s. 7A(8), s. 8(5) & s. 21 (2), Police and Criminal Evidence Act 1984, ss. 11, 13 & 14 and Criminal Procedure Rules Part 15.3 | Civil Evidence Act 1968, s. 17 and Civil Procedure Rules Part 31.19 Justice and Security Act 2013, Part 2 | *R v H and C* [2004] UKHL 3 | *Ashworth Security Hospital v MGN Ltd* [2002] UKHL 29 |
| *Competence and Compellability of Witnesses* | Youth Justice and Criminal Evidence Act 1999, ss. 53–55 (**non-defendants' evidence**), Criminal Evidence Act 1898, s. 1(1) (**defendant's evidence**), Police and Criminal Evidence Act 1984, s. 80 (**spouses' evidence**), Youth Justice and Criminal Evidence Act 1999, ss. 16, 17 & 19(6) and ss. 23–30 and Criminal Procedure Rules Part 18 (**special measures**), Coroners and Justice Act 2009, ss. 86–97 (**anonymity orders**) and Criminal Procedure Rules Parts 16 (**witness statements**), Crown Court Compendium, section 10, Youth Court Bench Book, (**children and vulnerable witnesses**) | Children Act 1989, s. 96(2) (**children**) and Civil Procedure Rules Part 32 (**all witnesses**) | *R v F* [2013] EWCA Crim 424 (**vulnerable witnesses**), *R v Mayers* [2009] EWCA Crim 2989 (**anonymity orders**) | *J v B* [2002] EWCA Civ 1661 |

| | | | | |
|---|---|---|---|---|
| *Improperly Obtained Evidence* | Police and Criminal Evidence Act 1984, s. 78 and s. 82(3) | Senior Courts Act 1981, s. 31 and Civil Procedure Rules, Part 32.1 | *R v Looseley* [2001] UKHL 53 | *Mustard v Flower and Others* [2019] EWHC 2623 |
| *Identification Evidence* | Police and Criminal Evidence Act 1984, Code D and s. 61 & s. 63 | Crown Court Compendium, s. 15 | *R v Forbes* [2000] UKHL 66 | N/A |
| *Confessions and Admissions* | Police and Criminal Evidence Act 1984, Code C, Code E, s. 76(2)(a) & (b), s. 77, s. 78 & s. 82(1), Criminal Justice Act 2003, s. 118 and Criminal Procedure Rules, Part 24.6, 25.13 | Civil Procedure Rules, Part 14, Part 32.18–19 | *R v Mushtaq* [2005] UKHL 25 | *Sowerby v Charlton* [2005] EWCA Civ 1610 (**pre-action admissions**), *Woodland v Stopford and Others* [2011] EWCA Civ 266 (**withdrawal of admissions**) |
| *Hearsay* | Criminal Justice Act 2003, ss. 114–126, Criminal procedure Rules, Part 20, Crown Court Compendium, s. 14 | Civil Evidence Act 1995, ss. 1–7 and Civil Procedure Rules, Part 32.1, Part 33 | *Riat and Others v R* [2012] EWCA Crim 1509 | *Shagang Shipping Company Ltd v HNA Group Company Ltd* [2020] UKSC 34 |
| *Character Evidence* | Criminal Justice Act 2003, ss. 98–108 and Criminal Procedure Rules, Part 21, Crown Court Compendium, ss. 11 & 12 | Civil Evidence Act 1968, ss. 11 & 13 and Civil Procedure Rules, Part 32.1 | *R v Hunter and Others* [2015] EWCA 631 (**good character**) and *Brewster and Cromwell v R* [2010] EWCA Crim 1194 (**bad character of a non-defendant**) *Stanton v R* [2021] EWCA Crim 1075 (**Defendant's bad character**) | *O'Brien v Chief Constable of South Wales Police* [2005] UKHL 26 |

*(Continued)*

(Continued)

| Trial Evidence | Criminal Legislation and Rules | Civil Legislation and Rules | Criminal 'Synopsis Case' | Civil 'Synopsis Case' |
|---|---|---|---|---|
| Silence and Denials | Criminal Justice and Public Order Act 1994, ss. 34–38, Crown Court Compendium, ss. 16 & 17 | Civil Procedure Rules, Part 12, Part 15 and Part 32.1 | Beckles v UK [2002] ECHR 661 | Andreewitch v Moutreuil [2020] EWCA Civ 382 |
| Opinion Evidence | Criminal Justice Act 2003, s. 118, s. 127 and Criminal Procedure Rules Part 19 (Experts), Crown Court Compendium, s. 10 | Civil Evidence Act 1972, ss. 1–3 and Civil Procedure Rules, Part 35 | R v Reed and Others [2009] EWCA Crim 2698 | Meadow v General Medical Council [2007] 1 All ER 1 |
| Supporting Evidence | Criminal Justice Act 1988, s. 34(2), Criminal Justice and Public Order Act 1994, s. 32(1), Perjury Act, s. 13, Treason Act 1945, s. 1, Road Traffic Regulation Act 1984, s. 89(2). Crown Court Compendium, s. 10 | Civil Procedure Rules, Part 32.1, Part 33.6 | R v Makanjuola [1995] 3 All ER 730 | O'Brien v Chief Constable of South Wales Police [2005] UKHL 26 |
| Lies | Perjury Act 1911 Crown Court Compendium section 16.3 | Contempt of Court Act 1981, and Civil Procedure Rules, Part 32.14, Part 81 | Murray v The Queen [2016] EWCA Crim 1051 | Liverpool Victoria Insurance Company Ltd v Zafar [2019] EWCA 392 |

# PART C
## Knowledge Revealed

This section provides suggested answers and guidance for approaching exercises, problem questions and case studies within this textbook. The case study answers are intended as a starting point for developing arguments and should not be taken as the definitive list of possible answers for each scenario. The author welcomes any constructive feedback, comments and suggestions from practitioners, academics and students on refining the text exercises and case studies for future editions.

# Suggested Answers for Chapter 1

## Exercise A – Problem Question

- This is an example of where there is possibly be a clash between the SRA Principles and the SRA Code of Conduct. Under Code 3 you have a duty of confidentiality to your client; to inform the prosecution about the missed convictions would be a breach of the duty of confidentiality. In addition, Code 2 states that you must "draw the court's attention to relevant cases and statutory provisions, or procedural irregularities of which you are aware, and which are likely to have a material effect on the outcome of proceedings" (2.7). It could be argued that the prosecution's failure to disclose all convictions could be regarded as a procedural irregularity under the duty of disclosure found in CrimPR Part 15 and Criminal Practice Direction IV. Also the Criminal Practice Direction 2015 (as amended) places the responsibility of the prosecution to ensure that the police national computer printout of convictions is up to date (see 8A.8). However, it could be argued that failing to pass on important information that you are aware of might be regarded as a failure to act with honesty under Principle 4. The way to resolve this conflict is to follow the one that best serves the public interest. It could therefore be argued that the public interest would best be served by preserving the fundamental principle of law that the prosecution must prove their case and the defendant remains innocent until proven guilty. There is not a reverse burden of proof on the defendant in these circumstances or a requirement to assist the prosecution in building its case against the defendant. To inform the prosecution of the missed convictions would arguably serve to assist the prosecution in preparing its case. The advocate's duty of confidentiality remains intact against the prosecution. However, the duty not to mislead the court is an important one and so if you were called upon in court to confirm whether the list of convictions was correct, you could not lie to the court and state that they are correct. This is because the wider public interest would be to assist the administration of justice to enable the court to function effectively.

# Exercise B – Multiple Choice Tests

## Test One

**The correct answer is 4.** This is because although there is a clear conflict of interest between your duty of confidentiality to the client/acting in your client's best interests and your duty not to mislead the court, observing the duty to the court is the one that is likely to best serve the wider public interest. The SRA Code of Conduct chapters 2.2 and 2.4 state that you could not seek to influence the evidence or help to generate false evidence. In particular, you could not make false assertions or put forward, statements, representations or submissions to the court that are untrue. The duty to the court is to only present facts and information that you know to be true. It does not, however, require you to reveal weaknesses in your client's case. As such, as long as your client does not expect you to mislead the court about the extent of his injury you are not required to immediately tell the court what you know.

## Test Two

**The correct answer is 3.** This is because whilst it is true that in a criminal case an expert must disclose the nature of their evidence in the form of reports, which have been served on all parties concerned before the trial, an expert may still be called to give testimony in court. In addition, an expert has an overriding duty to the court (see Criminal Procedure Rules Part 19.2) and this duty overrides their obligations to those who instruct them. As such, if the expert has reservations about her findings in her earlier report, then she must draw this to the court's attention, regardless of whether the evidence has not been previously disclosed or whether you raise any objections. As such, the sensible way to proceed is to test the strengths of those reservations through your questioning of the expert. At this stage, it is far too early to advise your client to change their plea as you do not have all the facts available to make an assessment as to whether this would be the best advice for your client. You cannot lie to the court by stating that the expert is ill.

# Suggested Answers for Chapter 2

## Exercise A – Problem Question

Section 319(2)(g) of the Communications Act 2003 states that any advertisement that contravenes the prohibition against political advertising contained in s. 321(2) shall not be included in any television or radio services.

Section 321(2)(a) defines political advertising as including an advertisement by or on behalf of a body whose objects are wholly or mainly of a political nature.

Section 321(b) defines political advertising as also including an advertisement directed at a political end.

Some suggested arguments in support of IMA's case might be:

1. Using the **literal rule**, it could be argued that in relation to s. 321(2)(a) an App containing just one political meme out of 50 memes cannot be said to show that IMA's objects are of a 'wholly or mainly' political nature. If 'wholly' or 'mainly' are given their ordinary meaning this would suggest the App should have at least over half of the memes as political memes.
2. Using the **literal rule**, whilst it could be argued that a meme about the voting system has the potential to influence public opinion, it cannot be said for the purposes of s. 321(3)(f) that the voting system in the UK is a matter of 'controversy'. If one gives the word 'controversy' its ordinary meaning it would denote a prolonged contentious public debate or disagreement rather than a mere difference of opinion or political divide about how the current voting system operates.
3. Using the **golden rule**, it could be argued that for the purposes of s. 321(2)(b), if we take the sentence as a whole then the words "an advertisement directed towards a political end" would focus on the product that is being advertised (the App) rather than the political meme which is not itself the purpose of the advert. The App is directed towards humour and is a collection of humorous messages and therefore does not have a political end. 'End' in this context should be interpreted to mean 'outcome' or 'goal'.
4. Using the **golden rule**, if one were to read s. 319 and s. 321 together and consider them in the context of the whole statute then these sections would seem to be

aimed at preventing political activities that might influence the public to, for example, vote for a particular political party or lobby for changes to the law. The sections were not intended to prevent politics being the object of humour.

5.  Using the **purposive rule** to argue that memes are an internet practice that was not around at the time of the passing of the 2003 Act but are commonly used to communicate satire for all aspects of life including political life but do not necessarily have the ability to 'influence' the outcome of elections or referendums as required by the wording of s. 321(3)(a) unless the internet was flooded with such memes during the election period. The internet has become a much more effective way of reaching and influencing people than radio.

# Exercise B – Multiple Choice Tests

## Test One

The correct answer is 3 this is because the Practice Directions (Judgments: Form and Citation) states that where a case has a neutral citation this should be used first followed by the law report citation - see discussion in Chapter 2, 2.4.3.

## Test Two

The correct answer is 2 and 4 because they are both false. Two is false because any opposing party or a court is likely to object to the use of the client's own accountant as experts must be independent. 4 is false because an expert's duty is to the court not the instructing party (see Chapter 2, 2.3.1).

# Suggested Answers for Chapter 3

## Exercise A – Problem Question

The errors that would have occurred during the hearing relate to court etiquette and arguments. These are as follows:

1. It is your opponent's interim application and therefore they should have started and spoken first instead of you.
2. A District Judge in the County Court who is hearing an interim application is addressed as Sir/Madam.
3. You should avoid referring to your client in court as 'my client' and instead refer to them by their litigation status or their name.
4. You should not present your argument based on what your client thinks. Instead, your arguments should be based on the law.
5. Your argument that CPR 6.1 is simply unreasonable is not a valid argument and is instead merely opinion. You should make clear arguments supported by law. For example, does the district judge have a discretion to disapply the required time period? If so, where is this to be found in the civil procedure rules? Why should the district judge exercise his/her discretion in your client's favour?
6. You should ideally refer to a barrister as 'my learned friend'.

You could therefore have selected any three from the above list.

## Exercise B – Multiple Choice Tests

### Test One
The correct answer is 2, 3, 4 and 5 (4 is wrong because you would not ordinarily address a new client by their first name).

### Test Two
The correct answer is 2 (because this is false, as Aristotle called the ability to prove 'logos').

# Suggested Answers for Chapter 4

## Exercise A – Problem Question

The scenario firstly raises issues around competency and secondly in relation to the ability to exercise rights of audience. It is important to ensure that when performing a legal task that your legal knowledge is current and that it is of sufficient depth and detail to enable you to properly advise and make representations or put forward legal arguments. As you do not have the requisite knowledge of possession actions you should not have agreed to handle this case. Given that your professional body's competency framework would expect you to be able to perform the task of advocacy to an acceptable standard, you could not do this given your limited knowledge of possession actions. The correct approach would have been to apply to the court for the case to be adjourned until such time as an appropriately qualified advocate could attend.

You will recall that in this chapter we looked at rules governing rights of audience. As a trainee solicitor you would not, at this stage, have completed the requisite training and been registered to obtain a practising certificate that would enable you to exercise rights of audience – see the Legal Services Act 2007, Part 3, s. 12 and Schedule 2. It is a criminal offence for someone who does not have rights of audience or the right to conduct litigation to exercise that right (see Legal Services Act 2007, s. 14). This offence carries a maximum sentence of 12 months (Magistrates' Court) or two years (Crown Court). However, it will be a defence if the person did not know, or could not have known that they were committing such an offence. It may be less difficult to argue that you were not aware that you did not have rights of audience given that it is part of your responsibility to acquaint yourself with your professional body's rules and guidance and codes of conduct.

By attending court and failing to explain your professional status to the court clerk it could be argued that you have acted unethically by being dishonest and/or that your actions lack integrity. It is also likely that your actions will be viewed as undermining the public trust and confidence in the profession. Although the application was successful it was not a risk worth taking given the alternative of adjourning the hearing.

# Exercise B – Multiple Choice Tests

## Scenario One

The correct answer is 3 because this is the only part of the report that has complied with CPR PD 35 para 3.

1 is incorrect because CPR PD 35 para 3.1 states that an expert's report should be addressed to the court.

2 is incorrect because whilst the report should include the substance of instructions it should also include details of the expert's qualifications (see para 3.2 (1)).

4 is incorrect because the correct wording for a statement of truth in an expert's report is:

> I confirm that I have made clear which facts and matters referred to in this report are within my own knowledge and which are not. Those that are within my own knowledge I confirm to be true. The opinions I have expressed represent my true and complete professional opinions on the matters to which they refer. I understand that proceedings for contempt of court may be brought against anyone who makes, or causes to be made, a false statement in a document verified by a statement of truth without an honest belief in its truth.

5 is incorrect because para 3.2(2) states that literature or other material that is being relied upon should be included rather than simply unread literature.

## Scenario Two

The correct answer is 2 because children under 14 are permitted to give unsworn evidence in court.

1 is incorrect because the age of criminal liability is ten and so a 13-year-old child can be charged with an offence.

3 is incorrect because the case will be heard in the Youth Court of the Magistrates' Court rather than an adult court.

4 is incorrect because the Mental Capacity Act 2005 does not apply here because capacity under the Act is defined as mental incapacity not incapacity due to age. There is nothing to suggest that the client lacks mental capacity.

5 is incorrect because anonymity orders are reserved for situations where a witness will not give evidence without an order protecting their identity and the interests of justice require such an order to be made (see s. 88 of the Coroners and Justice Act 2009). Children are in any event entitled to reporting restrictions in the Youth Court which would prevent their identity being revealed in the media. This is not the same as an anonymity order.

# Suggested Answers for Chapter 5

## Exercise 1 (Bail)

You are acting for the defence in a crown court bail application and so it is important to use the correct address for the judge (Your Honour). The first issue to be addressed is whether s. 25 of the Criminal Justice and Public Order ('CJPOA') 1994 applies given that the defendant does not have any previous convictions for the offences listed in s. 25(2). Whilst it is true he has been charged with attempted murder, this is the current charge; s. 25 would only apply if he had a previous charge or conviction for one of the offences mentioned.

The court should be informed that the CPS has failed to provide a list of the defendant's previous convictions despite repeated requests. Even if it could be established that the defendant had previous convictions, he could still come within the 'exceptional circumstances' of s. 25 and be entitled to bail because the case of *O (FC) v Crown Court at Harrow* [2006] UKHL 42 defines 'exceptional circumstances' as meaning no more than that if one were to take into account all the circumstances of the case that there is nothing to suggest the defendant would fail to surrender to custody, commit a crime, interfere with witnesses or obstruct the course of justice. The 'exceptional circumstances' in s. 25 was therefore taken to mean no more than the normal way bail applications would be determined under the Bail Act 1976.

However, s. 25 does contain a presumption of no entitlement to bail which can then be rebutted by a defendant showing exceptional circumstances. According to the case of *O (FC)* the court has to be persuaded that the arguments in favour of the existence of 'exceptional circumstances' outweigh the arguments against. Although s. 25 reads as if the burden of proving the exceptional circumstances lies with the defendant, in fact this case and others used statutory interpretation to 'read down' the provisions. This means the burden of proof remains with the prosecution.

Assuming the judge who hears the bail application accepts that s. 25 of the CJPOA 1994 does not apply, then the arguments can then proceed on the basis of para 2 and 2ZA of Schedule 1 Part 1 of the Bail Act 1976; see below:

a)   Fail to surrender to custody, or
b)   Commit an offence while on bail, or
c)   Interfere with witnesses or otherwise obstruct the course of justice, whether in relation to himself or any other person (para 2).

Note: these para 2 grounds may be more difficult to argue against because the defendant faces charges that carry a custodial sentence; however, the defendant has never been convicted before and so this should be stressed to the court. The risk can be alleviated by offering conditions of bail relating to reporting at the police station and/or the defendant surrendering his passport to the police (see CrimPR Part 14.14).

d)   The defendant would engage in conduct that would or is likely to cause physical or mental injury to an 'associated person' or cause them to fear physical violence (para 2ZA).

Note: this ground may be more difficult to argue given the allegation of violence by the defendant against his wife. An 'associated person' is defined by s. 62(3) of the Family Law Act 1969 as the defendant's relatives, spouse, civil partner, cohabitee or person the defendant is in an intimate relationship with. The risk can be alleviated by offering conditions of bail that require the defendant to reside away from the matrimonial home (see CrimPR Part 14.11).

In terms of submissions, it is easy to consider all four grounds (para 2 and 2ZA) with reference to all the charges as a whole and by using the Schedule 1 Part 1 para 9 factors as a checklist (as the defendant is not a child, one of the para 9 factors has been removed):

1.   **Nature and seriousness of the offence** (including the likely sentence) – *You might for example try submissions along the following lines*: "Whilst it is true that these are all violent offences that include attempted murder and wounding, the defendant denies the allegations. There are no witnesses to the alleged attack itself and the defendant told police officers that the victim (who is the only witness to the events) inflicted the injuries upon herself. This is clearly a troubled marriage and the background to the events need to be explored in more detail and in time more witnesses are likely to come forward, this may change the nature of what is alleged. The defendant is an upstanding member of the community who has a prestigious award of an OBE for his contribution to business. He wishes nothing more than to clear his name in court."
2.   **Defendant's character, antecedents, associations and community ties** – *You might for example try submissions along the following lines*: "We are instructed that the defendant does not have any criminal offences and the prosecution have not produced evidence to contradict this. There is no evidence to suggest that he would fail to surrender to bail. The defendant cannot therefore be said to pose a risk under Schedule 1 Part 1 of failure to surrender to bail or commit

offences whilst on bail. Whilst we accept the defendant faces charges that carry a custodial sentence, this alone is not a reason to suggest that he is a flight risk. However, if Your Honour takes the view that there is such a risk, the defendant would be prepared to surrender his passport and report to the police station each day as part of his bail conditions. In terms of interfering with witnesses, the defendant currently resides at the matrimonial home which is also the home of the alleged victim. The defendant would be prepared to accept a condition attached to his bail that he should reside elsewhere. He is able to reside at his mother's address."

3.  **The defendant's previous record of fulfilling any obligations on previously being granted bail** – *You might for example try submissions along the following lines*: "The defendant does not have a history of bail or failure to surrender to custody in the past. There is no evidence that he would not fulfil any bail conditions imposed on him today."

4.  **The strength of the evidence against the defendant (except where a defendant's case has been adjourned for inquiries or a report)** – *You might for example try submissions along the following lines*: "As mentioned, Your Honour, the majority of these offences will rest on the word of the defendant against that of the main victim. There were no witnesses to the alleged murder itself or even to the alleged theft of £500. Much of the evidence is circumstantial. The defendant does not deny that he was at the Moonrise Guesthouse and that he went there to find his wife. He denies that he harmed her or that he stole money from the premises."

5.  **If the court considers there is a bail risk, whether the risk would be by engaging in conduct that would, or is likely to, cause physical or mental injury to a person other than the defendant** – *You might for example try submissions along the following lines*: "We accept that the victim may allege that she is afraid of our client and that he poses a continuing risk to her. This is denied but if Your Honour considers that there is a risk of the defendant contacting the victim and that a residence condition is not sufficient, he would be willing to accept a condition of electronic monitoring but only as a last resort. We ask Your Honour to take into consideration the fact that the defendant has a place in society that would be greatly affected if he were to appear at important events wearing an electronic monitoring device. We would argue that any risks the defendant poses can be controlled by the imposition of conditions relating to residence and surrender of passport."

6.  **Any other factors that appear relevant** – *You might for example try submissions along the following lines*: "Although the defendant faces serious charges, it is important to note that no weapon was found either at the guesthouse or at the matrimonial home. The defendant was also arrested at the matrimonial home and there was no attempt by him to flee and evade arrest even though he was not arrested for a few hours after the incidence. Those are my submissions Your Honour."

If the bail application is successful, an application for wasted costs against the prosecution might be possible under the Prosecution of Offences Act 1985, s. 19A(2) if it can be shown that costs were incurred due to "unnecessary or improper act or omission". This might be because the prosecution adopted the procedure as if the charge were one of murder. Section 19(2)(a) allows costs order to be made at any time in the proceedings. It could be argued that bail should have been applied for at a first hearing in the Magistrates' Court rather than waiting for the matter to be sent to the Crown Court under s. 115 of the Coroners and Justice Act 2009. This is because s. 115 does not apply as this was not a murder case but an attempted murder case. Also, there was no evidence that the defendant had previously been charged with attempted murder or any of the other offences. Section 115(3) requires a Crown Court to hear bail decisions within 48 hours after a defendant is brought to the Magistrates' Court but because of delays in the Crown Court the bail application was not heard until five days later. This means the defendant spent longer in custody than he needed to.

# Exercise 2 (Specific Disclosure)

For this type of application, you will be making submissions based on arguments that the disclosure requirements of the Criminal Procedure and Investigations Act 1996 have not been properly followed and that this has placed the defendant at a disadvantage.

You might start by explaining the nature of your application and that it is made under CrimPR Part 15.5. It will be necessary to explain the nature of the material for which you are seeking specific disclosure. This will be all documentation relating to the company 'Global Ethical Trading' that was discovered as a result of searching 41 Tennyson Avenue on or about the early hours of 5 January. It is necessary to also explain why there is reasonable cause to think the prosecution will have that material and so this is where it is important to refer to the witness statement of Simon Montiana and the facts in that witness statement.

It might be appropriate to remind the court that s. 3 of the CPIA 1996 places a duty on the prosecution to disclose any previously undisclosed material which might be capable of undermining the case for the prosecution. The witness statement of Simon Montiana can be said to undermine the credibility of a key prosecution witness and therefore is capable of undermining the prosecution's case. The witness statement should have been disclosed much earlier than it has been (see s. 7A of the 1996 Act).

A reference to the Attorney-General's Guidelines on disclosure would also bolster your arguments, particularly para 6 that states that when deciding whether material satisfies the disclosure test the prosecution should consider factors that include the use that might be made of that evidence on cross-examination. Certainly, the defence would want to cross-examine Mrs Vermont about the truthfulness of her story, particularly the allegation that her husband attacked her to stop her revealing that he had falsified the company accounts.

The prosecution also has a continuing duty to keep disclosure under review (see s. 7A CPIA 1996). Also, the Code of Practice to the 1996 Act sets out a duty to retain material (5.1) and this includes any material casting doubt on the reliability of a witness (5.4) and in particular a prosecution witness (5.5). Such material should be retained until the accused is convicted or acquitted (5.8).

Even if the material (the company documents) was not retained, your firm has made the prosecution aware that it is relevant and the Code of Practice (5.3) places a duty to take steps to obtain it.

You can strengthen your arguments by using a quote from *R v H and C* [2004] UKHL 3. Although this case is primarily about disclosure of sensitive materials, it makes some helpful observation about disclosure generally. A helpful quote can be taken from the case as follows:

> Fairness ordinarily requires that material held by the prosecution which weakens its case or strengthens that of the defendant, if not relied on as part of its formal case against the defendant, should be disclosed to the defence. Bitter experience has shown that miscarriages of justice may occur where such material is withheld from disclosure. The golden rule is that full disclosure of such material should be made.

*[14]*

# Exercise 3 (Hearsay and Character Evidence)

For this application you will now look at the facts of the case from the prosecution's point of view. The prosecution intends to make two applications at the hearing and so the submissions should explain to the judge the nature of each application and which application will be addressed first in the submissions.

## Hearsay Evidence of Callum Proustin

Before s. 116 of the Criminal Justice Act ('CJA') 2003 can be used to admit hearsay evidence, the pre-conditions under s. 116(1) must be met and so the prosecution case might start by confirming to the court that:

1. If Callum Proustin had given evidence in court his evidence would have been admissible as evidence of the matters contained in the statement (i.e. Callum Proustin would have been a competent witness and there is nothing in the evidence that would have been excluded if he had given that evidence in person at court).

2.  That the prosecution is able to identify the person who made the statement as Callum Proustin and that Callum Proustin's identity can be established to the court's satisfaction. This provision is clearly satisfied as the prosecution is not seeking to admit Callum Proustin's evidence as an anonymous witness. It has his name and address.

The prosecution should then set the relevant ground under s. 116 (2) that it will be relying on, namely s. 116(2)(c) – Callum Proustin will be outside the UK at the time of the trial. The issue however is whether is it reasonably practicable to get him to attend. This ground must also be proved to the standard of beyond reasonable doubt.

The prosecution will need to explain what efforts have been made to get Mr Proustin to attend trial. The prosecution should explain that a witness summons was served on him. However, this will not necessarily guarantee his attendance at the trial as he may still refuse to attend or inform the court that he is unable to attend. Whilst technically he could be found in contempt of court by refusing to appear, it may be more difficult to enforce any penalty or sanctions as he is now living outside the UK.

A pre-CJA 2003 case which is still relevant to this area of law is *R v Castillo* [1996] 1 Cr App R 438. In that case, the court set out guidance on what might amount to 'reasonably practicable' steps to take to secure an absent witness's attendance at court. The judge will need to consider how relevant Callum Proustin's evidence is to the issues and how prejudicial it would be to the defence's case if the witness statement were admitted.

The defence may argue Callum Proustin is a central witness and that they would be disadvantaged by being denied an opportunity to cross-examine him if the court relies just on his witness evidence. The defence may ask the judge to exercise his/her discretion to exclude the witness statement under s. 126 CJA 2003.

The prosecution should pre-empt such arguments and so may argue that as Callum Proustin did not witness the attempted murder or the theft that is related to the allegation of burglary, he is not a material witness in that sense. He is important merely to place the defendant at the scene. The defendant does not deny that he was present at the Moonrise Guesthouse and that he went upstairs without permission to see his wife, June Vermont. As such, there would not be any prejudice to the defence in admitting Mr Proustin's evidence as hearsay evidence. The difficulty with this is if the prosecution is relying on the part of his evidence about the criminal damage and theft to suggest that the defendant carried out these offences then the defence would want the opportunity to cross-examine Mr Proustin.

The Court of Appeal in the case of *Castillo* also stated that the expense and inconvenience of securing a witness's attendance should be taken into account by the judge. One option that might be suggested by the prosecution is for the court to consider the use of video-link technology from a court in Dunedin to enable Mr Proustin to give evidence at the trial in the UK. This is permissible under s. 51 of the Criminal Justice Act 2003 either as live audio link or live video link. The court can allow a witness (who is not the defendant) to give live link evidence; this provision could therefore apply to Mr Proustin. The judge must be satisfied it is in the interests of justice to make such an order to allow Callum Proustin to give evidence (see s. 51(4)). The case of *R v Gyima (Edward)* [2007] EWCA Crim 429 confirms that whether a witness should be allowed to give evidence by video-link is at the discretion of a judge as it involves considerable cost in arranging the video evidence. This may not be regarded as a 'reasonably practicable' means to get Mr Proustin to attend.

Even if the prosecution cannot show it has taken all steps 'reasonably practicable' to ensure Mr Proustin's attendance, it could ask the judge to use his/her inclusionary discretion to include the evidence in any event. However, this would require the prosecution to satisfy the 'interests of justice' test (see s. 114 (1) (d) CJA 2003). The prosecution should consider whether there are any other witnesses who could corroborate what Callum Proustin says in his evidence (e.g. other guests and staff who were present and saw the defendant). If so, the evidence becomes less relevant and there may be justification for admitting it as hearsay evidence because the evidence then becomes less prejudicial.

Equally, if the evidence is not regarded as important evidence and if other witnesses can give similar evidence, then the court might feel that the trial can proceed without Mr. Proustin's evidence at all.

The prosecution should be mindful of the fact that Mr Proustin's evidence also contains evidence about the state of mind of the defendant at the time of the attack as he describes the defendant as 'agitated'. If the prosecution intends to rely on this evidence to show that Mr Proustin was agitated it would need to admit such statements as part of the '*res gestae*' under s. 118(4) CJA 2003 as statements that relate to a physical sensation or a mental state. The statement may therefore contain multiple hearsay within the meaning of s. 121 CJA 2003. As it does not fall under s. 117, s. 119 or s. 120, it will only be admissible if the defence agrees (s. 114 (1)(c)) to its admission or if the judge admits it under the interests of justice test (s. 114 (1) (d)).

The case of *Riat and Others v R* [2012] EWCA Crim 1509 states that the court should consider whether the admission of the evidence of the absent witness poses a risk of unreliability and if so to what extent and whether the reliability of the evidence can be tested and assessed (see paras 6–7 of the judgment). The prosecution may seek to rely on arguments that the evidence of Mr Proustin is reliable evidence that can be tested by the evidence of other witnesses including June Vermont, the victim.

## Character Evidence of Simon Montiana

The starting point is that permission of the court is needed for the evidence of Simon Montiana's previous convictions to be used at trial (see s. 100(4) of the Criminal Justice Act 2003).

The evidence to be adduced falls within the definition of bad character under s. 98 of the Criminal Justice Act (CJA) 2003 because it is "disposition towards misconduct (other than evidence which has to do with the alleged facts of the offence for which the defendant is charged) or is evidence in connection with the investigation or prosecution of that offence." Misconduct means previous convictions or other reprehensible behaviour (s. 112 of the CJA 2003).

Under s. 100(1)(b) of the CJA 2003 the evidence of Simon Montiana (a non-defendant) must have 'probative value' in relation to a matter in issue in the proceedings and be of substantial importance in the context of the case. It is within the judgment or discretion of a judge to decide if the previous convictions of Simon Montiana have probative value.

It could be argued that a matter in issue in the proceedings is who was responsible for the company fraud as it is alleged that the motivation for the attack on Mrs Vermont was to silence her and stop her revealing the fraud. However, if evidence suggests that she was in fact involved in the fraud and not the defendant, this will remove a motive for the attack upon her. The prosecution wishes to use the evidence of the previous convictions to discredit Simon Montiana during cross-examination so that its main prosecution witness's evidence remains intact. Therefore, Mr Montiana's evidence may be regarded as material to the case.

In deciding whether the evidence has probative value and is of substantial importance, the court will consider the factors in s. 100(3). One way of structuring submissions is therefore for the prosecution advocate to address the factors in s. 100(3).

The relevant factors based on the facts of the case are:

a) **The nature and number of the events to which the conviction relates** – there are two convictions.
b) **When those events are alleged to have happene**d – the speeding conviction is more recent (2020) than the fraud conviction (2010).
c) **Where the evidence suggests a person's misconduct and that person is responsible for the misconduct charged and the identity of the person responsible for the misconduct charged is disputed** – the prosecution may try to tie in some knowledge on the part of Mr Montiana about the company fraud as he has a conviction for fraud in the past (although this is insurance rather than company fraud) to suggest he is also tied into the misconduct.

The difficulty with this application is in showing that Mr Montiana's convictions are of 'substantial importance'. This is because they may be unrelated to the actual question of his credibility as a witness. The case of *Brewster and Cromwell v R* [2010] EWCA Crim 1194 is authority for stating that if evidence of misconduct is to be used to attack a witness's credibility it must undermine the credibility directly and not indirectly. The speeding conviction (2020) is largely irrelevant as it only indirectly undermines credibility. The conviction for fraud is more relevant as it is insurance fraud and shows Mr Montiana is capable of making false statements. However, the conviction might be regarded as 'stale' in the sense of very old. It will be necessary to convince the court that a sole conviction, which is relatively old, can still be of substantial importance. The defence may ask the court to refuse permission for the prosecution to rely on s. 100(1)(b) due to its prejudicial nature to the witness who is merely trying to assist the court in its administration of justice function.

# Suggested Answers for Chapter 6

## Exercise 1 Memorandum A – Setting Aside a Default Judgment

The action is in the High Court and so the interim application will be heard by a Master and so the appropriate mode of address to use is 'Master' (for both male and female judges).

Part 13 of the Civil Procedure Rules ('CPR') is the rule that governs this application together with Part 23 which governs interim applications generally. The rules should be read in conjunction with any accompanying practice direction. Whilst Part 23 has an accompanying practice direction, there is not an associated practice direction for Part 13.

Under Part 13.3 it will be necessary to persuade the judge that if the default judgment is set aside, the defendant has a real prospect of successfully defending the action. It is also necessary to show, according to *Core-Export Spa v Yang Ming Marine Transportation Corporation* [2020] EWHC 425 (comm) that the application to set aside judgment was made promptly and without substantial delay. The witness statement supporting the application is dated three days after the default judgment and so it can be argued that the defendant acted promptly. This is not therefore a situation where the application to set aside is likely to be denied because the application itself was not made promptly as occurred in *Cranfield and Another v Bridgegrove Ltd* [2003] EWCA Civ 656.

In terms of the process for making an interim application, the Part 23 requirements appear to have been adhered to as we are told in the memorandum that both an application notice and a witness statement have been filed in court and copies served on the claimants' solicitors. The defendant's solicitor's witness statement also follows the format under Part 32.6, 32.8 and PD 32 paras 17–23. The witness statement also contains a statement of truth with the correct wording under PD 32 para 20.2.

The witness statement of Margrit Munsted identifies the particular grounds under Part 13 on which the application is being made. You should therefore match the facts to each ground in your submissions, for example, the defendant has a real prospect of success because it is alleged the defendant was speeding and also the defendant denies making an admission.

When analysing the grounds for setting aside the judgment in default under Part 13, attention should also be paid to any procedural irregularities with regard to the claim as a whole. The claimants' solicitors do not appear to have followed the relevant pre-action protocol for personal injury claims or the Practice Direction on Pre-action Conduct and Protocols and it could be argued that this is an important failure (see paras 15 and 16 of the practice direction and CPR Part 3.1(4)–(6)).

A case that may be helpful here is *Denton and Others v TH White Ltd and Others* [2014] EWCA Civ 906. In this case (which was largely about relief from sanctions) the Court of Appeal considered the issue of setting aside due to failure to comply with court orders. This can equally be applied to failure to comply with procedural rules. The court held it was important to consider whether the failure was of a serious or significant nature, whether there was good reason for the failure and lastly whether taking into account all the circumstances, the default judgment should be set side.

Whilst the claimants' solicitors have sent a letter of claim as required by para 5 and Annex B of the protocol, they have not given the required 21-day period to allow the defendants to submit a response or allowed for a three-month period of investigation (see paras 1.6 and 6 of the protocol). There are no limitation issues regarding the claim (the action has ample time within the three-year limitation period under s. 11 of the Limitation Act 1980). The particulars of claim states that the claim is worth more than £50,000 and so the main personal injury pre-action protocol (rather than the Pre-Action Protocol for Low Value Personal Injury Claims in Road Traffic Accidents) is the one to consider. It is worth referring to CPR Part 3.4 which provides that when giving directions the court will also have regard to whether or not a person has complied with a pre-action protocol. This failure to comply with the pre-action protocol is therefore an important consideration.

The claimants' solicitors also failed to file a certificate of service in court in accordance with CPR Part 6.17(2)(a). This is an important point as CPR Part 6.17(2)(b) goes on to state that judgment in default cannot be entered where a certificate of service has not been filed. As such, there is a strong argument here that the judgment in default has been wrongly entered.

However, this defect may not be regarded as serious as in *Henriksen v Pires* [2011] EWCA Civ 1720 the court held that the defendant had not suffered any meaningful prejudice because of the claimant's failure to properly file a certificate of service. The defendant admits receiving the letter of claim and the particulars of claim and therefore had ample time to instruct solicitors and file an acknowledgement of service and/or defence before judgment in default was entered. The facts of this case can, however, be distinguished from the matters in this fact pattern because the defendant's tenants may have played an active role in knowingly failing to pass on important documents. It is also important to note that whilst the case of *Henriksen* makes it clear that the absence of a certificate of service will not automatically lead to an order to set aside the default judgment, it remains a matter that is at the discretion of the judge.

It is important to pre-empt your opponent's arguments and it may be that the claimant's solicitors will remind the court that they have the power to cure any procedural irregularities under CPR Part 3.

When arguing whether there are good reasons for the court to set aside the default judgment it is also worth referring to relevant parts of the overriding objective in CPR Part 1 such as Part 1.2(a) (ensuring parties are on an equal footing) and CPR Part 1.2 (f) (ensuring compliance with court rules); these are relevant to the fact that the claimants have breached court rules.

It is important to also ask the court for directions about the future progression of the action if your application to set aside the default judgment is successful. Directions for service of a defence are important as well as directions regarding obtaining medical expert reports (perhaps from joint experts – see CPR Part 35.4).

It is worth noting that if there were to be any procedural irregularities in your client's case that you should make the court aware of this at the earliest opportunity and not wait for your opponent to do so. This is because the SRA Code of Conduct Code 2 states that an advocate should "draw the court's attention to relevant cases and statutory provisions, or procedural irregularities of which you are aware, and which are likely to have a material effect on the outcome of proceedings" (2.7).

It would also be fair to question (privately to your supervising solicitor rather than in any court submissions) whether it is appropriate for your firm to act for both the first and second claimants. You should always be mindful of any potential breaches of the SRA Principles or SRA Code of Conduct found in the SRA Standards and Regulations (see Principle 7 and Code 6). Whilst there does not appear to be a conflict of interest at present because an admission is alleged to have been made by the defendant, this is contested by the defendant who claims it was in fact the first defendant who made the admission (see witness statement of Assiah Proctor). The defendant also alleges negligence on the part of the first claimant who was driving. If this is proved then the second claimant would have a claim against the first claimant for damages (which would in reality be met by the first claimant's insurance company). This can happen despite the first claimant being the second claimant's mother. A conflict of interest could therefore arise in the future which would mean the firm could risk breaching the SRA Standards and Regulations 6.

At the end of a successful application, it is usual to make an order for costs (known as summary assessment of costs). We have considered this in Chapter 4.

# Exercise 2 Memorandum B – Summary Judgment

Summary judgment is an interim application in the High Court and so will be heard by a Master. Again, the appropriate mode of address to use is 'Master' (for both male and female judges).

For this application, the arguments will be based on whether the defendant has a real prospect of successfully defending the claimants' action.

The case of *Swain v Hillman and Others* [1999] EWCA Civ 3053 interprets the word 'real' in this test to mean the opposite of fanciful. The legal principle arising from this case is also that in meeting this test, the court should not attempt to conduct a mini trial. Therefore, it would not be appropriate to explore whether admissions of liability were made and/or the legal effect. This is because the defence itself does not make any admissions other than that the accident occurred. CPR Part 14 has a formal process for admissions which requires the admission to be given in writing.

However, the case of *Royal Brompton Hospital v Hammond (no 5)* [2001] EWCA Civ 550 states that whilst it may not be appropriate for the court to conduct a mini trial, it does not preclude some consideration of the available evidence or the lack of evidence, if this goes to the question of prospects of succeeding at trial. However, the case must be more than merely arguable and must, according to the decision in *ED & F Man Liquid Products v Patel* [2003] EWCA Civ 472, carry a degree of conviction about it. Some further guidance can be found in *Three Rivers District Council v Governor and Company of the Bank of England* [2001] UKHL 16 which reminds us that the 'real prospects of success' test gives the judge a discretionary power and this discretionary power involves exercising judgment about whether a trial should take place or not. This is an assessment rather than a fact-finding exercise (which would be based on calling evidence). The issue is whether there is an absence of any reality of success. If evidence is not to be found in the pleadings but will be available at trial the case should be allowed to proceed to a fuller investigation of the facts according to cases such as *Doncaster Pharmaceuticals Group Ltd v Bolton Pharmaceutical Co 100 Ltd* [2007] FSR 63.

The witness statement of Assiah Proctor also invites the court to strike out the defence under CPR Part 3 as an alternative measure. Whilst the application itself has only been made under Part 24, the court has the power to make alternative orders of its own initiative (see CPR Part 3.3).

Strike out is sought on the basis that the defence does not disclose reasonable grounds for defending the action. CPR PD 3A para 1.6(1) gives examples of where a case discloses no reasonable grounds for defending a case, including where the defendant files a bare denial.

In terms of pre-empting what arguments the defendant may raise, be mindful that the defendant could argue that he has a right to plead his case in general terms until disclosure has occurred, at which point, he can apply to amend his defence to plead specific denials. This was an approach approved in *Arsenal Football Club Plc v Elite Sports Distribution Limited* [2002] EWHC 3057.

In terms of procedural irregularities, it is important to note that whilst the defence contains a statement of truth, it is incomplete and does not contain the full wording required by CPR Part 22(1)(a) and the practice direction to PD 22 para 2.1 (see document 2 for an example of the correct wording). It is possible to argue that the court should apply CPR Part 22.1(b) and preclude the defendant from relying on any evidence in the defence or CPR Part 22.2 which provides that a statement of case (which includes a defence) can be struck out if not verified by a statement of truth.

It is important to pre-empt your opponent's arguments especially on the question of procedural irregularities relating to the statement of truth. The defendant may argue that the statement of truth is merely defective rather than absent altogether. As such, the defendant may ask the court to apply CPR Part 22.4 and order that the defendant amend the defence to contain the correct wording for the statement of truth. The court can deal with a summary judgment by giving further directions rather than dismissing the defence (see CPR Part 24.6).

As a counterargument to this, it could be argued that under CPR Part 3.1(m) the court should be making orders that further the overriding objective. It could be argued that the overriding objective under CPR Part 1.2(b) of saving expense would best be served by dismissing the defence or argued that CPR Part 1.2(f) requires the court to be mindful of its overriding objective to enforce compliance with rules.

This application will always be a difficult one to win if the defendant appears as a litigant-in-person. This is because CPR Part 3.1A(2) recognises that an unrepresented litigant may require a degree of assistance from the court. Litigants-in-person will not always be familiar with court rules and procedure. In *Barton v Wright Hassall LLP* [2018] UKSC 12 the Supreme Court held that whilst allowances should be made for the fact that a party is unrepresented when conducting hearings (including interim hearings), that does not mean the procedural rules should be applied with a lower standard for litigants-in-person. However, as the procedural irregularity can be easily corrected under the rules, and the rules permit this, the argument about procedural irregularities may be more difficult to win if the judge decides to give the defendant an opportunity to correct.

If the application is successful, then the next stage is to ask the court to make an order for costs. As discussed in Chapter 4, the court can make a summary order for costs. The advocate should before attending the hearing file a costs schedule with details of the costs claimed. This will be based on the hourly charging rate identified in the memorandum to this exercise.

Note: The Civil Justice Council Costs Committee ('CJCCC') Guidelines 2021 set out suggested hourly rates for lawyers depending on seniority. The hourly rate of £186 is based on Grade D for London (1) for junior lawyers such as trainee solicitors and paralegals. In its January 2021 consultation paper, the CJCCC suggested these rates should be reviewed regularly in future. Therefore always check to see if the rates have been updated!

# Exercise 3 Memorandum C – Interim Payments

The issue to be argued on this application is whether the claim for £105,000 by way of an interim payment can be considered as a reasonable proportion of the likely amount of the final judgment.

As a starting point, the application can be approached by considering whether CPR Part 25.7(1)(c) is met and this has to be proved to the civil standard of 'on a balance of probabilities' according to *Test Claimants in Franked Investment Income Group Litigation v Revenue & Customs Commissioners (No 2)* [2012] EWCA Civ 57. This means showing on the evidence that if the matter went to trial, Rose Landice (the second claimant and applicant) would obtain judgment for a substantial amount of money. The case of *Test Claimants* defined 'a substantial amount of money' as meaning substantial rather than negligible amounts. It would be wise to therefore refer to the figures in the schedule of loss showing that the total claim exceeds £1 million (see instructions in Memorandum C).

One of the difficulties, however, is that the applicant is alleged to be contributorily negligent due to a failure to wear a seatbelt. It cannot therefore be certain what percentage of contributory liability the judge will determine at trial and therefore, if the applicant succeeds at trial, by how much the damages will be reduced. The defendants might therefore use the same *Test Claimants* case to argue that the applicant is unable on a balance of probabilities to show that the substantial sums claimed in the schedule of loss would actually be recovered at trial. They may refer to the judgment of *Heidelberg Graphic Equipment Ltd v R & C Commissioners* [2009] EWHC 870 (Ch) to argue that the standard of proof, although on a balance of probabilities, still has a high threshold as it is necessary to show the action will succeed at trial rather than that it is likely to succeed at trial.

It is important to note that the *Test Claimants* case criticises the assessment of the standard of proof as set out in the *Heidelberg Graphic* case. Arguments on behalf of the applicants can therefore be found by applying the interpretation placed on the standard of proof as found in the *Test Claimants* case per Aikens LJ (para 38) that the court must be satisfied based on the material before the court at the time of the interim payment application that the claim is likely to succeed at trial.

The court would be assisted by referring to similar cases that have applied a contributory negligence reduction of damages due to a failure to wear a seatbelt. The case of *Froom v Butcher* [1975] EWCA Civ 6 is still the leading case. The guidelines provide for a 25% reduction where the injuries could have been avoided if a seatbelt had been worn. If the injury would have occurred in any event but was made worse by a failure to wear a seatbelt then a reduction of 15% is advised. However, if the injuries would have occurred if no seatbelt had been worn then damages will not be reduced.

It could be argued in rebuttal that there is an evidential burden on the defendants to put forward evidence of contributory negligence. Even if we assume that it can be proved and (as a worst-case scenario) a 25% reduction would be made at trial, the resulting reduced damages could arguably still be considered substantial and the interim payment represents only a small proportion of what would be obtained as damages at trial.

The defendants may take another direction and argue that as the case as a whole involves difficult questions of law, there cannot be any certainty that the applicant will succeed at trial because causation is in issue and therefore the court should not exercise its powers under CPR Part 25.7(1)(c) as the defendant has an arguable defence.

In response to this it could be argued that there is an evidential burden on the respondents to raise any matters in evidence that they feel would show the applicant is unlikely to obtain substantial damages at trial. The defendant was entitled to file evidence under CPR 25.6(4) but has chosen not to do so. It is not enough for the defendants to simply point to their statement of case (the defence) and expect the court to accept this as proof that the applicant's claim will not succeed at trial.

Perhaps the strongest argument that the defendants will have is that the estimate about the house adjustments has come from a medical expert rather than, for example, a surveyor, and therefore the court does not have adequate evidence to assess whether the amount of the interim payment is a reasonable one. Also, the estimate in the medical report is lower than the amounts claimed.

This may be where it is necessary to assess the mood of the court on the day of the application. If the judge seems swayed by arguments that the application is premature or unsupported then perhaps give a concession (after consultation with the litigation friend) that the applicant might be prepared to accept a reduced interim payment in the first instance to allow work to begin whilst final costs are explored. A further application can be made at a later date if further sums are needed.

Again, reference to the overriding objective in CPR Part 1 would be helpful in any arguments made on behalf of the applicant. It could be argued that dealing with the case justly and at proportionate cost could be achieved by making an interim payments order as it would ensure that the case is dealt with expeditiously and fairly (see CPR Part 1.2(d)).

# Suggested Answers for Chapter 7

## Exercise 1

In this exercise you were asked to prepare a 'plea in mitigation'. Based on the relevant sentencing guidelines detailed in your instructions, your arguments might be structured in the following way:

1) **the offence** (including minimising aggravating factors and emphasising mitigating factors)

This is an offence that arguably falls within the lower range for sentencing based on the Sentencing Guidelines: Violent Disorder. This is because none of the category A factors are present as the defendant did not use any firearms or other weapons or incendiary devices during the incident and did not carry out a leading role or target particular individuals or groups. Whilst the jury found that the defendant started the fight, the defendant is adamant that he did not instigate the actual altercation and can be said to have been provoked rather than taking a lead role in starting the argument or disorder.

Category B factors are not present in that whilst the defendant did participate in an incident involving acts of violence and whilst two members of the public were injured as a result of the disorder this was by another defendant who has been found guilty at a separate trial.

This offence therefore should fall into category C for the purposes of the sentencing guidelines and the defence can take issue with the recommendations in the pre-sentence report that places the offence within Category B. The offence involved a lower level of violence as far as the four men who were convicted are concerned.

In terms of harm, it is accepted that some aspects of category 2 are present in that the incident did result in physical injury and led to fear and distress to bystanders who witnessed events and also possibly had an impact on the local community and costs were incurred by a business (the cinema) in terms of damage to a glass door. However, it is argued that none of these events, in terms of the involvement of the defendant can be categorised as 'serious' or 'substantial' as required by the wording in category 2 and therefore should be dealt with at the lower-level category 3.

2)  **the offender** (including the offender's personal circumstances as set out in any pre-sentence report)

The defendant does not have any previous convictions and only has a caution for an offence that he denies committing. The defendant is an individual who has previously held a job requiring responsibility and honesty, and prior to this incident had never been involved in any violent acts. He is a carer for his elderly mother who has Parkinson's and partly due to this and losing his job due to the charges brought against him, has been unable to find work.

3)  **the offender's conduct**

The defendant was not the instigator of the altercation and attempted to walk away when first confronted by Mr Thomas Lennon. It is Mr Lennon who was charged with the more serious offence of wounding. The defendant was involved in the fight that followed but the injured parties sustained minor bruising only compared to the defendant's more serious injury of a fractured jaw.

4)  **the offender's capacity to reform**

The defendant accepts his role in the fighting which led to property damage and injuries to others. He is remorseful and regrets that he was unable to walk away from the fight. Whilst he does not accept that he started the fight he respects the jury's verdict and now just wishes to put matters behind him and to get on with his life.

5)  **relevant sections of the pre-sentence report** that assist your arguments about the appropriate sentence

With reference to step 2 of the Sentencing Guidelines this would mean that for the starting point custodial sentence would be at least 26 weeks' custody but with a category range of a medium level community order or up to one year in custody.

The offence carries a range of possible sentences including a fine and/or community service. It is arguable that the custody threshold has not been met here as the offence cannot be said to be so serious that a community sentence cannot be justified (see s. 230 of the Sentencing Act 2020).

If the court considers that the offences are serious enough for a community order and that the threshold under s. 204 of the 2020 Act has been met, then this should be considered before any custodial sentence. Under s. 203 the court has the power to make a community order because the defendant is over 18 and faces an imprisonable offence. When referring to the community order requirements table at s. 201 of the Sentencing Act 2020 a requirement of a curfew may be appropriate. This would provide sufficient restrictions on the defendant's liberty without the need to impose a custodial sentence. Given that the defendant is a carer and needs to be present during the day a programme requirement would not be appropriate.

In addition, the court may feel that the imposition of a fine would also be an appropriate deterrent in terms of future misconduct. The court has power to impose a fine under s. 125 of the Sentencing Act 2020 at a level to reflect the seriousness of the offence. The Sentencing Guidelines Overarching Principles set out the level of fines from Band A–F. The court must take into account the financial circumstances of the defendant. As the defendant is unemployed, it is arguable Band A would be the most appropriate in these circumstances (50% of relevant weekly income). This would still have a significant economic impact on the defendant.

In addition, the court may feel that a compensation order should be made in terms of the damage to the cinema glass door. The court has the power to make an ancillary order for a compensation order in respect of the property damage to the cinema and the Crown Court Compendium Part II (Sentencing) S3.4 states that the court must consider making a compensation order in every case where there is personal injury, loss or damage (if it has the power to do so). However, applying the principles in *R v York* [2018] EWCA Crim 2754 it is argued that such an order is not realistic given the defendant's limited means unless the repayments were stretched across a long repayment period. The compensation could not, and should not, be payable based on a relative or friend's financial assistance. Based on the Sentencing Guidelines Overarching Principles, if the court is considering imposing both a fine and a compensation order then preference should be given to the compensation order where a defendant is of limited means.

Finally, consider whether there is a realistic prospect of rehabilitation, if so, it would be appropriate to address the judge about exercising his/her discretion to suspend the custodial sentence (assuming one is to be imposed). See Sentencing Act 2020 s. 286.

## Exercise 2

In this exercise you were required to read an extract from a summing-up by a judge towards the end of the trial. This summing-up is the subject of an appeal. You are asked to consider possible grounds of appeal.

The following wording from parts of the summing-up of the trial judge in this fictitious case gives some possible grounds for appeal as follows:

1.  "This is because the prosecution also had supporting evidence from a witness, a Ms Lowden, who claimed to have seen the defendant running from the scene.

The defence deny that the defendant has been correctly identified as the perpetrator of the crime. The prosecution however state that Mrs Lowden's evidence is recognition evidence" – the trial judge has not given a proper 'Turnbull warning' regarding the identification evidence of Ms Lowden.

Refer to this chapter (7.7.5) and the Crown Court Compendium (15). The identification evidence is contested and unsupported and the prosecution is relying wholly or substantially on it to prove the theft. The judge should have given a 'Turnbull warning' to the jury of 'a special need for caution' – see *R v Turnbull* [1977] QB 224. This warns the jury of the dangers of relying on such evidence because a convincing witness might still have made an honest mistake. The judge therefore directs the jury to examine, assess and evaluate the identification evidence in a number of ways. The two parts of the warning which might be problematic from the facts are:

a)  Assessing the quality of the evidence – the fact that Ms Lowden only saw the defendant running from the scene could be problematic. How long did she have the defendant under observation? If it was only a 'fleeting glimpse' the jury should never have been allowed to consider the visual identification evidence.

b)  Looking at the circumstances that led up to the identification evidence being made – it is relevant here that Ms Lowden knows the defendant. However, the judge should still have reminded the jury that recognition evidence can still be mistaken.

The next part of the summing-up that gives cause for concern and might justify grounds for appeal is the following:

2.  "You have been permitted to consider evidence of the defendant's previous conviction for theft of a bicycle which took place 8 years ago. This evidence was admitted because the defendant made an attack on the truthfulness of Ms Lowden's evidence during the trial. The evidence of the defendant's previous conviction can be used to decide whether you consider it likely that the defendant committed the present crime".

The judge appears to have admitted bad character evidence under the gateway of s. 101(1)(g) of the Criminal Justice Act 2003 because the defendant made an attack on another person (a prosecution witness). This may form one ground of appeal. Refer to the relevant discussion of character evidence in Chapter 5 and also read the Crown Court Compendium (12-9). If the ground of appeal is that the bad character evidence should have been excluded under s. 101(3) it is important to remember this is a discretion as the wording is "it appears to the court" and so it is a matter for the court's judgment and not easily appealable unless the judge's decision can be said to be 'Wednesbury unreasonable'. If the court decides that the admission of the evidence would have such an adverse effect on the proceedings that it ought not to be admitted, then it must be excluded. Section 101(4) also states that in deciding whether to exercise its discretion the judge should consider the length of time between the previous convictions and the current offence. It might be possible to argue that the offence of theft committed eight years ago is 'stale' but this may not be accepted by an appeal court. A ground of appeal might lie in the fact that the judge may have wrongly directed the jury as to how to treat the evidence and that it should have gone towards credibility only and not propensity as an offence for theft of a bicycle committed eight years ago does not mean the defendant has the propensity to commit the current offence of robbery. *R v Hanson* [2005] EWCA Crim 824 confirms that to show propensity a single conviction will usually not be enough unless the conviction shows "a tendency to unusual behaviour or where its circumstances demonstrate probative force in relation to the offence charged" [9].

In addition, *R v Highton* [2005] EWCA Crim 1985 suggests that a distinction needs to be drawn between the basis for admitting the evidence and the use that may be made of it once admitted. For this reason, the judge will generally have to give the jury a 'clear warning' during his/her summing-up 'against placing undue reliance' on the evidence and explain why it has been admitted and the ways in which it is relevant. This does not appear to have happened.

Another section of the summing-up that may contain grounds for appeal can be found in the following passage:

3.    "Ms Lowden struck me as a truthful witness, one who is to be believed."

It is arguable that the judge has shown a bias in favour of Ms Lowden. The appeal case of *Derek William Bentley (Deceased)* [1998] EWCA Crim 2516 considered the fact that the original trial judge appeared to be biased towards the prosecution witnesses who were police officers as they were described as showing "the highest gallantry and resolution; they were conspicuously brave". He then posed the question to the jury "Are you going to say they are conspicuous liars?" This summing-up was held to be biased and prejudicial. In the same way, the comments about Mrs Lowden's truthfulness might be regarded as biased and prejudicial as it is for the jury to decide whether or not they believe the prosecution witness Ms Lowden. This may form one ground for appeal.

Another section of the summing-up that may contain grounds for appeal is as follows:

4.    "She later changed her story and said a friend had given her the £10 but did not produce the friend as a witness to support this story. You may decide that this constitutes a lie that the defendant has been found to have told and this lie may be causative when deciding guilt or innocence".

The judge has failed to give a proper 'Lucas Direction' in relation to the lies told by the defendant.

Refer to the Crown Court Compendium (16.3). The lie must be a deliberate lie (rather than arising from confusion or mistake) and relate to a material issue. The jury must be sure that there is not an explanation for the lie which does not suggest guilt. Whilst there is no standard wording that the trial judge should use the judge should not tell the jury it is definitely proof of guilt as this is a matter for the jury to decide after weighing up other possible reasons why the lie was told.

5. "Remember that it is for the prosecution to convince you of the defendant's guilt and this must be done to a very high standard indeed. You must examine the evidence and decide which evidence you believe based on its credibility and certainty of truth" – the judge has failed to correctly sum-up the burden and standard of proof in this section.

Refer to 7.2.1 in this chapter and Crown Court Compendium (5). As the judge has correctly indicated the burden of proof rests with the prosecution. However, he has not correctly summarised the standard of proof. The standard of proof is 'beyond reasonable doubt', which has been expressed by Lord Goddard in *R v Summers* (1952) 3 Cr App R 14 as the jury members asking themselves whether they are satisfied so that they are sure. This has become known as 'the sure test'. The case of *R v Miah* [2018] EWCA Crim 563 confirms that the use of the word 'sure' is sufficient, but no particular words are needed. The judge can use the words 'beyond reasonable doubt' but this usually requires an explanation of its meaning. Beyond reasonable doubt does not mean absolute certainty.

# Index

Note: Page numbers in **bold** refer to tables